To Love
and to Cherish

365 Devotional Readings for Wives

To Love
and to Cherish

BARBOUR
PUBLISHING

ISBN 978-1-60260-221-2

Scripture quotations marked KJV are taken from the King James Version of the Bible.

Scripture quotations marked NIV are taken from the HOLY BIBLE, NEW INTERNATIONAL VERSION®. NIV®. Copyright © 1973, 1978, 1984 by International Bible Society. Used by permission of Zondervan. All rights reserved.

Scripture quotations marked NKJV are taken from the NEW KING JAMES VERSION®. Copyright © 1982 by Thomas Nelson, Inc. Used by permission. All rights reserved.

Scripture quotations marked NLT are taken from the *Holy Bible*, New Living Translation, copyright © 1996, 2004. Used by permission of Tyndale House Publishers, Inc. Wheaton, Illinois 60189, U.S.A. All rights reserved.

Scripture quotations marked NASB are taken from the New American Standard Bible, © 1960, 1962, 1963, 1968, 1971, 1972, 1973, 1975, 1977, 1995 by The Lockman Foundation. Used by permission.

Scripture quotations marked MSG are from THE MESSAGE. Copyright © by Eugene H. Peterson 1993, 1994, 1995, 1996, 2000, 2001, 2002. Used by permission of NavPress Publishing Group.

Scripture quotations marked ESV are from The Holy Bible, English Standard Version®, copyright © 2001 by Crossway Bibles, a publishing ministry of Good News Publishers. Used by permission. All rights reserved.

Scripture quotations marked CEV are from the Contemporary English Version, Copyright © 1991, 1992, 1995 by American Bible Society. Used by permission.

Scriptures marked ASV are taken from the American Standard Version of the Bible.

Scripture quotations marked AMP are taken from the Amplified® Bible, © 1954, 1958, 1962, 1964, 1965, 1987 by The Lockman Foundation. Used by permission.

Scripture quotations marked TLB are taken from *The Living Bible* copyright © 1971. Used by permission of Tyndale House Publishers, Inc., Wheaton, Illinois 60189. All rights reserved.

Published by Barbour Publishing, Inc., P.O. Box 719, Uhrichsville, Ohio 44683 www.barbourbooks.com

Our mission is to publish and distribute inspirational products offering exceptional value and biblical encouragement to the masses.

Member of the
Evangelical Christian
Publishers Association

Printed in the United States of America.

Introduction

Nobody has to tell a wife that marriage is a continually evolving relationship, filled with highs, lows, and lots of in-betweens. You're already well aware of that.

What you might need to hear, though, are some regular reminders of God's love for you. . .of the vital importance of the "oneness" you're a part of. . .of the incredible blessings of being a wife, in spite of the daily struggles. That's what *To Love and to Cherish* is all about—providing encouragement to help you face your challenges with confidence, hope, even joy.

These 365 devotional readings will turn your thoughts to the unchanging wisdom of the Bible and its heavenly Author—who longs to write a success story for you. You'll find insights into the emotions you face and practical ideas for keeping your marriage strong and alive. You'll be refreshed by the real-life triumphs of other wives and gently challenged at times to make beneficial changes to your own attitudes and actions.

Being a wife is a huge undertaking, and keeping your marriage strong, healthy, and whole presents its own unique challenges. With your heavenly Father by your side, you have access to all the wisdom, resources, and strength you need to accomplish everything He's called you to do—to be the best wife you can be. We hope *To Love and to Cherish* is an encouragement along the way!

The Publishers

Blessings for the
New Year

Day
I

So teach us to number our days,
that we may apply our hearts unto wisdom.
PSALM 90:12 KJV

The passing of another year is often a time of reflection. Looking back on the old year with its triumphs and failures . . .looking ahead to the possibilities and promises of the future. It's a time to set goals and make resolutions. And while you're making plans to tackle your weight and get organized, don't forget to evaluate your marriage.

Whether you are aware of it or not, your relationship with your spouse has changed since the day you were wed. You are not the blushing bride you once were. Married life has transformed you from a starry-eyed newlywed to a woman of experience. The same is true of your husband. Your lives together have made you what you are. . .for better or for worse.

Even happy marriages need work, and today is the best day to decide what part of your relationship could use some shoring up. Sit down with your husband and compare notes on the strengths and weaknesses of your marriage. Confess any faults you may have noticed about yourself. Discuss your goals for the new year. And most importantly, pray that God will bless you with your best year yet.

Dear God, thank You for another year together with my husband.
Help me to do all I can to make this one our best ever. Amen.

Spiritual Blessings

*Praise be to the God and Father of our Lord
Jesus Christ, who has blessed us in the heavenly
realms with every spiritual blessing in Christ.*

EPHESIANS 1:3 NIV

*D*iscouraged? Dejected? Disillusioned? Sometimes life leaves us feeling downtrodden. Although the Lord has abundantly blessed us, at times it's easy to forget that truth. We may be struggling financially. We may be dealing with marital strife. We may be experiencing health issues. Is it possible to respond with praise when our earthly life appears to conflict with spiritual truth?

Regardless of our circumstances, God has blessed us with every spiritual blessing in Christ. We are not lacking anything in the heavenly realm. The problem is that many times our focus is on the earthly realm. Instead, we can purpose to turn our thoughts heavenward and count the spiritual blessings that are at our disposal. The Lord's indwelling presence guides our minds and comforts our hearts. His resurrection power enables us to persevere triumphantly. His sustaining peace imparts encouragement for today and hope for tomorrow. When we meditate on eternal blessings, our momentary struggles are put into the proper perspective. Earthly trials are temporary. Spiritual blessings are forever. Let's embrace the eternal gifts we have been given and praise Him for His abundant provision!

Dear Lord, regardless of my circumstances, help me focus heavenward. Allow me to praise You for the spiritual blessings I have been given. Amen.

Walk in Love

Therefore be imitators of God, as beloved children.
And walk in love, as Christ loved us and gave himself up for us.
EPHESIANS 5:1–2 ESV

*S*ince marriage itself is a living thing, it moves and changes all the time. Sometimes it is like a dance, so seamless and sublime we are dizzy from excitement. Other times it is a game of emotional tug-of-war, each side pulling the other over a great expanse. We normally don't notice this drifting until we find ourselves worlds apart. With our feet planted firmly on the ground and our hands seized tightly on a rope of needs, we pull and pull until we realize the small ground we've gained has simply moved us even further apart. Marriage is the dance that continually takes us in one of two directions—toward or away from each other.

So how do we make it back across the great divide? Jesus commands us to love, but remember that He is never going to ask us to do what He cannot do through us. We don't need to cover the distance alone. Walk to Him. He is standing at the center of our struggles, waiting for us to draw near. His love is enough to carry us over the precipice of our pride that is keeping us at the fringe of our marriage. We don't have to have all the answers now—just move toward Jesus. Drop the rope and walk in love.

Father, You are my guide. Help me learn to draw close to You
so I can grow in love and move closer to my husband. Amen.

Precious Moments

> *. . .to whom God willed to make known what*
> *is the riches of the glory of this mystery among the Gentiles,*
> *which is Christ in you, the hope of glory.*
> COLOSSIANS 1:27 NASB

*D*o you ever lose sight of just how much you enjoy the presence of God? It's easy to become preoccupied with life's duties. When you finally find a moment to shut out the voices of the day, you quickly discover how little anything else matters but God. He is your light and your salvation. No one knows the path He's chosen for you quite like He does. He points to the truth and brings about the results He destined for you before the beginning of time.

Imagine—you were a thought, an idea with grand purpose, before He ever breathed life into the first man. Compare that to the things that penetrate your mind and cause you concern. In God's presence, there is little to worry about. The truth—freedom from everything—rests in time with Him. The more you lean into His higher purpose, the less you'll try to work it out on your own.

Why spend that precious time telling God all your worries— things He already knows? Instead give Him minutes of silence and moments of praise, and allow His wisdom to penetrate your heart and direct everything that concerns you.

Lord, help me to never lose sight of how much I enjoy spending time with You. Help me to take time each day to hear what You have to say. Amen.

Abide in Christ

*"I am the vine, you are the branches; he who abides
in Me and I in him, he bears much fruit,
for apart from Me you can do nothing."*
JOHN 15:5 NASB

o we want the blessing of God on our marriage? Of course we do. But how do we do it? By abiding in Christ. This means we are to remain, continue, and sink deeper into our relationship with Him. In doing so, we will bear much fruit.

In John 15:12, Jesus inspires us with the words, "Love one another, just as I have loved you." That means loving sacrificially, selflessly, totally, regardless of the other person's behavior or how we "feel" each day. When we apply that truth to our marriage, we will have an outgrowth of fruitful love we never dreamed possible.

Wives can be greatly encouraged by reading the entire text of John 15:1–17. Over and over Jesus tells us to remain or abide in Him. He assures us that apart from Him, we can't do anything. We can't be a good wife, mother, daughter, or sister unless we remain in Christ and seek His will for our lives.

Take time this evening to read through John 15:1–17, slowly and carefully. Think of ways you can implement all that Jesus is saying to you in these verses. Then pray for the blessing of God on your marriage as you sink deeper into Him.

*Dear Jesus, I want Your blessing on my marriage.
Show me how to abide in You. In Jesus' name, amen.*

The Love Letter

*This is love: not that we loved God,
but that he loved us and sent his Son as
an atoning sacrifice for our sins.*
1 JOHN 4:10 NIV

In the back of her closet, behind sweaters and boxes of seldom-worn shoes, was a carved wooden box. Every so often, she took out the box and slid off the lid. She sat on the carpeted floor in her bedroom and gently lifted out one sheet of paper after another. Each was wrinkled and stained, creased, and worn smooth with reading. Each was written in the same handwriting: her husband's.

Life was busier now; he didn't often tuck love letters under her pillow before he left for work in the morning or wedge a note between the milk and orange juice in the refrigerator. But his heart had not changed. Rereading his old letters helped her remember.

How would her husband have felt if he poured out his love to his wife in a letter and she was too busy or didn't care enough to read it? The same is true with God. And He hasn't just written us a few letters—He's written an entire book! If we want to show Him how much we love Him and desire to understand His heart, we need to read His words.

The Bible is our love letter from God, from the one true Lover of our souls. Read it; wear it out!

*Dear God, thank You for loving me so much.
Thank You for Your living, breathing, life-giving Word.
Help me to crave it as I crave food and drink. Amen.*

Everyday Miracles

Day
7

The Lord said unto him, What is that in thine hand?
And he said, A rod. And he said, Cast it on the ground.
And he cast it on the ground, and it became a serpent.
Exodus 4:2–3 KJV

For forty years Moses cared for his father-in-law's sheep. For forty years he carried a rod as he worked. He knew everything there was to know about rods. But that was before Moses encountered God in the burning bush on Mount Sinai.

God commanded Moses to return to Egypt, where he had killed a man. As if that weren't unreasonable enough, God also wanted Moses to tell Pharaoh to free thousands of Hebrew slaves whose unpaid labor enhanced the Egyptian economy.

Moses suggested many excellent reasons why he should not do this. He doubted even his fellow Israelites would believe him. But God turned his walking stick into a snake to jar Moses out of his comfort zone. God used this everyday rod to convince Moses and the Israelite elders He meant business.

Like Moses, we serve God with gifts and tools He has given us. After years of faithful routine, we may think we know everything there is to know about them.

But God may use the car, the business, the pie recipe, the backyard, the computer, the scrapbooking, or the saxophone for His kingdom in ways we never imagined.

Lord God, we often forget that You have bigger, better ideas for our lives than any we might conceive. Help us reach for adventure! Amen.

We're in This Together

And God blessed them, and God said unto them,
Be fruitful, and multiply, and replenish the earth, and subdue it:
and have dominion over the fish of the sea, and over the fowl of the air,
and over every living thing that moveth upon the earth.
GENESIS 1:28 KJV

When God placed Adam and Eve in the garden, He gave them a mandate. He told them to be fruitful, to responsibly care for the earth, and to have dominion over the animal kingdom.

The key word here is *them*.

God's mandate was given to the couple so that both the husband and wife would work together as a team in a common mission.

Sometimes a wife will catch a vision apart from her husband, and she'll plow ahead alone. The result—a busy schedule, too many outside commitments, a divided house—will be detrimental to the family.

If you have a desire for ministry, talk to your husband. If he doesn't share that desire, wait. God will lead you and your husband together. He will give you both the right vision for you as a couple and a family.

Then, when you are both ready, you can move forward— together.

Father, if it be Your will, give us a vision for
ministry so we can work together for You. Amen.

The Right Help

*And the LORD God said, It is not good that the
man should be alone; I will make him an help meet for him.*
GENESIS 2:18 KJV

*E*llen pinned the "honey-do" list to the bulletin board and grimaced. She wondered if Walt would even notice. Lately it seemed as if she spent more time nagging than her husband spent accomplishing. It was really putting a strain on their marriage. Why was it so difficult for him to empty the trash or put his laundry in the hamper?

Ellen grumbled inwardly as she headed into their bedroom, where she found Walt's clothes strewed across the floor. Sighing in frustration, she picked up a pair of his jeans and tossed them into the hamper. Then it struck her. *That really wasn't difficult,* she thought. *Why have I been so specific about* his *jobs and* my *jobs?*

She thought about how she'd been given by God to her husband. She had intended to be a good helper to Walt. Lately she'd been more of a taskmaster. It was no wonder there was such tension in their home. From now on she'd do her best to be a helpmeet for her husband. Ellen realized that as she was obedient to God, He would bless her home. Walt would have more time to spend with her, and their love would grow.

*O God, let me be the helpmeet You intended me to be.
I desire to bring joy to my husband.*

Delilah's Nagging

Then she said to him, "How can you say, 'I love you,'
when you won't confide in me? This is the third time you have made
a fool of me and haven't told me the secret of your great strength." With
such nagging she prodded him day after day until he was tired to death.
JUDGES 16:15–16 NIV

Delilah wouldn't let it go. She wanted something from Samson—information—and she was determined to cajole and wheedle it out of him. Three times he tried to put her off! But he underestimated her greedy nature. Delilah was not a woman who could be deterred, not when a generous sum of money was at stake.

Eager to rid their country of Samson, some Philistine rulers offered Delilah 1,100 shekels to discover the secret of his strength. Delilah never loved Samson, but he loved her. That love gave her an advantage of power. She used it to cause his downfall and, ultimately, his death.

Delilah's role in this sordid tale is a dire warning to wives. Can our husbands trust us with their weaknesses and vulnerability? Or do we use that private knowledge to hurt or embarrass them? Most likely, Delilah withheld affection from Samson until he caved in and gave her what she wanted. She knew that a cold shoulder would accentuate her point. Does that ever seem like a familiar scene?

Being loved is a privilege and a responsibility. We need to be good stewards of our husband's affection. Love is not a game.

Lord, make me a safe haven for my husband
and a good steward of his love.

Consolation amid Conflict

Our bodies had no rest, but we were troubled on every side.
Outside were conflicts, inside were fears. Nevertheless God,
who comforts the downcast, comforted us by the coming of Titus.
2 CORINTHIANS 7:5–6 NKJV

Sometimes we feel so beaten down by life, battered by outside circumstances over which we have no control. During these unwelcome storms, fear begins to permeate our inner being. Seeing no way out, we may fall into depression and enter into self-preservation mode by withdrawing into ourselves. But in doing so, we cut ourselves off from those who would give us aid and comfort.

Fortunately, God has other plans. He knows what we need and lovingly provides it. He comforts the downcast by sending earthly angels to help us. These people of God, Tituses among us, give freely of God's love and fill us with the healing balm of His comfort.

In the midst of distress, we are not to withdraw from God's helping hand but immerse ourselves in His Word and reach out to others, allowing both to give us love and comfort in our time of need. And then, whole once more, we in turn can be a Titus for another.

Dear God, You know my frame, my circumstances, my outlook, my troubles.
Comfort me in this situation through Your Word and the love of others.
Give me consolation in the midst of this conflict. Amen.

God's Purposes

*Though I walk in the midst of trouble,
you preserve my life. . . .
The LORD will fulfill his purpose for me.*
PSALM 138:7–8 NIV

*I*t's hard to see that the Lord is fulfilling His purpose in our lives when bad things happen, especially when it relates to our marriages. These "bad things" usually happen when we place unreal expectations on our spouses—expectations of security, peace, contentment, or fulfilled needs.

In Psalm 138 David praised God for guiding him through the rough times in his life. As David looked back, he saw God's goodness to him through the good times as well as the bad. And he realized that God would continue to guide his life in the future as He had in the past.

What can we do when life derails our plans, desires, or expectations? First, remember how God has led through difficult circumstances in the past. Looking back helps us see how God has fulfilled His purpose for saving us—molding us into the image of Christ. Second, thank Him for His guidance and protection as He brings us through hard times. Third, look forward, knowing that God does not allow anything into our lives that isn't for our good. We can trust Him to do what is best for us.

*Dear God, help me to not place expectations on my husband that only You can fulfill. Help me to remember that You are working Your purpose in my life.
Amen.*

Never Give Up

*And the second time the cock crew. And Peter called to
mind the word that Jesus said unto him, Before the cock crow twice,
thou shalt deny me thrice. And when he thought thereon, he wept.*
MARK 14:72 KJV

Today, do you feel like Peter—a failed disciple, worthless to God, who's been faithless multiple times? Maybe you've gone astray into busyness, making your marriage less than wonderful. Or courage and dependence on God haven't been hallmarks of your marital relationship.

Our flaws and failings often leave us weeping at our own weakness. Self-disgust runs deep in our hearts when we recognize how much God offers us and how little we've done in return. Though we love Him, like Peter, we don't always obey Him.

Let's remember that God didn't end the story with Peter's tears. Peter lived to fight another day and, in Christ's power, won the battle of spreading the gospel to the world. This seriously unfaithful disciple ultimately became the church's outstanding leader.

Our marriages are testimonies to God's faithfulness, if we continue the fight against sin and grow together in Him. Like Peter, we are not living our final moments, though our hurting hearts might tell us so. Our mission is not finished, and until God calls us home, we must never, never, never give up.

*Forgive me for my sin and turn my eyes toward Your glory, Lord.
When I fail, help me not to give up but to seek strength in You.*

Anticipation

*Let your waist be girded and your lamps burning. . .
like men who wait for their master. . .that when he
comes and knocks they may open to him immediately.*
LUKE 12:35–36 NKJV

The clicking of the dog's claws startled Kim until she glanced at the clock. Every day the retriever greeted her husband at the door, eager to show affection. Looking out the window she watched as Mike trudged up the drive. She knew the instant he saw his pet waiting for him. His whole attitude brightened.

How simple it is to crush or uplift. Changing a person's day can take only a moment. As wives, we have the ability to make our husband's homecoming something for him to anticipate—or dread. When he knows we are waiting to greet him with a hug or kiss to listen as he talks about his day, he is more anxious to come home. Likewise, his evident enthusiasm to see his wife makes us anticipate his homecoming more.

And we should all be ready and waiting for Christ's return. His coming for us is a sure promise. As we rest in that truth, we can allow ourselves to feel the excitement. We can be figuratively at the door, ready to meet the Lord when He comes—to fling open the door and rush to meet Him, our arms stretched wide.

*Jesus, thank You for Your promise. Help me to be eager to see my husband
and to view this as a forerunner of the time I will see You. Amen.*

Unexpected Treasures

Don't fall in love with money.
Be satisfied with what you have.
HEBREWS 13:5 CEV

When Dave asked Jen to marry him, he promised her love, faithfulness, and a lifetime of chocolate. He never said anything about money.

As years passed, Jen became increasingly frustrated with broken appliances, calls from bill collectors, and budgets strained to the ripping point. As her family struggled from paycheck to paycheck, she watched friends living comfortably. Discontent and envy stirred in her innards.

The Bible tells us not to fall in love with money, but it's incredibly hard to do—especially if we don't have enough. Money becomes a pseudo-savior, a way to rise above problems and enjoy the good things of life. We lose sight of the immeasurable wealth God *has* provided and become lost in the woods of discontent that border our blessings.

Jen recognized the brewing storm in her soul and stepped back to take inventory of the *needs* God had provided for her family, rather than focus on the *wants.* She knew the Lord was imbedding gratefulness in her heart the day she found herself dancing with the ailing washing machine as it mamboed across the floor.

Giver of all good things, quench my insatiable thirst for the comfort money provides. Teach me that my security is in You alone. When I fret about money, remind me that Your beloved Son was born on a bale of hay in a barn. Amen.

Day
16

Caring for the Temple

Honor God with your body.
1 CORINTHIANS 6:20 NLT

Our bodies are amazing gifts from God. Without any thought or effort on our parts, our hearts beat life-giving blood throughout our veins, providing us with the energy to accomplish the thousands of tasks we do each day. Our brains give the commands, our bodies obey. But these incredible structures aren't maintenance-free. Just as we are to be good stewards of our resources of time and money, we should also be good stewards of our bodies. God's Word calls them temples.

When we are busy meeting the needs of others, we often neglect to care for ourselves. But God wants us to treat our bodies with care and respect. This means exercising regularly, eating good food, getting enough rest. These are simple things but the dividends are high, for when we treat our bodies right they treat us right in return.

Father, thank You for the amazing body that You have given me, for all the things it does that happen without my knowledge. Help me to care for my body in a way that brings honor and glory to You. Amen.

One Hundred Percent

*"And remember the words of the Lord Jesus,
that He said, 'It is more blessed to give than to receive.'"*
ACTS 20:35 NKJV

*M*ore than half the marriages today end in divorce. There is a good reason for that! When asked how much each partner should give to their marriage, most people will logically answer that the contribution should be 50/50. However, God's way is for each to give 100 percent so that there will never be a moment when anything is lacking.

When you expect a certain level of commitment or participation from your spouse and base your happiness on that, you are sure to be disappointed when he fails you. Guard your heart from disappointment by focusing your joy on what you give to your husband and what you receive from your heavenly Father. Never let your happiness be dependent on your husband lest you begin to count and measure his flaws.

If you expect to give 100 percent, you will feel blessed when you see your husband responding and giving to you. Disappointment, resentment, anger, and self-righteousness in your marriage will fade away as joy takes its place.

*Father, forgive me for demanding more than I am willing to give.
Help me to give 100 percent to my marriage so that my joy
will increase and crowd out the disappointments. Amen.*

Repent and Be Restored

*And I will restore to you the years that the
locust hath eaten, the cankerworm, and the caterpillar,
and the palmerworm, my great army which I sent among you.*
JOEL 2:25 KJV

Throughout scripture we encounter a divine paradox, an apparent contradiction in the way God intervenes in human history: The same God who chastens His people is the same God who turns around and blesses them.

We see this over and over in the history of Israel. God directs Israel; Israel follows for a while but then turns away and commits sin. God chastises His people, destroying their crops or sending them into exile. When they repent, He has pity on them and blesses them again.

The key is repentance.

Our hearts must turn from ourselves to our Lord. God is so gracious, forgiving, and loving, that a mustard seed of repentance grows a whole tree of blessing. God restores what was lost even when He knows there will be future failures.

Have the locusts been eating away at your marriage? Have there been mistakes and failures? Has your pride caused contentions in your house? If so, repent. Turn from your foolish ways and obey Him.

He will cause His face to shine upon you and restore the years the locusts ate.

*Father, although I have a good marriage, I've made some mistakes.
Help me turn away from myself and obey You.
Please give us back the lost years and bless our lives. Amen.*

Selfish Ambition

Do nothing out of selfish ambition or vain conceit,
but in humility consider others better than yourselves.
PHILIPPIANS 2:3 NIV

*B*eing selfish can damage your relationship with your husband. Marriage is about commitment and putting your spouse's needs above your own.

God wants us to honor our husbands, and our husbands are to love us as they love themselves (Ephesians 5:28). This means that each needs to put the other first in all things.

If you and your mate are having problems in this area, go to God in prayer. Then, if you feel so led, have a long heart-to-heart talk with your spouse. Let him know how you are feeling. Discuss how you can better meet each other's needs. If forgiveness is in order—on either side—seek or give it, whichever may be the case. Pray and ask the Lord to bless your desire to be unselfish and meet each other's needs. Afterward, if you find you are still having problems, perhaps it's time to seek help from your pastor or a professional counselor.

Although you may not have control over the actions of others, you do have control over yourself. So in all things be selfless. Stay strong in your faith. Seek God's help and guidance as you honor and love your husband as you honor and love yourself.

Dear heavenly Father, help my husband and me to meet one another's needs. Give us the desire to honor and respect each other. In Jesus' name, amen.

The Shunammite

When he [Elisha] saw her in the distance, the man
of God said to his servant Gehazi, "Look! There's the Shunammite!
Run to meet her and ask her, 'Are you all right? Is your husband all right?
Is your child all right?' " "Everything is all right," she said.
2 KINGS 4:25–26 NIV

*E*verything wasn't all right. The Shunammite's cherished son was dead, his body lay out at home. In the midst of a tragedy, this faith-filled mother didn't panic or fall apart. She didn't even stop to cry. She saddled up her donkey and headed out to track down Elisha, the prophet. She went to find God—and in those ancient days, Elisha had access to God's ear.

She might have heard how Elijah had raised the son of the widow in Zarephath. The circumstances were similar. She, too, had generously opened her home to Elisha, knowing that he was a prophet of the Holy One. Years earlier, Elisha had given her the message that God would bless her with a child. Today, she was determined to bring Elisha back to her home to restore life to that promised child.

Elisha agreed to return with her and prayed earnestly over the boy. The boy sneezed! Not once but seven times! He was alive! This nameless woman led her family to God. Everything did turn out all right.

The Shunammite gave us a wonderful example of what godliness really looks like even in the midst of a tragedy.

Lord, thank You for this model of a woman who first sought God's kingdom, trusting completely that everything else would be given to her.

No Matter Where

This is my command—be strong and courageous!
Do not be afraid or discouraged. For the LORD
your God is with you wherever you go.
JOSHUA 1:9 NLT

After the death of Moses, God called Joshua to lead the Israelites into the Promised Land. Imagine how Joshua must have felt, taking over for Moses. Moses—the man through whom God performed mind-boggling miracles, the man who stood up to Pharaoh, who received the Ten Commandments and oversaw the building of the tabernacle. Not only that, but Joshua had worked side by side with Moses; he had seen firsthand how fickle and capricious the Israelites could be.

Joshua did not know what would happen after he took over for Moses, and he certainly did not know how the Israelites would react to God's leaving him in charge. He simply had to trust that God would, indeed, be with him wherever he and the Israelites went.

In our own lives, we experience new responsibilities, change, and fear of the unknown. Whether it is a promotion at work, a new baby, a cross-country move, or simply learning to love our spouses better, we experience our fair share of fear and discouragement. When we don't know what to do or where to turn, God speaks to us just as He did to Joshua. *Be strong and courageous! Don't be afraid or discouraged!* God promises to be with us wherever we go, and we can certainly trust Him to keep His word.

Dear Lord, thank You for Your promise to be with me wherever I go.
Teach me to let go of my fear and trust in You. Amen.

Godly Love

Love is kind and patient, never jealous, boastful,
proud, or rude. Love isn't selfish or quick tempered. It doesn't keep
a record of wrongs. . . . Love rejoices in the truth, but not in evil. Love
is always supportive, loyal, hopeful, and trusting. Love never fails!
1 CORINTHIANS 13:4–8 CEV

*S*arah wept as she confessed that she had a mental record of the wrongs her husband had committed toward her. She knew it was sin to harbor an unforgiving heart, but her pain was so deep that she had difficulty laying it down and loving him.

God defines *love* in 1 Corinthians 13:4–8. God proved His love in giving us Jesus (John 3:16). Jesus modeled godly love by laying down His life and exhorts us to do the same for our husbands (1 John 3:16; John 15:12–13). In our own power, it is impossible to give this unworldly, sacrificial, godly love to our husbands. However, God makes it possible (Jeremiah 32:17; Mark 9:23).

Ask God to forgive you for your own sins (1 John 1:9). Then follow the Lord's example of forgiveness (Colossians 3:13) and forgive your husband. Lay down any pride, anger, record of wrongs, and self-seeking desires, and invite the Lord to empower you to take up patience, kindness, and truth.

Trust God that, through the power of the Holy Spirit, God "can do far more than we dare ask or imagine" in our marriages (Ephesians 3:20 CEV). He will help us to always protect, trust, hope, and persevere in our marriage when we desire to give godly love to our husbands.

Lord, I trust You to transform my marriage. Empower me
with the godly love that You intended me to have for my husband.

First Love

*"'You have abandoned the love you had at first.
Remember therefore from where you have fallen; repent,
and do the works you did at first. If not, I will come to you and
remove your lampstand from its place, unless you repent.'"*
REVELATION 2:4–5 ESV

*Y*ou've heard the expression "God has no grandchildren."
Truly, each of us must choose to love Him—and to
rekindle that love each and every day! As the church of Ephesus
discovered, churches also need to revive their love daily. Churches
fail in many ways, but all that failed had lost the thrill of loving
Jesus.

Like churches, our marriages can become old and stale if we
become forgetful of the joy of our relationship. Just because we
had wonderful honeymoons doesn't guarantee our marital success.
A strong marriage requires both members of the couple to draw
close to each other. They need to spend time together and to put
their marriage before many other undermining distractions. And a
husband and wife need to draw close to Jesus, too.

No matter what relationship we're in, it's love that holds
it together. Whether it's our love for Jesus, our church, or
our spouses, let's not abandon that first love. If we do, like a
lampstand, we'll be easily removed from our usual spot.

*Lord, we want our marriage to shine brightly for You.
Show us how to keep alive our first love—for You and for each other.*

P.S. I Love You

My beloved is mine, and I am his.
Song of Solomon 2:16 kjv

When was the last time you sent a love note? Not just a card for the appropriate holidays, birthday, and anniversary, but a genuine note, penned by your hand, to your one and only? Chances are you have a shoe box full of old love letters written on pretty, scented paper, just waiting to be sifted through on a rainy afternoon. Relics from the days when your head was spinning and your heart was throbbing with romance.

Marriage has a way of pulling our heads out of the clouds and into the lackluster world of the mundane. The excitement of being a newlywed begins to ebb and you are merely a wife trying to keep up with your required tasks.

Maybe it's time to revisit the romantic days of your courtship. Dust off that scented stationary and write a long love letter, telling him all the things you cherish about your marriage. Tuck a love note in the pocket of his work slacks. Use soap to write a romantic message on the bathroom mirror that will fill his thoughts with nothing but you. Remind him that he's not just your husband. He's your *beloved*, and you are forever his.

Dear Father, teach me how to keep the romance alive in my marriage, and help me to cherish my husband as my one and only beloved. Amen.

Receiving God's Embrace

How great is the love the Father has lavished on us,
that we should be called children of God! And that is what we are!
1 JOHN 3:1 NIV

Some people are born "huggers." They greet family members or complete strangers in the same way—with a hug. They just can't help themselves. They must lavish love on those around them. They must demonstrate affection. Most of us would agree that the closer the relationship, the more meaningful the hug. Can you imagine receiving an embrace from our heavenly Father, the God of the universe?

God lavished His love on us when He sent Jesus to earth. Jesus' sacrificial death on our behalf paved the way for adoption into God's family by faith. When we receive the gift of Jesus, we become children of God. We are no longer strangers. We are no longer alienated from a holy God. We have become family!

As you ponder God's great love for you, picture Jesus hanging on the cross. With arms outstretched, He not only came to embrace the world with God's love, He came to embrace you! Will you receive God's hug? The unconditional love of our Creator is the greatest gift we could ever receive. Will you allow His love to be lavished upon you? Receive the embrace of your heavenly Father today!

Dear Lord, I need Your embrace. May I receive the abundant
love You desire to lavish upon me because I am Your child. Amen.

More Than a Beauty Queen

> *"If you persist in staying silent at a time like this, help and
> deliverance will arrive for the Jews from someplace else;
> but you and your family will be wiped out. Who knows?
> Maybe you were made queen for just such a time as this."*
> ESTHER 4:14 MSG

Queens usually begin their lives in royal palaces, living in the
lap of luxury all their lives.

If someone had told Hadassah, Mordecai's orphaned cousin,
that she would become Queen Esther of Persia, she would have
laughed in his face! But God had big plans for the lovely Jewish
girl. She won an empire-wide beauty contest and King Xerxes's
love.

At this point, most fairy tales end with "they lived happily
ever after." But even a queen had no guarantee of protection from
powerful enemies. Mordecai discovered that Haman, the king's
closest advisor, had engineered the genocide of the Jews scattered
throughout the empire. While his heart yearned for Esther,
whom he regarded as his daughter, Mordecai realized that Esther
might play a role in saving her people—if she agreed to take the
risk.

Few of us live the exotic, thrilling life of a queen, but all
women possess power within their spheres of influence—home,
work, school, community. God has brought us to this place in
history for a purpose. Will we take the risks?

*Father, I cannot imagine the plans You have for me.
But I know I can trust You with my hopes, dreams—and life. Amen.*

Let Your Joy Shine!

But let all those that put their trust in thee rejoice:
let them ever shout for joy, because thou defendest them:
let them also that love thy name be joyful in thee.
PSALM 5:11 KJV

*I*f there is anything that is missing from the Christian home these days, it's a smile.

Weighed down by unreasonable expectations, impossible schedules, and just the daily grind of life, we become stressed and sullen. Smiles disappear at the first hint of tension.

Why do we open our homes to the thieving pressures that rob us of joy? Why do we so easily forget the great things that God has done and is doing for us?

God is our redeemer. Our defender. Our rock. Our high tower. Our hope. Our deliverer. Our shield. Our strength. Our salvation.

We are forgiven. Justified. Sanctified. Made holy.

Our bodies are the temples of the Holy Spirit. He is *in* us, and we are in Him. Nothing—death, life, angels, principalities, powers, the future, the past, things in the heavens or the deep, or any other creature (even our faithless selves)—absolutely *nothing*, can separate us from the love of God in Christ Jesus, our Lord.

If we would truly grasp just *one* of these truths, our lives and our faces would be light and cheerful.

Our burdens have been lifted!

Praise His name!

Be joyful!

Smile!

Oh Father! How foolish I can be when I let the little irritations of life get me down so easily. Christ has won the victory over sin and death! Christ has saved me! How can I do anything but smile?

Honor God with Healthy Habits

When you eat or drink or do anything else, always do it to honor God.
1 CORINTHIANS 10:31 CEV

The statistics are grim. Sixty percent of Americans are overweight or obese. Only about a third of us get the minimum recommended amount of exercise each day. Health problems that were once reserved for elderly people, like diabetes and high blood pressure, are now affecting us at younger and younger ages. In spite of living in a society obsessed with diet and exercise, many of us are becoming increasingly unhealthier. Yet the Bible says that whatever we do we are to honor God, and that includes with our bodies (1 Corinthians 6:20). We often think of this in relation to sexual purity. And it certainly applies. However, we also have an opportunity to honor God with our bodies by taking good care of them—by getting enough rest and enough exercise.

Take a look in the mirror. You probably need at least eight hours of sleep each night so that your body can function optimally. Do you make it a priority to get enough rest, or do you stretch yourself to the limit all week and then try to make up for it on the weekends? The surgeon general recommends that adults get thirty to sixty minutes of physical activity most days of the week. Is there time in your day for fresh air and exercise? Particularly as you age, healthy habits are an investment that will pay enormous dividends down the road. It sounds like a cliché, but you only get one body—make it a priority to honor God with it.

Father, thank You for blessing me with a body that does so much for me. Please help me to make it a priority to care for it in a way that honors You. Amen.

Follow the Leader

Follow after charity.
1 CORINTHIANS 14:1 KJV

*T*rue love is a wonderful leader because it always has its recipients' best at heart. Christ is the greatest giver of true love that there is. In fact, He embodies true love. Following His lead is the best way to ensure that you have the proper kind of love.

The ultimate gift of love is the sacrifice of one's self—a gift our Lord gave without hesitation because His heart is undefiled. We are to follow His example—not to the cross most likely, but in any way that puts others' needs and desires before our own. This goes against human nature in so many ways. In our flesh we want to fulfill our own desires—or better yet, to have someone else fulfill them.

As wives we want to be spoiled and pampered by our husbands. At the least, we don't want them to get in the way of our goals and plans for our lives. Women have become more and more independent in recent years, and that can be a very good thing—God expects us to use the brains He has given us. He does, however, intend for us to do this within His instructions. It is still His plan that we do everything with a heart filled with love. Ultimately, if the love we have toward Him is what it should be, we won't have any trouble in expressing our love in other relationships.

So get ready to follow the Leader!

*Thank You, Jesus, for leading in the area of love.
I know if I follow You, I will do right.*

Strength in Christ

*I can do everything through
him who gives me strength.*
PHILIPPIANS 4:13 NIV

*B*eing a wife comes with a unique set of challenges. Whether you stay at home with children, go to work all day, or use your time to volunteer—whatever it is that you do—you are probably often tired at the end of the day. At night you have dinner to make, dishes to wash, cleaning to do, plans to make for the weekend, groceries to buy, and the list goes on. On top of all that, you have a husband to love.

While we face our challenges with willingness, sometimes we experience trials that overwhelm us. Bills are coming due that we cannot pay; we are forced to move for a job and leave our friends behind; we have a fight with our spouse in which hurtful words leave us confused and feeling discouraged about our marriage.

Paul's words in Philippians can be a true comfort when life seems to be falling apart. God will give us strength for *everything* through Jesus Christ. When we feel hopeless and when our struggles overwhelm us, God is there. God loves us and wants to see us through our challenges. We simply must trust Him, placing our faith entirely in His hands, and believe that He will see us through.

*Dear Lord, thank You for Your promise to give me strength.
Help me to rely on You and believe in Your promises today. Amen.*

He Is Here

And Jacob awaked out of his sleep, and he said,
Surely the LORD is in this place; and I knew it not.
GENESIS 28:16 KJV

No matter where we are, no matter what we are going through, God is with us. Whether we are on the run or rooted in the mud, in conflict with our husbands or reaching a compromise, deep in dreams or fully awake, He is here. He is in this place.

Jacob discovered this when he awoke from a dream of angels ascending and descending on a ladder. Having just stolen his brother's blessing, Jacob was on the run. But he could not outrun God. He was still with him, reassuring him: Behold, I am with you and will keep you wherever you go. . . . I will not leave you (Genesis 28:15 NKJV).

Jacob's God is our God. He has been, is, and always will be with His people. He is the Rock that never moves.

God holds us by the hand, telling us not to be afraid. Through thick and thin, amid dreams and waking hours, while at home and at work, amid laughter and tears, He leads, loves, speaks to, and cares for us. He is here.

Call to Him. He is listening. Love Him. He adores you. Pray and praise Him. He wants to hear your voice. Reach out and grab His hand. He wants to touch you. Never, ever let Him go.

Dear God, my heart overflows with joy and peace in Your presence.
You are here—hallelujah! Your Spirit is with me wherever I go,
whatever I am going through. Thank You, Lord, for never leaving me.

Deepening the Roots

*Your roots will grow down into God's love
and keep you strong. . . . Then you will be made complete
with all the fullness of life and power that comes from God.*
EPHESIANS 3:17, 19 NLT

*M*any times, the longer a husband and wife are married,
the deeper their love grows for each other. Many are
amazed that it could be this way. On her wedding day, a bride
finds it difficult to imagine herself more in love than she is at the
moment. Yet as the years pass and the couple shares both pain
and joy in their lives together, they often look back and see how
those experiences strengthened and deepened their love for each
other.

But this growing love doesn't automatically happen. To love
someone when he makes it difficult to love takes commitment.
It's not easy to obey God's command to love our neighbor—in
this case our husbands—as we love ourselves. Just as God chose
to love us while we were still in sin and enemies with Him, we
must love our spouses even when they don't make it easy to love.
When we do, we mirror God's love, which is deeper, wider, and
higher than any human love.

As we grow in His love, we grow in love for others. As His
love strengthens us and enables us to do His bidding, so our love
for our husbands enables them to be the men God intended
them to be.

*Father, I will never fully comprehend Your love.
But it enables me to love my husband unconditionally as
I choose to demonstrate Your love to him. Thank You.*

Proper Thoughts

For out of the heart come forth evil thoughts,
murders, adulteries. . .
MATTHEW 15:19 ASV

Have you ever seen something you wanted but didn't have? As you think about that item, you begin to visualize yourself with it. The more you think about what you desire, the more you convince yourself it is essential. Wanting that object consumes your thoughts.

Impure thoughts in a marriage can have the same effect. At first, only a flicker of a thought may tease at us as we consider how nice divorce or separation might be. Maybe we only start with wishing our husband would be away for a short time, giving us time to breathe. As time passes, we think more and more about how incompatible we are. Eventually the thought of divorce begins to consume our thoughts, and we become sure this is right for us.

When dissatisfaction first rears its ugly head, we must be on our knees before God, asking for a loving, forgiving heart and healing in our marriage. The longer we put off restoring relationships and purifying our thoughts, the harder it is to set everything right. Whether the relationship is between us and our spouse or us and God, we must work to keep it pure.

Even if time has passed and things look bleak, remember that all is not lost. God is a worker of miracles. He is also the biggest encourager for us in our marriages.

Lord, thank You for my husband. Please, restore my
marriage to a God-designed work of wonder. Amen.

Never Forget

Remember Lot's wife.
LUKE 17:32 KJV

*T*here is one wife—and only one wife—whom we are told to remember from scripture.

It wasn't Eve, the mother of all living.

Nor was it Sarah, whose daughters we should be.

It wasn't Noah's wife, faithful Ruth, unfaithful Bathsheba, or the grieving, bitter wife of Job.

Jesus tells us to remember Lot's wife.

Who was this nameless woman?

Scripture doesn't tell us anything about her origins, but it is likely she was a heathen from the plains. When Lot separated from his uncle and went toward Sodom, he apparently was not married.

She likely did not know the God of Abraham, and instead of following Lot's faith, she compromised his testimony in the home to the point that her daughters and sons-in-law thought Lot was joking when he warned them of impending doom.

She was a stubborn, disobedient woman. She had direct revelation from God to leave her house, but she, as well as her husband, lingered. She was told not to look back, but she did.

While we are not likely to be turned into a pillar of salt for our disobedience, we can become hardened in mind and spirit. Let's strive to support our husbands, obey our Lord, and remain pliable.

And never—ever—forget Lot's wife.

Lord Jesus, be with me as I strive to support my husband and obey Your commands. And let me never be like Lot's wife. Amen.

Love Past a Lifetime

This shall be written for the generation to come:
and the people which shall be created shall praise the LORD.
PSALM 102:18 KJV

"Why do you keep those cards?" Corinne shook her head at the boxful of Valentine's Day, anniversary, and birthday cards her twin sister had collected over the years. "What are you going to do with them? I'm the pack rat of the family." She knew Carly hated clutter.

"I love to look at Michael's cards." Carly's fingers almost caressed a few favorites. "And I like to reread the ones I've given him. Some days when I'm sick of paying bills or cleaning bathrooms, they remind me of what we're all about. But that's not the only reason I don't toss them." Carly chuckled as she read a short, silly note her husband had written. "I keep a couple on the mantel so the kids can see we love each other. And one day, when Jack and Jasmine are looking for spouses, they can read *some* of the really mushy ones." Her eyes twinkled then grew serious. "I want them to know how good the Lord has been to their dad and me."

Do you have a few special cards or notes that proclaim the love you share with your spouse? If so, encourage the next generation's marriages with love, faithfulness, and fun by passing them down.

Lord Jesus, thank You for what You have given my husband and me.
May we hand down a marriage legacy that will bless
our children and grandchildren. Amen.

Who Gives This Woman?

*"Here is Rebekah; take her and go.
Yes, let her be the wife of your master's son,
as the LORD has directed."*
GENESIS 24:51 NLT

Perhaps the hardest thing for a father to do is to give his daughter away on her wedding day. The little girl he has cherished since she was a tiny infant now belongs to another man, and Daddy's role as her protector and guide has been forever replaced. Yet a good father will only allow the finest suitor to wed his child, and your heavenly Father is no different.

For thousands of years, God has specialized in matchmaking. Just as Rebekah was chosen especially for Isaac (Genesis 24:42–44), so you were chosen for your husband! God knew exactly what each of you needed in a spouse. Which personality would best complement yours. . .which qualities would bring out the best in him. He put the two of you together for a purpose, and He delights in watching what His careful plans have produced.

Whether you've known your husband since childhood or met unexpectedly as adults, you can rest assured that you didn't come together by chance. God had His hand in it from the beginning. You were *given* to your husband and he to you, and there is no greater gift than the one that God gives.

*Father, thank You for giving me the husband best suited for me.
Help me to ever be the wife that he needs and to always
remember that it was You who put us together. Amen.*

Read It. . .Then Do It!

Day
37

*But the man who looks intently into the perfect law
that gives freedom, and continues to do this, not forgetting what
he has heard, but doing it—he will be blessed in what he does.*
JAMES 1:25 NIV

It is so important to read scripture together as a couple. God's Word is "living and active" (Hebrews 4:12). It has the power to change lives. However, you can read the Bible all day long and it won't mean a thing unless you start practicing what you've read! The Bible says that if we keep looking into and reading God's Word. . .and then *do* it—we will be blessed! It doesn't say that if we just read the Word, we'll be blessed. We have to actually get up and do something about it!

The next time you sit down to read scripture, have a plan. First, pray that God would open your eyes and heart to His Word. Then begin reading the Word slowly, prayerfully, carefully. Write down the verses that speak to your heart, mind, and spirit. Then consider how you can apply them to your marriage and your everyday life.

And if your husband is open to sharing this special time with you, by all means, do it together. The main thing is to make an effort to prayerfully read, study, and apply God's Word to our lives each and every day. For when we do, the blessings will follow.

Dear Lord, thank You for giving us Your Word. Give us the desire to read it each day and then help us to do what it says. In Jesus' name, amen.

Bad Encouragement

*And when the woman saw that the tree was good
for food, and that it was pleasant to the eyes, and a tree to be desired
to make one wise, she took of the fruit thereof, and did eat,
and gave also unto her husband with her; and he did eat.*
GENESIS 3:6 KJV

The fruit was so tempting. It was beautiful; it was perfect. And to Eve it was irresistible. So when the serpent encouraged her to take a bite, she did so willingly. Then she took it to her husband. We don't really know why. Maybe it really did just taste delicious. It could be that she wanted to lessen her own feeling of guilt and thought that if Adam ate, too, it would justify her own sin. Whatever the case, we know that Eve encouraged Adam to do wrong. It was the start of trouble and sadness.

While our bad encouragement isn't likely to affect the whole world, it will affect those we love the most—family, friends, church, etc. Be careful how you encourage your husband. Eve encouraged Adam to sin, but bad encouragement isn't always sin. For example, buying a new car isn't wrong unless you can't afford it or don't need it. If you talk your husband into buying something beyond your means, that's bad encouragement and can be just as detrimental as something that is specifically sin.

So be careful how you encourage your man. It can make or break your marriage and testimony.

*Father, let me be a positive,
helpful encouragement to the man I love.*

The Silent Treatment

*When I kept silent, my bones wasted away
through my groaning all day long.*
PSALM 32:3 NIV

The argument began with a simple question. Greg merely asked his wife, Julie, what time he should tell his parents to come for Christmas dinner. Julie's angry response surprised them both. They talked in circles for almost an hour before the real issue came to the surface. Julie felt threatened by Greg's mother. The two women had initially enjoyed one another's company, but over the past few years Julie felt more and more like there was nothing she could do to please her mother-in-law. Julie became bitter, resenting any time she had to spend with her in-laws. This was news to Greg—he always felt his wife and mom had a good relationship. He was surprised and more than a little hurt when Julie revealed her true feelings.

It can be risky to share your feelings with your husband—especially when you're not sure what those feelings are or are afraid the truth might hurt him. However, God's Word says that keeping silent about our feelings can be detrimental to us and our relationships. Stifling our feelings doesn't make them go away. Instead it makes them build up and simmer to a slow boil, eventually causing us to explode in anger, saying things we later regret. While it's not realistic or beneficial to say everything that pops into our heads, it is a wise practice to share feelings as they arise. Both your marriage and your emotional health will benefit when you share your feelings in an honest and loving way.

*Father, help me not to confuse holding my tongue with holding in my feelings.
Teach me to be honest and authentic with my husband, ultimately trusting
You to help me sort out my sometimes confusing feelings. Amen.*

Rejoicing in a Parking Lot

*Be glad in the LORD and rejoice, you righteous ones;
and shout for joy, all you who are upright in heart.*
PSALM 32:11 NASB

*M*aybe she'd been beautiful twenty years earlier, but she certainly wasn't now. Her face was wrinkled. Her hair looked as though she'd pinned it up in the dark with one hand tied behind her back. But there she was, riding on the front of the shopping cart like a kid, grinning from ear to ear as her husband pushed her across the parking lot. He grinned back and leaned forward to plant a proud kiss on her lips. It was obvious that he didn't notice her wrinkled skin and messy hair. Her joy made her beautiful to him.

Working a stressful job or being at home all day with small children can take its toll on our joy and our faces. We don't always have the time to look our best when we see our husbands at the end of the day. But we can steal a minute or two to do a "joy" makeover. Why not try it right now? Praise the Lord for His goodness, think about the beauty of His creation, and thank Him for His many blessings.

Makeup, tooth whiteners, and hair dyes can cover up a lot of flaws, but the joy of the Lord will really make us glow from the inside out.

*Dear Lord, You are so good that I can't help but rejoice.
Fill me with Your joy as I go about my day. Help my face reflect Your glory.
Amen.*

Natural Beauty

*She makes her own clothing, and dresses
in colorful linens and silks.*
PROVERBS 31:22 MSG

*H*ave you let down your guard a bit since you've been married? When you were dating you wanted to look your best at all times, so you chose the perfect outfit, applied impeccable makeup, and even used perfume. But after marriage, it may have been easy to slip into a lazy pattern of comfy sweats, a scrubbed face, and Ivory soap as perfume.

Yes, natural beauty is great, and inner beauty is most important. But God did create our husbands to be motivated visually. They take notice when we honor them by taking a little extra time on ourselves. Femininity and womanly things make them feel strong and help to more clearly define the beautiful differences between men and women.

Today, take a little extra time to put on some makeup, pick out a nice outfit, and show your husband that you think he is worth the effort.

*Father, please forgive me for taking my husband for granted by not taking
time to make myself physically appealing to him. Help me to want to please
him and to remember that one way I can do that is by taking care of myself.
Amen.*

That Dreaded "S" Word

Wives, submit to your husbands as to the Lord.
EPHESIANS 5:22 NIV

Emily braced herself. Yikes—a sermon on submission, her least favorite biblical topic! After ten years in a Christian marriage, it was a subject about which she was still in the learning process.

Emily had always prided herself on her independent thinking. Successful in business, she was regarded as a community leader. Her husband, Kyle, respected her judgment and sought her opinion in decisions concerning the family. So why did she chafe when this subject arose? Why did wifely submission seem so. . .*unfair*?

Emily's mind drifted to the wedding reception she'd attended the night before. She and Kyle had attempted ballroom dancing, but in their inexperience, they'd succeeded only in stomping each other's feet, butting noggins, and pushing each other around the floor, wrestling for the lead.

Marriage is like dancing, Emily decided. *There must be a leader and a follower. If both partners try to lead, they fall out of sync, inflicting wounds, and creating resentment.*

Submission doesn't mean we're weak or any less capable than our husbands. It simply means we choose to let him lead the dance.

Lord of the dance, help me remember that when I'm submitting to my partner, I'm really submitting to You. I value my marriage and trust You enough to follow Your leadership so that my beloved partner and I can continue dancing until the last note resounds. Amen.

Bending Hearts

*Praise be to the God and Father of our Lord Jesus Christ,
the Father of compassion and the God of all comfort.*
2 CORINTHIANS 1:3 NIV

There is a sadness that settles into our heart when we realize that the dreams we brought into our marriage are often different from the way things really are. The loss of those expectations is as great as any other. This sadness can spill into the rest of our lives and fool us into thinking that somehow our marriage has failed us.

We all suffer when our expectations are not met. The challenge for us, then, is to mourn their passing without falling into despair. Surprisingly, the death of what we want can leave a space for what we still need. So even though our expectations may have died, our hope has not.

God quietly waits through our struggles until we invite Him in. He empathizes with our grief, for He has suffered, too. He hears prayers whispered on tearstained pillows after angry words are said. He is the reason we feel less troubled when morning comes. Day by day, He offers a new vision for our marriage, where He is the center of peace and understanding. He soothes our souls with gentle hands so when we do face disappointment, our hearts and those of our husbands will bend toward each other rather than break apart.

*Father, sometimes I feel lonelier in my marriage than I ever did by myself.
Help me to release my grip on my expectations, realize my hope that things
will get better, and trust that You will bring me closer to my husband. Amen.*

Day
44

Beloved

I am my beloved's, and my beloved is mine.
SONG OF SOLOMON 6:3 KJV

On Valentine's Day, how do you plan to celebrate your love for your husband? You could start by reading all or part of the Song of Solomon together. Maybe you are one of those couples who goes all-out for Valentine's Day—you know, romantic dinners, thoughtful gifts, and sentimental cards. On the other hand, you might be rather cynical about the commercialism of the holiday. Be honest with yourself, though. You *can* find a way to make this day extra special for your husband and yourself.

The Song of Solomon really is a beautiful story of love—not just between Solomon and his beloved but also between Christ and His beloved. That is *you*, if you've accepted Him as Savior. As Christ's bride, your earthly marriage is to be a reflection of your spiritual union. All the love and commitment that you enjoy with your husband is multiplied with Christ. How He adores you! How deep is your love for Him? He has such powerful ways of showing His commitment to you. Will you requite?

As you celebrate Valentine's Day with your own beloved, be sure to include your heavenly Groom. He, too, will rejoice in your love for each other.

Lord Jesus, thank You for this love of my life.
Join us as we celebrate this special day together.

In-Laws!

"The two will become one flesh."
1 CORINTHIANS 6:16 NIV

There are many times in marriage when well-intentioned family members get too involved in your marriage. This is especially hard for young couples who have always taken Mom and Dad's advice on everything. It's often just as hard for the parents as it is for the newlyweds! The Bible is very clear that a newly married couple has become one and needs to become independent of their parents. Now, this certainly doesn't mean that you cut yourself off and disregard all advice from your parents. But it does mean that you need to consider your spouse's opinion and take things to him *first*! There isn't anything that will harm your marriage faster than a spouse who still "lives at home" emotionally, financially, or sometimes even physically (when you are spending more time at your parents' home than with your spouse).

If you feel like there is tension in your marriage over the "in-laws," now is the time to talk this out. Sit down with your spouse and find out where this tension is coming from. Then work out a plan to becoming more independent so that you truly become "one flesh."

Father, we want our marriage to honor You. Please help us to become one flesh and work at becoming independent of our families. Amen.

Deep Roots

*"And he said to the vinedresser, 'Look, for three years
now I have come seeking fruit on this fig tree, and I find none.
Cut it down. . . .' And [the vinedresser] answered him, 'Sir, let it alone this
year also, until I dig around it and put on manure. Then if it should bear
fruit next year, well and good; but if not, you can cut it down.'"*
LUKE 13:7–9 ESV

As we read this parable, we may ask ourselves, Why did God call us to Himself? After all, we often think we'll never win any awards for fruit-bearing. Our marriages often seem fairly ordinary, our testimonies less than exciting, our ministries faithful but limited.

Yet in the same way God did not chop down the barren tree, He has not cut us down. Looking to the future, He digs at our comfortable roots, challenging us to change. Then He fertilizes us with His Word, causing our roots to go deep into faith's soil.

Because God hasn't finished with us yet, let's put ourselves in the path of growth through study, prayer, and fellowship. One day, we'll see that long-awaited fruit and rejoice with God at what He's done through us.

Are we ready to grow? Let's put our roots deep into His Word today.

*Lord, thank You for Your gracious love that builds me up instead of cutting
me off at the roots. Help my roots go deep in faith today.*

A Request for Wisdom

*Now, O LORD my God, you have made me king
instead of my father, David, but I am like a little
child who doesn't know his way around.*
1 KINGS 3:7 NLT

This prayer occurs one evening after Solomon has replaced David as the king of Israel. God appears to Solomon in a dream and offers to give him whatever he wants. Instead of asking for wealth or long life or triumph over his enemies, Solomon asks for wisdom. Solomon wants to rule wisely but, as he says, he feels like a little child. Therefore, Solomon asks for the ability to decide between right and wrong and to lead his people as a true follower of God.

Solomon's example stands out for us today. We need wisdom in our relationships, particularly as we strive to grow in godliness and love with our spouses.

At some point in your marriage, perhaps you have felt like a little child. A new situation arises an argument you've never had before, a life-altering change, the death of a loved one. God is waiting for your prayer, and He desires to guide you in His unsurpassed wisdom. Like little children, we must ask God for help; He will help us find our way.

*Dear Lord, You are wise beyond understanding.
Grant me Your wisdom today in my relationships and in my current
situations. Thank You for Your love and guidance. Amen.*

Day
48

Soulful Connection

There is a time for everything. . .
a time to embrace and a time to refrain.
ECCLESIASTES 3:1, 5 NIV

Sometimes couples grow apart because of sheer busyness. Details of daily life can crowd out the time required to keep a marriage healthy.

Kara and Jim, a two-career couple, were concerned at the growing distance between them. A friend recommended having a once-a-week date night. It was a good idea but not for Kara and Jim. Conversations at night quickly soured due to fatigue. Instead, they switched their date night to a date morning. They woke up early on Saturday mornings to go out for coffee together, before their teenagers were awake. They felt fresh, rested, and discovered that their communication skills flowed more easily in the morning. So did their listening skills.

Date mornings became a small but significant effort that started to impact other parts of Kara and Jim's marriage. Through something as simple and doable as good timing, they found a way to connect again.

Good timing seems like a small thing, but it is actually a very big thing. A biblical thing. "There is a time for everything," Solomon wrote thousands of years ago. That wisdom holds true today.

Lord, all good relationships take time. Today, help me to set aside the demands of daily living and spend time with You, the source of my blessings.

But Seek First

But seek ye first the kingdom of God,
and his righteousness; and all these things shall be added unto you.
MATTHEW 6:33 KJV

Times were tough. Her husband's business was slowing down. Bills were beginning to mount. She was torn. Should she seek full-time employment or continue in volunteer ministry? Prayerfully, she and her husband sought the Lord's wisdom. They sensed the Lord asking them to trust Him financially while she served in ministry. By faith they followed the Lord's leading. Soon afterward, an unexpected check came in the mail to cover current expenses. Gradually, her husband's business began to prosper. God supplied their needs as they sought and followed His will.

Many times we are called to make difficult choices. We must glean God's wisdom for discernment. After seeking His wisdom, we must trust Him in obedience. That may require following our heads rather than our hearts or exercising faith rather than succumbing to fear. When we trust and obey, the Lord will take care of the rest. He will reward our faith. He will confirm that His way is indeed the best. He will meet our needs as we follow His will, despite the difficulties. Seek His kingdom and watch the Lord provide for you!

Dear Lord, may I seek You above all else
and trust that You will meet my needs. Amen.

Reverse the Curse

*Unto the woman he said, I will greatly multiply thy
sorrow and thy conception; in sorrow thou shalt bring forth children;
and thy desire shall be to thy husband, and he shall rule over thee.*
GENESIS 3:16 KJV

After Mother Eve had fallen to the devil's deception and led her husband to sin, God cursed her in her primary area of ministry—the home.

She had been designed to help her husband and bring forth children. But now God told her she would suffer during childbearing. And worse than that, the relationship between her and her husband would be a constant struggle. As she had taken the lead to eat from the forbidden tree, so she would always want to lead, but her husband would rule over her.

Fortunately for Eve and us, the curse has a cure. But it cannot be achieved by our own will alone.

We must be in a right relationship to our Creator, having been saved by His Son, Jesus Christ, and having His Spirit within. As we allow the Spirit to rule in our hearts, we will find the power to honor our husbands and lovingly submit to their leadership, rather than chafe beneath their rule.

Through Christ, marriages can return to the Garden and find peace.

Through Him, we can reverse the curse.

*Lord Jesus, show me when I am caught in the curse.
Open my eyes to the areas where I am most prone to disobey my husband.
Remind me always that submission is Your will for me. Amen.*

*Examine yourselves as to whether you are in the faith.
Test yourselves. Do you not know yourselves,
that Jesus Christ is in you?*
2 CORINTHIANS 13:5 NKJV

How many times do we almost drown in the floodwaters of fear? How often are we overcome by waves of discontent or pulled by currents of doubt? How often do we forget that Jesus Christ, the Master of the Universe, is within us? He has already saved us from doubt, disappointment, dread, and death. In His strength, we can move mountains. We can change the world. We can be His representative of peace, strength, and love within our family, our neighborhood, and our workplace.

Jesus, the One with the power to rebuke the winds and calm the waters, is our lifesaver. The knowledge that He is within us boosts us up above the waves of fear and into the peace of His presence.

When caught up in the riptides of life, we are to examine ourselves to make sure we are acknowledging the *fact* that *Christ resides within us.* Buoyed by His presence, we can withstand the storm and rise up in the power of His strength.

Jesus, You are the one who has saved my life, the one who resides within me. Give me the wisdom to keep this in my mind throughout my day, and give me the power to do Your will in this world, knowing You have overcome it. Amen.

In the Arms of a Friend

But we all, with unveiled face, beholding as in a
mirror the glory of the Lord, are being transformed into the
same image from glory to glory, just as by the Spirit of the Lord.
2 CORINTHIANS 3:18 NKJV

Shanna found the weeks following the birth of their second son emotional and a true test of faith. Finally, God had proven faithful and restored her newborn to health in spite of the doctor's words, "He only has a fifty-fifty chance of survival." Yet he completely recovered and was home.

The crisis over, Shanna's emotions were more than she could handle, and she found herself at the front door of her friend Barbie. As the door opened, Shanna fell into Barbie's arms.

Fighting to gain her composure, Barbie spoke the words Shanna needed to hear. "It's over. The baby's fine. Now get ahold of your emotions, girl! You're a woman of faith! With God at your side—you won!"

Tears turned to laughter. "I know," Shanna said, "but I needed to hear what you just said."

Have you ever found comfort from God through a friend? God brings His comfort to our hearts in many ways, but often He touches us most through the compassion of our brothers and sisters in Christ. Perhaps God wants to use you to touch someone today. Are you willing?

Thank You, Lord, for friendships.
Give me compassion and a willingness to be
used as Your hand in someone's life. Amen.

Expectations

Day
53

My soul, wait only upon God and silently submit to Him;
for my hope and expectation are from Him.
PSALM 62:5 AMP

*E*xpectations—we all have them. No matter what the circumstances or which people are involved, we anticipate good coming our way. Marriage is no exception. Both husbands and wives enter the marriage with realistic and unrealistic hopes and dreams of what that marriage can be.

Wives want to feel loved, accepted, appreciated, secure; husbands want to be respected, loved, pampered, needed. Many marriage counselors and pastors warn us of having unrealistic expectations because it's human nature to think of self first, not others. And it's easiest to slip into selfish habits with the people we live with.

When our husbands fail to meet our needs, we feel hurt, and this can result in angry and bitter thoughts and words. Then our husbands react negatively, and often we're left wondering what happened to the rosy picture of marriage we'd clung to throughout our growing-up years.

Scripture tells us that the only One who can meet our every need is God. We can safely hang all our hopes and desires on Him. He never fails. As our Creator, He knows what we need even more than we can imagine. So let's give our husbands a break, look at our expectations realistically, and rest in God, waiting for Him to satisfy our deepest needs.

Father, give me the grace to accept my husband as he is, knowing that he will
fail me at times. You never fail. Only You can satisfy my deepest needs. Amen.

Deadly Poison

*Thou shalt not go up and down as a talebearer
among thy people: neither shalt thou stand against
the blood of thy neighbour: I am the LORD.*
LEVITICUS 19:16 KJV

Gossip is the favorite pastime of far too many Christian women. Probably all of us have been guilty of it at one time or another. The truth is that God hates gossip, and it doesn't matter if a person is a casual talebearer or a chronic one. God is not fooled when we attempt to disguise gossip as prayerful concern, and most people probably aren't fooled either.

The really sad thing is that often when we gossip, we focus our discussion on those we love—our husbands, close friends, or other family members. It's possible that this is because we know more about these people and are more likely to pick up on their faults. Still, it is not right. Gossip is often as deadly as murder.

Another area we fail to acknowledge as gossip is "discussion" with our husbands. It's true that our communication with our spouses should be more open than it is with other people. There are times when talking things over with our husbands is necessary, even though the same conversation with someone else would be gossip. Just be careful not to "over-discuss" something. Otherwise it begins to fester and boils into talebearing.

Remember: You will not please God if you are prone to gossip.

*O Lord, I can bring all things before You.
I don't need to spread gossip like a virus.*

Pretty Woman

Thou art a fair woman to look upon.
GENESIS 12:11 KJV

No matter how often men are admonished to seek the inner qualities of a potential mate, the fact remains that they are attracted to beauty. One fine day, you turned your future husband's head, compelled him to meet you, and to ultimately fall in love with you. It may have been your inner qualities that won him in the end, but it was your outward beauty that hooked him in the first place.

Now, after you have successfully captured your man and sealed your vows of marriage, is no time to leave your appearance by the wayside. Long after the honeymoon, your face and figure are still important to your husband. Remember how much time you took to get ready for a date? The pains you took with your hair? The outfit that had to be *just so*? Take the same care now that you are married. Time will take its inevitable toll on your body without your helping it along through neglect and carelessness.

Be beautiful for your husband! Dress up for him! Show him that years after your wedding, he's still worth the fuss. By doing so, you will ever be the woman that he can't wait to come home to.

Dear God, thank You for making me beautiful in the sight of my husband. Help me to take care of my body and maintain the beauty that You have created in me. Amen.

Day
56

*Looking Ahead to
Where God Is*

*But Jesus told him, "Anyone who puts a hand to the
plow and then looks back is not fit for the Kingdom of God."*
LUKE 9:62 NLT

We know that we shouldn't worry about tomorrow, but even worse is to worry and feel regret about the past, which can only cripple us for tomorrow. "I wish things could be the way they were." "I wish I were younger." "I wish my husband treated me like he did when we first met." "I wish I could fit into those jeans again. . . ." "I wish, I wish, I wish."

Although the Lord doesn't want us looking back at what once was, our enemy does. He wants us to feel discouraged and helpless over what we face today and drown in self-pity about how it was in the past. But God wants us to look ahead to the future. The future is where He is. He promises to give us hope in our futures. Let's claim that promise for ourselves, for our spouses, and for our marriages. Let's forget the past—it's long gone already and cannot be changed. Let's move ahead and press toward the new things that the Lord wants to do in our lives.

*Jesus, please help me to lay aside my past regrets and longings for the things
that have already faded away. Let me find contentment in the present and
hope for the future. Guide me into the future in accordance with Your will.
Amen.*

Marriage Disaster Kit

Those who marry will face
many troubles in this life.
1 CORINTHIANS 7:28 NIV

*S*mart homeowners have a disaster kit stashed away in case of emergency. Flashlights, extra batteries, drinking water, canned food. . . Having a plan for when disaster strikes is not only prudent, it saves lives. The same is true for our marriages. When the last of the wedding cake has been served and the punch bowl is empty, many new couples ride off into the honeymoon sunset, eagerly anticipating how they will live happily ever after. But couples who've been married for longer than a few years (or even a few months) know that "happily ever after" is the stuff of fairy tales. Marriage takes work. Hard work. Even Paul, who wasn't married, said that "those who marry will face many troubles in this life."

Crisis in marriage is inevitable. It makes sense to be prepared. How? By praying, studying, and applying God's Word. Learning how to communicate well—before you experience communication problems. Talking about anything and everything. Establishing a relationship with a godly counselor and scheduling regular "marriage checkups" when you're not in crisis. Finding accountability partners, both for you individually and as a couple. Then instead of being surprised when you experience marriage troubles, you'll be prepared and better able to face those troubles with strength and grace.

Heavenly Father, thank You for my husband. Even though
marriage is hard, it is a gift, and I pray that we will prepare
wisely so that when trouble comes, we will emerge victoriously.

Shared Ministry

*[Apollos] began to speak boldly in the synagogue,
but when Priscilla and Aquila heard him, they took him
and explained to him the way of God more accurately.*
ACTS 18:26 ESV

*T*alk about a shared ministry! From what we read in
scripture, Priscilla and Aquila worked together as a flawless
team.

Paul met the couple in Corinth, after they'd fled persecution
in Rome. The apostle lived and worked with this pair of
tentmakers, who founded a house church in Corinth. When
Apollos came to the Corinthian ministry team's hometown,
preaching an incomplete gospel, the couple took him in and
taught him more.

We'd probably all like to share such a ministry with our
spouses and imagine it would be smooth sailing. Yet doubtless
Priscilla and Aquila faced their fair share of challenges. Both
involved in a consuming ministry, they probably spent fewer
hours together than they would have liked. Finding time to
complete all the tents that were ordered may have been a
challenge. The Bible doesn't tell us such details—it records their
faithfulness, not their troubles. But every couple faces challenges,
and surely this couple didn't escape them all.

Are we facing ministry challenges—alone or with our
husbands? Let's not think that God does not approve of our
work. Let's remain faithful. Then, as with Priscilla and Aquila,
God can give us a good report.

*Lord, help us to serve others, as You have called us.
But help us to always bring glory to Your name.*

Diligent Hearts

*Above all else, guard your heart,
for it is the wellspring of life.*
PROVERBS 4:23 NIV

*E*llen pondered the better life she would have if she divorced her husband and married Charlie. Ellen pictured a peaceful life where they would grow old, living happily ever after. . . . After all, isn't that what God desires?

Well, sort of. God does desire for us to have a peaceful life, but He does not intend for us to divorce to have peace. God is able to work peace into our current marriages.

One of the means God uses to infuse peace into our marriages is by exhorting us to watch over or guard our hearts. This is of the utmost critical importance to the Lord, so much so that God tells us, "*Above all else*, guard your heart. . ."

Other Bible translations encourage us to keep our hearts with diligence or vigilance. Since our hearts are the source or wellspring for the abundant life God gives us (John 10:10), we are to be attentive and careful with what we allow into our hearts and consequently our marriages. We are to say no to fantasies of life with another. We are to shield what we watch on TV, read on the Internet and in magazines, and what we allow our minds to dwell upon. God tells us to think about whatever is true, honorable, just, pure, pleasing, commendable, excellent, and praiseworthy (Philippians 4:8). God will protect and provide peace in our marriages through our diligence in guarding our hearts.

*Lord, I desire an abundant, peaceful life with my husband.
Protect my marriage by enabling me to diligently guard my heart.*

Love and Respect

*However, each one of you also must love his wife as
he loves himself, and the wife must respect her husband.*
EPHESIANS 5:33 NIV

Husbands are called to love. Wives are called to respect. Why the distinction? What does R-E-S-P-E-C-T mean? Aretha Franklin emphatically defined the word in her 1960s song by the same name. According to Merriam-Webster's, to respect someone means "to consider worthy of high regard; esteem; to refrain from interfering with." Maybe loving our husbands would have been easier!

Respecting our husbands means we value what they say and what they stand for. We hold their opinions in high regard. We ask for their counsel because we truly believe it is wise and astute. We do not attempt to circumvent their plans or ideas. There is no room for manipulation or deception, conniving or contriving, to railroad our agenda.

As wives we yearn to be loved by our husbands. In the same way our husbands yearn to be respected by us. That's God's design. When our husbands are truly respected, they will be more compelled to respond with love toward us. God has a plan for marital relationships. Let's do our part by respecting our husbands. When we do, our marriages will thrive!

*Dear Lord, forgive me for not respecting my husband as I should.
Teach me how to esteem and value him. Amen.*

Loving Mercy

*He has shown you, O man, what is good;
and what does the LORD require of you but to do justly,
to love mercy, and to walk humbly with your God?*
MICAH 6:8 NKJV

We love the mercy God extends to us. No matter what we do wrong, God is so willing to forgive us and show His infinite mercy when we are repentant. The emotions this arouses are incomparable to anything else—that the God who created the universe would love us so much.

So what does God ask of us? He asks that we do our best to be like His Son, Jesus, or like Him. We are called to show mercy to those who offend or do wrong against us. Many times in a marriage our husbands will knowingly or even unwittingly hurt us. Sometimes those offenses leave deep wounds that take time to heal. Yet God calls us to show mercy. How? By walking humbly with Him.

Each time we feel we can't bear up under the hurt, we must remember the times and ways we have hurt God. How does He react? Does He lash out in anger? Does He turn His back on us and refuse to acknowledge our presence? Never. God is always there with His arms outstretched, love shining from Him like a beacon to our wounded souls. We need to learn to be likewise to our husbands, no matter what.

God, give me the grace to extend mercy as You do. Help me to be humble before You and to become an extension of Your love. Amen.

Day
62

Change

*Jesus Christ is the same yesterday
and today and forever.*
HEBREWS 13:8 NIV

*A*re you and your husband experiencing a lot of change in your life right now? Maybe a career change, a big move, or a child going off to college? Or maybe you aren't facing a huge change but every day seems to hold quite a few variations and challenges.

Change can be very unsettling and downright scary sometimes. Even the small daily changes tend to eat away at us and have us wishing for something predictable! If we aren't grounded in Christ, change can send us tumbling over the edge. Isn't it wonderful that He gives us the assurance that He will never change? He is the same yesterday, today, and forever! Jesus Christ is with you always. He sees all of the unpredictable moments that creep—or slam—into your life. Remember that these moments have passed through His hands before He allows them to greet you.

Change can actually be a good thing! It might not seem like it at the time, but the Lord will work all things together for your good (Romans 8:28) if you love Him. You can trust that God has a plan for your life and He will be with you through all of the changes you will face.

*Dear Jesus, help me to trust in You through all of the changes in my life.
Thank You for never changing and always being there for me.
In Your name, amen.*

Learning to Love

*Then the LORD said to me, "Go and love your wife again,
even though she commits adultery with another lover.
This will illustrate that the LORD still loves Israel, even though
the people have turned to other gods and love to worship them."*

HOSEA 3:1 NLT

God trained Hosea in what it meant to love an unrepentant wife. Through the prophet's selfless response to his wife's failings, all who read Hosea's book understand what it means to be truly loved by God.

Hosea isn't the only man who has had to learn how to love his wife. Most newlyweds find themselves in something of the same situation. Brides also quickly discover that the man they love has much to learn about loving them. But a faithful woman teaches her husband what pleases her—and seeks in turn to discover what makes her husband happy. The two have begun a lifelong lesson in godly love.

No one comes into marriage knowing how to love perfectly. But with time, consideration, and God's tutelage, we learn to make a happy marriage that glorifies our Lord. Comfortingly, we do not go into marriage alone. When we marry in Christ, we are part of a cord of three strands that binds our hearts together (Ecclesiastes 4:12).

With the help of our Lord, our marriage can become a testimony to His love.

Lord, help me learn to love my husband as You would have him loved.

*Moses:
Friend of God and
of His People*

*And the LORD said unto Moses, I will do this thing also that thou hast
spoken: for thou hast found grace in my sight, and I know thee by name.*
EXODUS 33:17 KJV

God talked with Moses on Mount Sinai while the Israelites gathered at the foot of the mountain, awestruck at His presence and accompanying fire, lightning, thunder, and trumpet blasts. God wrote the Ten Commandments on stone tablets with His finger and promised to dwell with them.

But when Moses did not return immediately, the people grew a little bored with God. They created their own excitement: a golden calf and a wild festival to celebrate their new deity. Moses set them straight, but because of their idol worship, the Lord informed Moses He would no longer accompany them.

Moses could have abandoned the Israelites, who had caused him endless headaches. But he pleaded for them and even asked God to blot out his own name in His book if He would not forgive them. God spoke with Moses "face to face, as a man speaketh unto his friend" (Exodus 33:11 KJV). God told His faithful servant He would accompany the Israelites because of Moses' intercession.

What an encouragement to us who intercede for family members who defy God and seem bent on self-destruction! Our prayers can make an enormous difference in their lives.

*Lord Jesus, I cannot control my loved ones' choices, but I choose to follow the
One who can rescue them. Thank You for the privilege of intercessory prayer.
Amen.*

Future Perfect

*Now unto him that is able to keep you from falling,
and to present you faultless before the presence of his glory
with exceeding joy, to the only wise God our Saviour,
be glory and majesty, dominion and power.*
JUDE 1:24–25 KJV

Will slammed the back door so hard that the house shook. Erica felt tempted to yank it open and yell after him, but she made herself a mugful of tea, trying to calm her angry thoughts and pounding heart.

Will always made fun of her preference for tea over coffee. The thought made her boil inside. "We can't even agree on beverages, Lord, let alone budgets!" Erica's eyes filled with tears. "And we thought we were perfect for each other!"

She saw Will in their garden, yanking weeds as if they were enemies. Erica almost giggled. He looked so funny, pitching clumps of ragweed into the vacant lot next door as if they were baseballs. In that moment, God's peace began to soothe her raw irritation. Yes, she and Will sometimes rubbed each other the wrong way. They had lots to learn. But both had committed themselves to Christ and to each other. He would help them work it out.

Erica drank her tea, bowed her head, prayed, and then headed for the garden. Will had slowed down a little, but she'd better apologize before he started on the radishes!

Father, help us get past our disagreements by the power of Your forgiveness. And please help us remember heaven's not here—yet. Amen.

Serving Together

*The churches of Asia greet you. Aquila and Priscilla
greet you heartily in the Lord, with the church that is in their house.*
1 CORINTHIANS 16:19 NKJV

*I*n the Bible, there are numerous references to men and
women who were followers of Jesus during His earthly life
or became believers after His death. Some of these women were
widows, singles, or wives.

At least one of those wives, Priscilla, did not serve Jesus
alone. Aquila, the husband of Priscilla, was also a believer.
Together, this couple started a church in their home.

It is a great joy when we can serve the Lord together with
our husbands, and this is the ideal plan for ministry. But the
husband must lead. A wife should help and follow.

A woman who leads in this area may trouble her own home,
particularly if her husband lacks faith. A husband who is not
walking obediently may be embarrassed by his wife's devotion
to the Lord. An unbelieving husband may become hostile to a
believing wife's ministry.

A wife's first ministry is to her husband. If you are faithful
here, you will encourage an apathetic believer, and you may see
your unbelieving husband saved.

Remain diligent in your home mission and someday you may
find yourself—and your husband—serving the Lord beyond the
house together.

*Father, whenever I hear of a need "out there," I want to meet it,
even if I must meet it alone. Yet I don't want to provoke my husband
by leading. I'll wait for You to lead him so I can follow. Amen.*

Giant Killers

Day
67

Go. . . . And may the LORD be with you!
1 SAMUEL 17:37 NLT

Feeling bullied? Discouraged? Are others trying to fit you into their mold? Are giant-sized problems looming before you?

Welcome to David's world. When he boldly claimed that he would fight Goliath, his brother Eliab assaulted him with dispiriting remarks. But David simply defended his position and then walked away.

King Saul told David he was no match for Goliath. But David, remembering how God had helped him in the past, responded with "The LORD who rescued me from the claws of the lion and the bear will rescue me from this Philistine!" (1 Samuel 17:37 NLT).

The resigned Saul then tried to fit David into his battle gear—an uncomfortable fit for a shepherd boy. So David shed the armor, along with Saul's sword, and picked up his usual weapons—a sling and some stones.

When the Philistine giant saw David, he mocked and abused him. David said, "I come to you in the name of the LORD. . . . Today the LORD will conquer you" (1 Samuel 17:45-46 NLT). Then he took out a stone and hurled it at Goliath. The stone sank into the giant's forehead, and the behemoth fell facedown.

Ladies, we, like David, can refuse to allow the words of discouragers, naysayers, molders, and giants to affect us. We, too, can walk forward in God's name and power. He will help us vanquish every negative word, thought, and deed and lead us to triumph!

God, give me the strength and the power to walk forth in Your name,
to turn away from the negative remarks of others,
to be who You've called me to be, and to conquer the giants of this world.

Expectations

So often we have expectations for our husbands. They aren't unreasonable in our eyes. The longer we're married, the more those expectations blossom until our poor husbands have a list of actions to adhere to that is so long they can't hope to accomplish it. If they don't do as we think they should, we get angry or petulant until they come back in line or there is a confrontation.

Instead of being free to be the head of the home, the husband often finds he is restricted by our expectations. He can no longer act in the manner the Lord has designed for him without incurring our displeasure. As loving wives, we must break the bonds of our expectations and allow our husband to be the way God made him.

Many times we expect God to act in a way we have already planned. We pray with that in mind and are disappointed when the answer to prayer isn't right in our eyes. We are so sure of what God's answer should be that we don't stop to consider our inability to see through His eyes. We must give God the freedom to work His way in our lives.

*Thank You, God, for Your patience with me.
Help me to love my husband, and You, without conditions. Amen.*

God's Delight

"The LORD your God is with you, he is mighty to save.
He will take great delight in you, he will quiet you with his love,
he will rejoice over you with singing."
ZEPHANIAH 3:17 NIV

Think of the joy you experienced on your wedding day as you walked down the aisle to meet your bridegroom. Your eyes met his, and you could see his love for you as he saw only you. His face shone in delight and joy. As you gazed into the eyes of your lover, your nervousness fled. You quietly basked in his love and calmly spoke your vows pledging to honor your husband and love him. Silently you vowed to do nothing that would cause that delight to fade.

The same is true of our heavenly Bridegroom. He loves us so much that He died for us to bring us into fellowship with Him. He delights in us, His chosen from before the foundation of the world. His face shines with a love so incomprehensible and deep that all fear flees and we quietly bask in His love. A song of praise bursts from us, harmonizing perfectly with the song of rejoicing that He sings over us. One day we will fully comprehend this great love that quiets us, rejuvenates us, and gives us reason to live for Him.

Jesus, may I rest in Your love today. May I hear Your song of rejoicing that You sing over me. May Your love quiet me no matter what I face today. Amen.

Letting Go

*As God's chosen people, holy and dearly loved,
clothe yourselves with compassion, kindness, humility, gentleness
and patience. Bear with each other and forgive whatever grievances
you may have against one another. Forgive as the Lord forgave you.*
COLOSSIANS 3:12–13 NIV

Christine knew she needed to forgive her friend Sandy. She valued the relationship and wanted to make things right. However, she couldn't stop rehearsing the ordeal in her mind. How could Sandy have been so thoughtless? The harder Christine tried to make herself forgive, the further away forgiveness seemed. Then Sandy's father died and Christine decided to take her a meal. As Christine prepared the casserole, she found herself praying for Sandy. Her heart broke in grief. She knew how it felt to lose a parent. As the day went on, Christine spent less time rehearsing the pain and more time simply praying for her friend. The feelings of injustice that seemed so deep-rooted were gradually replaced by feelings of kindness and compassion. By the time Christine arrived to deliver the meal, she realized she'd forgiven Sandy.

We speak of working toward forgiveness, but this effort can sometimes be counterproductive. Perhaps we would do better to work toward feeling genuine Christlike compassion for others, to think of ways to treat them with kindness and patience, to pray that God would help us to see others through His eyes. As we do these things, patiently and consistently, one day we will wake up and realize that forgiveness has replaced our pain.

*God, I cannot express how grateful I am that You have forgiven
me for the many things I've done to hurt You. Please help me to see,
through Your eyes, the person who has wronged me and to bestow
on him or her the same gift You've given me. Amen.*

Choose Laughter

Sarah said, "God has brought me laughter."
GENESIS 21:6 NIV

*U*h-oh. Geni felt that familiar quivering of the shoulder beside her. What would she do if her husband, Pete, got tickled at the goat lady in church again today?

The goat lady—Pete's name for the elderly lady who sat in back and sang her heart out in a reedy, bleating voice. It did sound an awful lot like barnyard praise, but Geni would have never thought of it until Pete explained why he'd been privately shaking with mirth during praise and worship.

Geni had always been a very serious person. . .until she met Pete. Her husband had a humorous way of looking at life that brought light and levity to even the most somber occasions. They were a good mix, the two of them, but Pete's funky sense of humor sometimes put Geni in an awkward situation. She had grown annoyed with his "silliness" on more than one occasion.

Geni remembered the story of Old Testament Sarah in an awkward situation, too, the most awkward of her life. God had just sent word that she would bear a child while in her nineties. Sarah could laugh, cry, or run away screaming. What was her response?

Sarah chose laughter. She even named her son Isaac, a name that meant *laughter*.

Author of humor, help us to lighten up. Like Sarah, remind us that we can choose laughter even in the most awkward of circumstances. Amen.

Your In-Laws

*It hath fully been shewed me, all that thou hast done unto
thy mother in law since the death of thine husband: and how
thou hast left thy father and thy mother, and the land of thy nativity,
and art come unto a people which thou knewest not heretofore.*
RUTH 2:11 KJV

Mother-in-law. What image does that phrase conjure up
in your mind? There are many jokes about mothers-in-
law in our society. Often there are negative attitudes attached to
women of this station. Maybe you are a mother-in-law yourself.
How do you view your child's spouse?

No doubt it is complicated when a man and woman join in
marriage. There are two families who have very different ideas
about how this new branch of the family should operate. This can
lead to some pretty strained feelings, but it doesn't have to.

While we don't know much about Ruth's parents, it does
seem that they were still living. Yet Ruth chose to leave them
and join her mother-in-law, Naomi. We don't know exactly
why this happened, but she and Naomi apparently had a good
relationship. We can see that they loved and respected each other,
and God blessed them both.

Wives, respect your husband's mother. Mothers, respect
your child's spouse. You don't always have to agree, but you can
respectfully disagree. You really can be a blessing to each other.

*God, I'm so thankful for the example of Ruth and Naomi.
Help me to have such love and respect for my in-laws.*

Smart, Brave, and Beautiful

*And it was so, when the king saw Esther the queen standing
in the court, that she obtained favour in his sight:
and the king held out to Esther the golden sceptre.*
ESTHER 5:2 KJV

Queen Esther, a lovely Jewish girl who married King Xerxes of Persia, found herself in desperate straits. Not knowing her ethnic background, Haman, her husband's advisor, plotted the annihilation of all Jews throughout the empire. Esther wanted to save her people, but the king had not invited her to his side for thirty days. Had he found a new trophy wife?

Nevertheless, Esther risked her life to connect with Xerxes. She fasted for three days, but Esther did not use a "spiritual" approach in dealing with her husband. Instead, she appeared in royal robes, looking her best. She did not blurt out demands but piqued the king's curiosity with dinner invitations that included Haman.

By the time Esther presented her request for mercy, Xerxes had offered her half his kingdom. Upon hearing of Haman's treachery, he dispatched him in no time flat.

Few of us win Miss America titles or compete with Martha Stewart's entertainment skills, yet God has gifted us with wisdom, beauty, and hospitality that impact our husbands and others. While we may not rescue an entire nation, we can make a difference in—and even help save—the lives of those around us.

*Lord, please help me recognize the gifts You have invested
in me and how I can best use them to help others. Amen.*

Well-Watered Gardens

*The Lord will guide you always; he will
satisfy your needs in a sun-scorched land. . . .
You will be like a well-watered garden.*
ISAIAH 58:11 NIV

Well-kept gardens are beautiful. The rows of plants are weed-free, the vegetables and flowers abundant, and everyone who sees such a garden admires it and wants the same.

When God is allowed to be our guide, our lives and marriages become like well-watered gardens. Even in the driest of times, God's beauty can shine through us. All we have to do is to allow Him the leadership in our home.

We do this by giving the reins to our husbands. This may sound easy, but often we want to take control. We want to be a subtle guide, ignoring God's blueprint and giving our husbands suggestions or bold statements as to how we should be living as a married couple.

This is not God's design and will lead to a garden full of weeds and haphazard rows. The fruit will be withered, the flowers stunted. If we want a garden that is a showcase, then we need to step back and let our husband lead. Even if he doesn't seem to be following God's path as we see it, we must trust God to bring His will to pass. He is a wonderful guide.

*Thank You, Lord, for Your guidance in my life.
Help me to trust You in all things.
Help me to believe Your word. Amen.*

Is Budget Just a Six-Letter Word?

Wisdom is better when it's paired with money, especially if you get both while you're still living. Double protection: wisdom and wealth!
ECCLESIASTES 7:11–12 MSG

How do you feel about the state of your checkbook and the pile of bills that sits beside it? Is there a comfortable balance, or does it prove that there is a need for you to get your finances under control? A budget is a scary thought because, like any resolution, it is so hard to stick to. But it's a critical move for every marriage.

The most important thing in the attempt to stick to a budget is to realize the need to limit yourself and not allow rationalization to creep in and undermine that resolve. Next, you need to prioritize the bills and decide who needs to get paid first and when—and don't leave out God when you consider the places where you need to allocate your funds. Then get organized. Have one place for bills and financial matters and keep it free of other types of clutter. Finally, surrender your budget, your finances, and your will to the Lord.

Heavenly Father, please help me to be a better steward of the gifts You have given me. Help me to prioritize and organize my finances and grant me self-control so that I can stick to my budget. Amen.

God First

*"You shall love the Lord your God with all your heart,
and with all your soul, and with all your mind."*
MATTHEW 22:37 NASB

Elizabeth was exasperated with her husband. No matter how clear her requests were, Jeff was not meeting her needs.

One of the hardest challenges in a marriage is to look to God rather than to our husbands to meet our needs. In scripture, the Lord repeatedly focuses our mind on Him by telling us to look to Him first (Matthew 6:33; 22:37). As we spend time with God every day, God tells us, "In everything by prayer and supplication with thanksgiving let your requests be made known to God" (Philippians 4:6 NASB). Since God is our Helper (Psalm 46:1), we can trust God that He will not forsake us (Psalm 9:10) but will meet our needs. In Genesis 2:18, God tells us, " 'It isn't good for the man to live alone. I need to make a suitable partner for him'" (CEV). Just as God, our Helper, meets our needs, as women, our husband's helper, we are called to meet his needs.

As we put God first, laying our needs before Him and trusting Him to meet them, we are encouraged to then meet our husband's needs. In putting God first, we are able to give back to the Lord. For we are serving and worshipping the Lord (Colossians 3:17, 23) when we meet our husband's needs.

*Lord, help me to put You first daily. It is only then that my needs
can be met and, most importantly, I can meet my husband's needs.*

A Penny for Your Thoughts

We use great plainness of speech.
2 CORINTHIANS 3:12 KJV

*H*ow much easier marriage would be if God had only granted couples the ability to read each other's minds! No more trying to figure out what prompted your husband's moody silence. No more indecision about where to dine. A mere probing of one another's brains would solve every mystery in marriage and life would be pure bliss!

On the other hand, if couples did possess mind-reading skills, there would be no need for communication. No need for honesty and trust. There would be no surprises and no adventure. In short, marriage would be dull. Perhaps that's why the Creator chose not to grace mortals with mind-reading abilities and instead gave them two ears and one mouth.

God expects husbands and wives to talk to one another. He wants you to share your fears and insecurities. Be honest and open, freely discussing your desires, needs, and disappointments. Don't clam up when something goes amiss in your relationship. Talk frequently and frankly about every aspect of your couplehood. After all, if you don't tell your husband what you're thinking, he'll never know. And communication is a two-way street, so don't forget to listen. There's a reason why we have two ears and only one mouth.

Dear God, help me to listen carefully to my husband's needs and to be honest and open about my own. Amen.

A Healing Confession

*In all that has happened to us, you have been just;
you have acted faithfully, while we did wrong.*
NEHEMIAH 9:33 NIV

*C*onfession is a powerful part of any relationship. Through confession, we are able to humble ourselves, admit our wrongs, and ask for forgiveness. Confession also marks the moment when healing can begin. Until we acknowledge our shortcomings, we can never begin to be restored. Confession is certainly never easy, but it is vital to a healthy relationship.

After the Israelites hear the Law in the book of Nehemiah, they are both brokenhearted and overjoyed; brokenhearted because of their sins toward God and overjoyed because of God's unfailing love. They admit that God has been just, that He has acted faithfully, and that they have wronged Him again and again. However, even as they wail, the Israelites see what a mighty God they serve, and they rejoice in His faithfulness.

Doing the right thing in our relationships is sometimes extremely difficult. Stress, fatigue, and demanding schedules can lead to short tempers, angry words, and careless acts. Confession is necessary for healing wounds made through thoughtless words and inconsiderate actions. Only through admitting our faults and asking for forgiveness can we repair the rifts in our relationships, and only through confession can we come to appreciate the love and faithfulness of our God.

*Dear Lord, please give me the strength to confess my sins to those I love today.
Show me when I sin against You by wronging others. Amen.*

His Water in Our Wilderness

*For waters shall burst forth in the wilderness,
and streams in the desert. . . . The ransomed of the LORD
shall return. . . . And sorrow and sighing shall flee away.*
ISAIAH 35:6, 10 NKJV

*D*uring her quiet time with God, so many thoughts intruded upon her mind: *Will Frank be laid off? How will we ever afford Annie's college tuition? Did I type up the minutes for the next church board meeting? What should I make for dinner tonight?*

Frustrated with her wandering thoughts and parched for God's presence, she struggled to center on Jesus. To calm her restless spirit, she attempted to shift her thoughts to a peaceful place in nature. Drifting back to childhood, she envisioned herself paddling a canoe down a shadowy creek and imagined the sound of water lapping against the boat. There, amid this pastoral scene, her body relaxed, her spirit calmed. Soon God's peace prevailed as His presence filled her heart.

Sometimes, to attain those quiet moments with Jesus, we must look for those waters in the wilderness of our minds, fragments of memories, scenes of nature that will quiet ourselves. There we will find God, the living water of our lives.

Lord, I come to You seeking Your peace. Show me the way to Your side. Ease my weary body, govern my thoughts, calm my spirit. I seek Your face now and pray that, in You, I will find the rest I so desperately need. Amen.

Queenly Listening

He who answers before listening—
that is his folly and his shame.
PROVERBS 18:13 NIV

Nebuchadnezzar's wife, the queen, had been widowed for some time when her grandson, Belshazzar, decided to throw a big banquet. The queen wasn't planning on attending the party, but then she heard voices, upset and frightened. She was told that a hand had mysteriously appeared and wrote words on the banquet wall.

No one could interpret the meaning of the writing, but the queen knew someone who could. She hurried into the banquet hall to find King Belshazzar. "This man Daniel, whom the king [Nebuchadnezzar] called Belteshazzar, was found to have a keen mind and knowledge and understanding, and also the ability to interpret dreams, explain riddles and solve difficult problems. Call for Daniel, and he will tell you what the writing means" (Daniel 5:12 NIV).

This queen had apparently listened to her husband throughout their marriage—really, really listened. She was raised in a pagan culture and was probably very young when she married King Nebuchadnezzar, yet she had the wisdom to pay attention to her husband's dramatic problems. On this fateful day, the knowledge she had gleaned was used to accomplish God's purposes.

Listening, really listening, is a rare trait. We all need to listen more attentively to our husbands, our children, our friends. We might learn something!

Father, sometimes I talk too much! Teach me to be a good listener to others.
Stop me as I start to interrupt someone so that I can hold back and just listen.

Expectancy

*"But of that day and hour no one knows,
not even the angels of heaven, nor the Son, but the Father alone."*
MATTHEW 24:36 NASB

Waiting for a baby to be born is a mystery—no one really knows the hour he or she will appear. The doctor can provide a due date as the time for the birth approaches, but it's only a guess as to that baby's arrival. The expectant mother prepares for her first few steps into motherhood. She is constantly aware of pending delivery, counting down each day closer and closer to her baby's birthday.

Even though the day the baby will arrive is unknown, the expectant father, mother, and even the grandparents prepare for that baby's appearance. They decorate the nursery, purchase the baby bed, and buy diapers, bottles, and things they know they'll need. They're preparing for the soon coming of that baby, and they celebrate the event with excited words, hopes, and dreams for that baby.

Likewise, Christians are anticipating Christ's return—but only the heavenly Father knows the hour. We must wait with expectation—doing what we know to do until that glorious day arrives. We must prepare daily by growing in the Word of God, continually building our relationship with God in prayer, and sharing with others the excitement of His return.

Approach eternity with excitement, forever looking forward to that glorious day!

*Lord, show me how to remain expectant,
never losing sight of the reality of Your return. Amen.*

Call on God

> " 'Call to me and I will answer you.
> I'll tell you marvelous and wondrous things
> that you could never figure out on your own.' "
> JEREMIAH 33:3 MSG

*W*here do you turn when life is going well? How about when life isn't going so well? Many times in scripture, God calls us to look to Him for the answers, for wisdom to deal with people and circumstances, not only when we're in trouble but also when life is good.

Very few marriages, if any, flow smoothly from the day "I dos" are exchanged. Differences of opinion and in personalities will eventually lead to conflict in any relationship. And the problems resulting from inevitable conflicts can escalate out of our control and even our wisdom to know how to "fix" them.

James 1:5 tells us that when we ask God for wisdom in anything, He will give it to us, gladly and without reproach. When God told Jeremiah He would restore Israel after a time of testing, He urged Jeremiah to call on Him, and He would answer in ways that would reveal His plan for Israel in ways that nation couldn't even conceive.

In the same way, God will answer our sincere call for help and restoration, and He will show us "things that [we] could never figure out on [our] own."

*Father, when my marriage hits a rough patch, help me
to diligently call on You for help, for wisdom. I know You will
give the answers to seemingly impossible questions. Amen.*

Leave and Cleave

*"For this reason a man shall leave his father and mother
and be joined to his wife, and the two shall become one flesh."*
EPHESIANS 5:31 NKJV

The young husband was so excited that he was about to burst! After years of hard work and sacrifice, he had been offered a job promotion. Enthusiastically he came through the door after work to share the fantastic news with his wife. She quickly responded, "I could never move to another state and leave my parents!" Her reaction pierced his heart.

I do are two very powerful words. They encompass promises that are seldom pondered at the altar. Yet when we are joined as husband and wife, a new bond is formed. We are pledged to our husbands. Our allegiance is to them. We have become a team. That means becoming one flesh in every sense of the word.

In God's design, a marital relationship should take precedence over a parental relationship. As wives, we should not allow the bond with our parents to hinder us from putting our husband's needs first. By the same token, parents must emotionally release their adult children to their respective spouses. Following the Lord is not always easy, but the blessings are worth it.

Purpose to be the wife that God intended for you to be. Cleave to your husband.

*Dear Lord, thank You for my husband and the bond that we share.
May I cherish and nourish our relationship. Amen.*

Every Marriage Needs a Jethro

After Moses had sent away his wife Zipporah,
his father-in-law Jethro received her and her two sons.
EXODUS 18:2–3 NIV

Like every couple, Moses and his wife Zipporah had some trouble in their marriage. In fact, the book of Exodus tells us that Moses sent his wife away. While the details of their conflict are not revealed, it appears that they needed some time apart. It might have been tempting for Zipporah's father, Jethro, to listen to her perception of the story and take her and the kids in to live with him. However, Jethro refused to blindly take his daughter's side. Instead, he packed them up and took them back to Moses.

Jethro warmly greeted his son-in-law. Then he listened and observed. Jethro discovered that Moses had been working too hard and needed a break. He didn't shame Moses or blame him for all the problems. Instead, he offered a practical solution. Objectively. Caringly. We can assume, then, that Moses and Zipporah got back together. A marriage restored.

Do you have a Jethro in your marriage? Someone who loves you both unconditionally? Someone who is not afraid to tell you the truth? From time to time, every marriage can benefit from an objective point of view. Entrust your marriage to a Jethro—you both will reap the blessing.

Father, thank You for the accountability and perspective
that our friends and loved ones can provide. Help us to not
be shy about seeking help from those we trust. Amen.

Forgiven Debtors

*And forgive us our debts,
as we forgive our debtors.*
MATTHEW 6:12 KJV

The wife stared at the scripture in her Bible. Although she'd read the verse many times, this morning the words took on a new impact. Was Jesus saying she would be forgiven as she forgave others? She closed her eyes as the memory of last night's argument with her husband washed over her. She'd flung so many accusations of past offenses at him. Was this what she wanted God to do with her?

We wives are great at storing a mental list of past grievances and then hauling it out every time our husbands are the least critical or argumentative. After all, if we don't tell him what's wrong with him, who will? At least, that's the common reasoning. How untrue.

God wants to be the one to work with our husbands and mold them to His image. He didn't put us here to nag our man and change him. We are here to be his helpmeet.

God has forgiven us for a multitude of sins. When He forgives, scripture says, God puts our sins as far as the east is from the west. He forgets what we've even done and won't haul out those past wrongs to ask us about them. We need to do likewise with our husbands. Forget what he's done. Forgive.

*Jesus, help me to follow the words You gave.
Help me to forgive and forget no matter the hurt. Amen.*

Temptation

*Submit yourselves, then, to God.
Resist the devil, and he will flee from you.*
JAMES 4:7 NIV

As a Christian wife, the devil will try to get you off track as much as he can. You will face countless temptations throughout your marriage. The devil is crafty and cunning. The Bible tells us he is a roaring lion looking for someone to devour. But he can also tempt you in ways that make it seem like you aren't doing anything wrong. He is a wolf in sheep's clothing.

You must be ready to guard your heart and your marriage against the father of lies. Be prepared to stand firm against him. You have to resist him, or he will make a mess of the love and commitment you and your husband share. But how can you manage that? By submitting yourselves and your marriage to God. Learn and obey His Word. When you are tempted by the devil, ask God to take away that temptation and fill your mind with His Word instead. If you submit yourself to the Lord in this way, God promises that the devil will flee from you! Praise the Lord for His faithful power, guidance, and protection!

*Dear heavenly Father, I know that the devil wants to tear
my marriage apart. Please fill my heart and mind with Your Word
so that I can resist the enemy's attacks. In Jesus' name, amen.*

First Labors

She is energetic and strong, a hard worker.
PROVERBS 31:17 NLT

No matter what our occupation, whether that of homemaker or career woman, God's Word urges women to be hard workers, leading productive lives, not unlike the amazingly fruitful yet nameless wife of noble character described in Proverbs 31:10–31.

Several examples of industrious women can be found in the Bible. In the Old Testament, we can read about Deborah, who was a leader, judge, and prophetess. Then there was the widow Ruth, faithful to her mother-in-law, who worked in the fields, gathering wheat and barley. In the New Testament is Lydia, who was a dealer in purple cloth. There was also Dorcas, who made clothes. And there was Priscilla, who, along with her tentmaking husband, Aquila, worked in ministry with the apostle Paul. All these women seemed to have energy and appeared to be strong, hard workers.

But our work—whether inside or outside of the home—should not come before our relationship with God or our husbands. In all things, faith and family must come before the deadline we need to meet, the business trip we need to take, or the garage that needs to be cleaned out. Faith and family are even more important than whatever church project we've agreed to direct or community charity drive we've volunteered to participate in.

So let's be good stewards of the time we have here on earth. Give the first and best of your effort, energy, and strength to God and your husband. And the Lord will bless all your labors.

Father, remind me that my first labors are to You and my husband.
Help me to be a good steward of my strength, time, and energy. Amen.

In Control

*Encourage one another daily,
as long as it is called Today.*
HEBREWS 3:13 NIV

*T*rials, troubles, doubts: We don't even have to go looking for them, because in its ordinary course, life drops many such things before us. Whether we face a single serious challenge or a barrage of minor ones, when we stand up against the world, discouragement can quickly become our portion.

Paul commands us to encourage and build up each other. It's good advice for a first-century church or a marriage, since both face the depredations of a world gone awry with sin. Without support, Christians easily get caught up in troubles and become discouraged and doubtful. For anyone who tries to stand against the world alone, faith, marriage, and life itself turns into a chore, not a joy.

It's wonderful to have someone in our corner when our careers become overly challenging, family dissensions take their toll, or health problems sap our energy. When two face a care together, they hold each other up and take courage from sharing opinions and solutions. Problems are solved more easily when two think them through.

Are we encouraging our husbands, whatever they face? Then we're building our marriages—and the church—right in our own homes.

*Lord, help my husband and me to encourage each other daily.
Remind me that You are still in control and working things out for our good.*

No Sweat

*. . .lest any root of bitterness
springing up cause trouble.*
HEBREWS 12:15 NKJV

*I*t's easy to sweat the small stuff. The toilet lid that he never puts down. . .the socks that he carelessly tosses across the bedroom. . .his inability to find anything, even when he's looking right at it. Such quirks are harmless and even humorous at times, but if you're not careful, they can become the first stones in a wall of resentment.

Little annoyances have a way of becoming big problems in marriage. They tend to pile up over time until all of your spouse's good qualities are buried under his faults. His sensitivity is obscured by his sloppiness. His sense of humor hidden by his absentmindedness. Your critical eye will see only his shortcomings, and you'll start to wonder why you ever married *that man*!

Your husband isn't perfect, and neither are you. That's why God expects spouses to be forgiving and long-suffering with one another. There are plenty of critical issues in a marriage that need to be taken care of without worrying about petty things. If you have a loving husband who is fulfilling his vows of marriage, consider yourself blessed indeed, no matter how often he forgets to pick up his socks.

*Dear God, help me to love and accept my husband in spite of his flaws and
to guard against the bitterness that the enemy would try to sow in my heart.
Amen.*

My Own Little World

Know therefore this day, and consider it in thine heart,
that the LORD he is God in heaven above, and upon the earth beneath.
DEUTERONOMY 4:39 KJV

*B*efore Erin opened her eyes each morning, challenges swarmed through her head like gnats. Bills. Groceries. Meetings at work. Kindergarten plays. She wondered if possessing multiple personalities would not be such a bad thing. Then she could delegate the impossible tasks she needed to accomplish.

Her husband, Chaz, on the other hand, focused on the business at hand, much like their five-year-old son. Take a shower. Brush teeth. Sit down to breakfast and wait for Erin to pour his juice. Chaz especially annoyed her when he switched on the morning news while she dashed around before work.

She wanted to scream, "Can't you think of anything beyond *your* needs?" Erin tried to talk to him about her frustrations. He always agreed but didn't change.

One day, as she slapped lunches together, Erin heard a TV newsman's voice as he reported on children starving in a third-world country. She looked up in time to see a young boy's face fill the television screen. He bit into a large piece of bread, his huge, dark eyes full of joy. Despite sticklike limbs, he danced in celebration of the meal he had received.

Erin's taut anger loosened; her to-do lists suddenly shrank to nothing. Yes, Chaz was wrapped up in himself; but Erin, too, often forgot anything outside her daily planner.

God, on the other hand, laughed with a happy little boy on the other side of the world.

Lord Jesus, please open my eyes and my heart to what You see. Amen.

Fox Traps

Catch all the foxes, those little foxes, before they ruin
the vineyard of love, for the grapevines are blossoming!
SONG OF SOLOMON 2:15 NLT

*G*rapes were a big deal in Solomon's day. Productive vineyards were the family's livelihood. When foxes snuck in and wreaked havoc, the family suffered.

Solomon compared the destructive little foxes daily eradicated from his vineyards to the annoying habits that sneak into a marriage and erode relationships over time. Every marriage is plagued with those wily little foxes hiding in the shadows, just waiting to sabotage marital intimacy: "*Must* you always..." "I hate it when you..." "I've always done it *this* way...."

So how do Christian wives set effective fox traps?

Infusing our marriages with God's Word and reading the Bible is essential. The Lord uses His truths to strengthen our relationship when those little foxes come gnawing. Only God can instill in our marriages the realities of 1 Corinthians 13:4–5: "Love is patient and kind. Love is not jealous or boastful or proud or rude. It does not demand its own way. It is not irritable, and it keeps no record of being wronged" (NLT).

Prayer erects a hedge around our vineyards and protects our blossoming grapevines from those vexing foxes. Dealing with the little foxes *before* they sneak in is a surefire way to keep our vineyards healthy.

Loving Father, thank You for choosing my beloved just for me.
Make me aware of the ruinous little foxes in my marriage
and give me wisdom to lay effective traps. Amen.

True Love

Besides that, they learn to be idlers, going about from
house to house, and not only idlers, but also gossips
and busybodies, saying what they should not.
1 TIMOTHY 5:13 ESV

*S*cripture connects gossip with idleness, and Paul warns
Christians against engaging in it.

Those who care deeply about their families may encourage,
praise, or defend them, but they do not gossip—especially about
in-laws—because they know the damage this causes to family
relationships. Gossip easily passes from one person to another,
usually because it contains damaging information or opinions.
Our base natures naturally revel in such things, and Paul did not
want us to encourage ourselves in sin.

That doesn't mean we don't occasionally become irritated
with loved ones, even our spouses, and slip up. In the heat of
emotion we may fail. But a proper Christian response is to
recognize gossip as sin, confess it, and seek to change.

Then we will truly be loving our families.

Lord, keep a guard over my mind and lips.
I don't want to fall to the temptations of gossip.
Help me love my family more than I love a juicy gossip tidbit.

How Are You Doing?

Let all your things be done with charity.
1 CORINTHIANS 16:14 KJV

*D*uring Summer and Kyle's prenuptial counseling, they had been asked to discuss what their domestic responsibilities would be within the marriage relationship. Kyle had admitted to having limited culinary ability, so he'd agreed to help with cleanup if Summer would be mostly responsible for meal preparation. She'd agreed because she'd seen no way around it. The truth was, she was capable of cooking, but she didn't much care to do it. At the time she'd thought her love for Kyle could overcome her distaste for the task. It soon became apparent that she was mistaken. Her mashed potatoes would be runny, her gravy way too thick. She'd scorch every other meal, and then she'd be mad. Kyle hadn't enjoyed the meals anymore than she had.

So they'd meet after work for dinner. They'd order pizza, and they'd spend way more money than they had available. Then the fights about money had begun and had escalated into a very unhappy situation.

Summer thought back to the beginning. She'd grudgingly agreed to do the cooking, but she had never done it with a loving heart. She'd certainly not put much effort into it.

"Lord, forgive me," she prayed. "Help me to become a better cook and to pour generous amounts of love into each recipe."

Dear God, of course I have tasks which I find a bit distasteful, but if I season them with love, You will help me to accomplish them with the right attitude.

Gossip Fuels the Fires Within

Where there is no fuel a fire goes out;
where there is no gossip arguments come to an end.
PROVERBS 26:20 CEV

*M*ost women have a few special girlfriends who are there for everything—the laughter, the tears, the successes, and the failures. Friendship is a treasured gift from God. But it's easy to let friendship cross the boundaries of the sanctity of marriage. When we trade stories about our husband's neglect or failures, we've crossed the line. When we share private things, rather than taking them to God and to our husbands, we've crossed the line.

Whether it's a habit that has developed or it's truly borne out of frustration, it's vital to your marriage that you bite your tongue *before giving in to the temptation of husband-bashing*. It serves no good purpose and, if we're honest, we'd have to admit that it *does* fuel the fire of resentment. A fire will only go out when it's not continually stoked.

If we honor our husbands by refraining from gossip, eventually the fires within us will go out and God will bless our marriages for the honor we show them.

Heavenly Father, please forgive me for the words I have carelessly spoken about my husband. Help me to replace my complaints with words that honor him and You. Please bless my marriage and let it give You glory. Amen.

Strength in Weariness

He gives power to the weak and strength to the powerless.
But those who trust in the LORD will find new strength.
ISAIAH 40:29, 31 NLT

As wives it seems our work never ends. While many husbands help to maintain a clean home, prepare meals, and care for their children, many do not. And today, many wives work outside the home, as well. Very few wives and mothers are totally rested each day. Many mothers are the first one up in the morning and the last one to bed at night. Then there are the interruptions and the added stresses of sick children, elderly parents, job-related responsibilities, and other problems.

Spending time with our husbands is a dream of the past at times. Then someone recalls the Proverbs 31 woman, and we feel that we are about to break from the pressure. Where do we turn for help?

As Christians, when we are weary and worn-out, when we have no idea where we will call up the strength to face another day, we still have hope. God promises that when our hope is in Him, we will receive the strength to fulfill all the duties He has given us. We will soar above the difficulties like eagles above the storm.

Father, may I lean on You today for strength to meet each challenge.
Let me never forget that all power comes from You,
that Your strength is perfected in my weakness. Amen.

Put On Your Armor

*Wherefore take unto you the whole armour of God,
that ye may be able to withstand in the evil day,
and having done all, to stand.*
EPHESIANS 6:13 KJV

Over the years, Satan has challenged God's people in different arenas.

He fought Israel on many battlefields. He fought Jesus, using puppet kings, a weak-willed governor, and religious leaders.

He has fought the church with the same determination, using governments to persecute true believers while pandering to the perverse.

In the last century, Satan has been waging an all-out attack on the home. He has easily penetrated our walls on airwaves, coming right into our living rooms with his demonic images and messages.

The Internet, too, has become his playground, where he lurks in cleverly disguised Web sites, just waiting to destroy the purity and innocence of our children.

The home is the last and most important battleground. As our homes and families go, so goes our nation. If Satan wins in our homes, he wins our nation.

Our greatest defenses as wives and mothers are the sword of the Spirit and the armor of God.

Put it on daily. Don't stay home without it.

Father, I thank You for the helmet of salvation, the breastplate of righteousness, the girdle of truth, the shoes of the gospel, the shield of faith. Above all, I thank You for the sword of the Spirit. Let me stand firm. Amen.

Feeding the Flames of Love

But you walked away from your first love why? . . .
Turn back! Recover your dear early love.
REVELATION 2:5 MSG

*D*orothy wondered why she and her husband seemed so
distant lately. Although they lived in the same house, they
seemed to be strangers, each going through their own routine,
barely acknowledging the other as they tried to keep up with
their hectic schedules.

Whatever happened to the man I married, Dorothy wondered,
*the man who brought me flowers, sent me cards just because, called me
just to tell me that he loved me? But then,* she thought with some
dismay, *when was the last time I did something special for him?*

Maintaining a relationship can be hard work. Although we
may never again feel that initial spark of love, we do need to feed
the flame, to stoke the embers, in order to keep our love and
marriages alive. And that takes time and energy.

This week make an effort to get to know your spouse again.
Check your calendars and agree on a date night, a time just for
the two of you. Work on keeping your love alive, and you will be
richly rewarded as you and your husband fall in love all over again.

And while you're at it, renew your passion for Christ. Don't
let your love for God turn to ashes. Instead, immerse yourself in
the scriptures, mediate on His Word, and rejoice in His presence.

Keep the home fires burning by feeding the flame of love for
your spouse and your God!

Lord, help me to keep my love for You and my husband alive by spending
more time with each of you. Thank You for blessing our lives together!

*The Secret to
Contentment*

*I have learned the secret of being content in any and every situation,
whether well fed or hungry, whether living in plenty or in want.*
PHILIPPIANS 4:12 NIV

We plan and dream. We imagine a life called *us*. And on
the wings of our hopes we see "happily ever after" just
over the horizon. The days come and go and dreams give birth to
other dreams until our very happiness is put on a shelf, just out of
reach. We wait for the day when our children are a little older or
our husband's work schedule changes.

But waiting for the right circumstances to make us happy
brings a tension all its own. Very often we mistake this tension as
a sign that we are lacking something, but it is actually a tension
born out of wanting what we do not have. Contentment, after all,
is an inside job, and no amount of rearranging our lives will bring
it to us. We must find it within ourselves.

The secret to contentment comes from understanding that
where we are now is exactly where God wants us to be. He has a
purpose for our lives, and He offers a peace that is separate from
our circumstances. When we open our hearts to this, love comes
rushing in the way the tide fills even the tiniest holes in the sand
and blessings are scattered around like seashells.

*Lord, help me grow in the holy habit of contentment
by seeking Your presence and purpose for my life. Amen.*

Do the Next Thing

*"My food," said Jesus, "is to do the will of
him who sent me and to finish his work."*
JOHN 4:34 NIV

*B*usyness is the curse of modern life. There are lawns to
mow, meals to cook, gutters to clean, gardens to weed—
enough chores to last a lifetime of evenings and weekends. Even
if you live in a tiny apartment and eat only take-out food, there
are still phone calls to make, floors to scrub, letters to write, and
errands to run.

But the Bible says that God has numbered our days as He
numbers the hairs on our heads. He knows how long we have to
live, and He knows best what we should do with the time He has
given us.

Christian author and former missionary Elisabeth Elliot
gives this advice about how to decide what to do amid a myriad
of necessary and useful things: "Just do the next thing." These
simple words are an echo of Jesus', and in this He is our model.
He did nothing that wasn't God's perfect will, and He was
perfectly content. When we feel harried and stressed, it is often
because we are trying to do more than God has asked us to do.

God always gives us enough time to do His will.

*Dear Father, help me see all the things I have to do and I want to do,
and order them according to Your will. Amen.*

Abigail

*And she was a woman of good understanding,
and of a beautiful countenance: but the man
was churlish and evil in his doings.*
1 Samuel 25:3 KJV

Abigail was an amazing woman. She was wise and beautiful, but she was married to a nasty, hard-hearted man. It must have been difficult for her to be married to such a selfish and inconsiderate person, but she stood by him.

Nabal made a foolish decision when he refused to give food to David's men, and David would have killed Nabal and Nabal's men. Many wives in Abigail's position would have seen this as an easy escape, but when she heard what Nabal had done, she set out to make things right. In doing so, she prevented a great slaughter. God rewarded her, of course, but she had no way of knowing what would soon happen. She merely knew that it was her duty to be a good wife regardless of how awful her husband was.

When you married, it was for better or worse. If you have a wonderful husband, praise the Lord. If your husband is a bit more like Nabal, turn your situation over to God. Either way, determine to be a good wife. It won't always be easy no matter what kind of husband you have, but with God directing you, it *is* possible.

*Dear Jesus, I look forward to the day I will be Your bride.
For now, let me be a good wife to the husband You've given me.*

Delight and Desires

Delight yourself in the LORD;
and He will give you the desires of your heart.
PSALM 37:4 NASB

Delight means to take great pleasure in or to give keen enjoyment to the object of our delight, either a thing or a person.
Most women going into marriage desire a solid, enduring marriage with their husbands. They don't plan on that marriage ending for any reason other than death. Their delight is in their husbands, and seemingly nothing can break that bond. Yet in spite of the deepest desires of our hearts, all too often marriages fail, even among Christians.

An anonymous author wrote this poem about marriage that sums up the biblical principle that, as a result of delighting in the Lord, He gives us the desires of our hearts:

I once thought marriage took
Just two to make a go,
But now I am convinced
It takes the Lord also.
And not one marriage fails
Where Christ is asked to enter,
As lovers come together
With Jesus at the center.
But marriage seldom thrives,
And homes are incomplete,
Till He is welcomed there
To help avoid defeat.
In homes where Christ is first,
It's obvious to see,
Those unions really work,
For marriage still takes three.

Putting Christ first, delighting in His presence, and welcoming Him into every area of your life will guarantee God's giving you the desires you hold most dear.

Jesus, help us learn to delight in You. Amen.

In-Laws or Outlaws?

*Then Rebekah said to Isaac, "I'm disgusted with living
because of these Hittite women. If Jacob takes a wife from among
the women of this land. . .my life will not be worth living."*
GENESIS 27:46 NIV

After all the mother-in-law jokes out there, there is a
refreshing element of humor in this Bible verse. Can you
imagine Rebekah complaining to Isaac about her daughters-in-
law? Who knows why Rebekah thought Esau's wives were so
difficult—maybe they only wanted to spend time with their own
families. Maybe they didn't keep Isaac and Rebekah in the loop
when making plans. We don't know the details, but whatever
they were doing, these women were making their mother-in-
law's life miserable. Sure, there are two sides to every story, but
it's clear that this relationship was less than ideal.

How is your relationship with your in-laws? Are you
difficult? Do you have unfair expectations of them? Do you
make it hard for them to visit you—or resent the time and
attention they give your husband or children? You certainly aren't
responsible for the behavior of your in-laws, but you can do
everything in your power to maintain a good relationship with
them. Regardless of how they treat you, they did raise the person
who you loved enough to be with for the rest of your life.

What can you do today to be a joy to your in-laws?

*Dear Father, family relationships are hard. But I know You created
us to live in community and harmony with one another. Help me
to do what I can to have a good relationship with my in-laws.*

Holding On

Scarcely had I passed by them, when I found the one I love.
I held him and would not let him go.
SONG OF SOLOMON 3:4 NKJV

*S*eeing the hurt in her husband's eyes before he walked out made the wife ache with regret. She wanted to go with him, but she had other responsibilities. The children needed her; there was always housework or laundry. She just didn't have the time anymore.

Remember those early days in our romance and marriage when we wanted to be with our husbands all the time? Nothing stopped us. We would drop everything to accompany him anywhere, even places we wouldn't go on our own.

As time passes, life interferes. We have children, church, housework. . . . Our desire to be with our husbands gets overrun by everyday cares. If we aren't careful, we forget that being a helpmeet to our husbands should be a priority. We must put him above everything else and cultivate our relationship.

When we first became Christians, we wanted to spend a lot of time with God. As the years passed, duties to family, church, and community interfered with our prayer and Bible study time. Our relationship with God became more of a passing interest than a consuming fire. We must make it our heart's desire to find the One we love and hold on to Him.

Lord, help me remember to seek You out, to put You before any other. Please help me to seek out my husband, as well, and love him by my actions. Amen.

A Little TLC

*Yet a little sleep, a little slumber,
a little folding of the hands to sleep.*
PROVERBS 6:10 KJV

You don't need a green thumb to keep a houseplant alive. You only need to pay attention to it. Anyone who has ever killed the geranium on the windowsill knows that the key to its demise was neglect. And anyone who has ever suffered a failed marriage knows that ignoring problems won't make them go away.

There are always kinks to work out of a relationship, no matter how long you've been wed. Each phase of your couplehood—from honeymoon to empty nest—has its own unique challenges. And each of those challenges must be confronted and conquered, no matter how unpleasant it is to do so.

Drooping leaves on a houseplant indicate that it needs some attention, and when the quality of your marriage begins to droop, it's time to focus on some TLC. Discuss your relationship over a candlelight dinner. Air your grievances. Reaffirm your commitment to one another.

Catching problems and nipping them in the bud before they can bloom into serious issues will go a long way to keeping your marriage lush and beautiful.

*Dear Father, thank You for my marriage. Help me to treasure
it as the precious union that You have joined together,
and may it never fail because of my neglect. Amen.*

What God Has Joined Together

"Therefore what God has joined together, let man not separate."
MARK 10:9 NIV

*M*arriage is a covenant ordained by God. He values our marriage relationship. We should, too. Yet we live in a society that attempts to redefine the word *family* and esteems cohabitation. The divorce rate has crossed over 50 percent. Adultery is culturally acceptable. What can be done to protect our marriages? How do we value the union that God has brought together?

We can only be responsible for ourselves. However, the good news is that we represent half of the marriage relationship. We must do our part to prevent a wedge from coming between our husbands and us.

Keep the lines of communication open. Do not sweep unresolved issues under the carpet, thinking they will vanish. Be quick to forgive and to extend grace. Develop similar interests and hobbies. Spend purposeful time together, laughing and enjoying one another. Do not take your husband for granted, but show love and appreciation often. Seek God's wisdom on a daily basis. Allow God to transform your heart, and leave your husband's shortcomings to Him. Respect and esteem your husband above others. Let us not separate what God has joined together!

*Dear Lord, help me do my part to protect my marriage.
Daily show me ways to strengthen what You have ordained. Amen.*

Know God,
Know Peace

Great peace have they which love thy law:
and nothing shall offend them.
PSALM 119:165 KJV

*M*any a woman can take criticism from friends, coworkers, bosses, and strangers. But let her husband mention her slightest imperfection, and she will feel hurt, maligned, or angry.

When it comes to a friend, she'll desire to know the sharpening of iron against iron (Proverbs 27:17). But let the husband be like iron, and the sparks will fly.

She will accept the faithful wounds of a friend and will humbly patch herself back together. But let a husband wound her, and she'll bleed to death.

She knows that a friend loves at all times, but when it comes to her own husband, she's not so sure.

Why is this? Why does a woman who is perfectly reasonable with strangers become so offended by her husband?

The answers would fill a book and then some—and already have. Volumes have been written on interpersonal relationships. But the answer is probably more fundamental than how men and women view life. The real reason we are offended is because we have forgotten or not applied God's Word. If we lived by His Word, we would not be offended by anyone—especially our husbands.

We who have been forgiven by a holy God have no right to be offended. The only "right" we have is to share the grace God has given us with others (Ephesians 4:32).

Where grace enters, peace abounds.

Father, let me be kind and tenderhearted and forgiving,
knowing that You have been kind and forgiving to me. Amen.

Lovin' It!

*"Then I was the craftsman at his side. I was filled with
delight day after day, rejoicing always in his presence,
rejoicing in his whole world and delighting in mankind."*
PROVERBS 8:30–31 NIV

*S*ome Christians view the earth as one big mess. Why did
God create people? And what was He *thinking* when He
invented marriage?

But in the book of Proverbs, Wisdom, personified as a
woman, describes God's joy as He crafted the earth and its
inhabitants. Gladness reverberated through His comments on
His work, as recorded in Genesis 1. God loved the mountains,
meadows, and rivers He designed. The lilies, pine trees,
sunflowers, and maples excited Him. He enjoyed the industry of
the beavers, the grace of the deer, and the cool independence of
the cats He created. We, who are made in His image, reflect our
Maker's goodness when we, too, make beautiful, useful things.
Like God, we can celebrate our own excellent work or that of
others: "It's good!"

God's deep satisfaction included man, woman, their
sexuality, and reproduction. Certainly, the tragedy of the Fall
affects mankind; our sin has resulted in the war of the sexes. The
precious products of our ultimate creative ability, our children,
suffer when we defy God. But as we obey Him rather than
our culture, we can bring a smile to His lips as He sees our
transformation. Once again, we'll hear God say, "It's very good!"

*Father, help my husband and me to use the creative abilities
You gave us and celebrate them in each other. Amen.*

Day
108

*Standing Firm
in the Faith*

If you don't take your stand in faith, you won't have a leg to stand on.
ISAIAH 7:9 MSG

The utilities bill is two weeks overdue, the mortgage is due on Friday, and the day care wants to know where its check is. Your job doesn't pay very well, your husband is in school, and money is tight to say the least. Tomorrow is Sunday, and you sit at the kitchen table, bills surrounding you, calculator on, checkbook in hand. Your pen is poised on the pay-to-the-order-of line, and you wonder—can I really afford to write this check to the church? Will God mind my skipping a month?

Perhaps money is not a faith issue for you. Maybe your faith issue is the woman at work you just can't make up your mind to ask to church. Perhaps it exists in the unknown future—where you and your husband will be living next month, next year. Whatever it is, however, the book of Isaiah tells us that we absolutely must stand firm in our faith. Faith is vital to our relationship with God. Without our faith, we have nothing; we are nothing.

Standing firm in faith, trusting in God to take care of us, and believing that God hears our prayers assures us that we will remain standing when the trials end.

Dear Lord, take away my fear and doubt and let me trust You. Give me the strength to stand firm in my faith. Thank You for Your faithfulness. Amen.

The River

*Consider it pure joy. . .whenever
you face trials of many kinds.*
JAMES 1:2 NIV

Finding joy in the trials of life is like finding a precious
stone embedded along a river's edge. As the water rages on,
it is almost impossible to spot the stone's vibrant colors, but when
the water is still, it is easy to see how it has been there all along.
These are deep lessons that, when gathered together, strengthen
our faith.

Turning away from trials is our natural response to life, but
if we remember the river and the treasures that await us, they
become easier to bear. Jesus tells us that throughout life we will
have many troubles. At the same time, He offers us strength by
reminding us that He has overcome them all (John 16:33). This
is of great comfort to us when life becomes the raging river and
we are struggling just to keep our heads above the water.

In time, as the water of our days ebbs and flows, eventually
the turbulence passes. We gasp and cough and cling to shore to
find that we survived not only the current that threatened to pull
us under but our own doubt, as well. And blinking to us in the
sunlight, caught along the riverbank, are pearls of wisdom and a
jewel called hope.

*Father, I fear the trials when they come, but I know that You are
always with me. Help me cling to You when troubles come, believing
that through faith there is a lesson waiting for me in the end. Amen.*

A Messy Marriage

*But when the Father sends the Advocate as my
representative—that is, the Holy Spirit—he will teach you
everything and will remind you of everything I have told you.*
JOHN 14:26 NLT

*I*s your marriage filled with the Holy Spirit? Can you feel
God leading and guiding you every step of the way? Or are
you wishing that somehow someone would come in and help you
sort out the problems in your marriage?

You will never know true joy and peace in your life or your
marriage until you've committed your life to Christ and given
Him control of all things. If you have never given your life to
Christ, take this moment right now and open your heart to Him.
Confess your sins and ask Jesus to be the Lord of your life and
your marriage. When you do this, God sends the Holy Spirit to
live inside you, teaching you His ways and leading all your steps.

Share this decision with your spouse and ask him to think
about trying life and marriage with God at the center. God is the
only one that can remedy your marriage!

*Dear Jesus, please fill my life and my marriage with Your Holy Spirit. I need
Your wisdom in all things. Lead me and guide me. In Your name, amen.*

Refilled and Refueled

*Hope does not disappoint, because the love of God has
been poured out within our hearts through the
Holy Spirit who was given to us.*
ROMANS 5:5 NASB

God said that it was not good for man to be alone, so He
created a woman to be his helper, his companion. Men have
done great things throughout the history of the earth, but many
of those accomplishments were achieved because a woman stood
behind him.

Married couples are one flesh, dreaming a destiny that God
has for them together. So many times when one is ready to quit,
the other cheers him or her on. When one wants to fight, the
other becomes the peacemaker. Marriage brings the strengths of
each to cover the weaknesses of the other. They share all things—
when they lose and when they win.

Are you your husband's cheerleader? Are you standing
behind him with words of encouragement that build him up
when the world has sucked the life out of him? Are you there to
speak truth when he's tempted to be deceived? And do you hold
him up in faith when no one else believes in him?

Make a commitment to be the one who refills your husband
with positive words and refuels him with hope to press on to the
dream and destiny to which God has called you both!

*Lord, help me to hold tightly to the truth of Your promise so that I am a
support and blessing to my husband no matter what we face together. Amen.*

Not My Fault!

*Hot tempers start fights; a calm,
cool spirit keeps the peace.*
PROVERBS 15:18 MSG

Does it seem like a sin to be irritable at our husbands or kids? Irritability certainly can't be compared to murder, stealing, or adultery. Besides, there can be physical reasons as to why we're irritable: lack of sleep or a certain time of the month. And some of us are just wound more tightly than others. It's not our fault! Irritability shouldn't really be classified as a sin. . .just a flaw.

Or *should* it?

The problem with expressing ourselves in an irritable way is that we don't see it as a sin. And usually, we're most careless with our families. We end up tolerating irritability, excusing it away. The truth is that it's wrong. It's hurtful. Usually, our family is not even the reason we're irritable! It starts with a bad commute and a crowded grocery store and the news that the car needs to have new brakes. We walk into a kitchen, find a sink filled with breakfast dishes and. . .the trigger is switched! Everyone gets a dose of our pent-up frustration.

We need to take irritability seriously, to call it for what it is: a sin. If we don't, we tolerate it. A better way is to go to God, confess it, and ask for His forgiveness and grace.

*Lord, I confess my habit of irritability.
Hold me accountable until this pattern is broken.*

Offering Strength

Bear ye one another's burdens,
and so fulfil the law of Christ.
GALATIANS 6:2 KJV

*E*cclesiastes 4:9–12 discusses in great detail the idea of sticking together, and the story of the Good Samaritan (Luke 10:30–37) is intended to show us how to treat our neighbors. The truth is that your husband is your closest neighbor. You, of all people, should recognize that he has burdens from time to time, and you should stick right there beside him and help him bear those burdens.

If he has a troubled workplace, endeavor to make sure his home is an oasis of peace. If he's lost his job for some reason, don't nag him. Instead, pray that God will lead him in the right direction. Listen to and acknowledge his concerns. Remember, you are one flesh. You are together in joy and in difficulty. You both have unique perspectives on situations, and when you allow God to join in, you have a very strong threesome.

God didn't intend for us to struggle through difficulties alone. That's why He commands us to bear the burdens of others. When we offer strength and support to others we, in some measure, uplift ourselves, too.

Examine your heart. Have you been doing all you can to encourage your husband? If not, renew your commitment to him today.

On my own, my strength is limited, but with the power You offer,
Lord, I can bear my husband's burdens.

The Lord Alone

"As for me and my house, we will serve the LORD."
JOSHUA 24:15 NASB

Heather admired her friend Jane's commitment to the Lord regarding her marriage. Jane sought the Lord's will daily in praying specifically for her husband and that the Lord would make her the wife He called her to be.

Joshua challenges God's people to make one of the most important decisions ever: "Choose for yourselves today whom you will serve" (Joshua 24:15 NASB). If we answer, as Joshua did, that we will serve the Lord alone, then our marriages must look differently than the world's marriages. As wives, the thoughts we have, the behaviors we model, the actions we take, must reflect a servant of God who chooses to worship the Lord alone.

How do we reflect to the world the wife God is creating us to be? We must know the Lord, confessing with our lips that Jesus is Lord and believing in our hearts that God raised Jesus from the dead (Romans 10:10). We must regularly study and know God's Word, memorizing scripture as the Lord leads. Daily we must commune with God through prayer, quiet time, and reflection, praying specifically for our husbands and our marriages.

Through daily choosing the Lord alone and abiding in Him, the Holy Spirit residing in us as believers empowers us to model to the world the wife God desires us to be.

*Lord, just as Joshua chose You, I also choose You.
For me and my household, we will serve You alone.*

Changeless

"I the LORD do not change."
MALACHI 3:6 NIV

*L*ife doesn't always go the way we expect. Just as everything's running smoothly, the washing machine dies or the furnace stops pumping out heat. The things of this world break down—they change. That includes people, who neglect or harm us or leave our lives. Sometimes even our spouses do not come through for us when we most need them. Other days we disappoint ourselves in a big way with our own lack of consistency.

But when situations or people, even ourselves, let us down, we need not despair: God never changes or fails us. Our Lord promised to save us, and He will. Everything in our lives, good or ill, points us toward our heavenly destination; all we face on this side of eternity has a purpose that ends in God's plan. Every changeable situation is designed to bring out holiness in us, though we may not see it as we're hauling dirty clothes to the laundromat or negotiating budget changes with our spouses.

Trust your life—and your marriage—to the unchangeable One. He will never let you down.

Thank You, Lord, for never altering. Help me trust in You,
no matter how often I fail You, myself, or my husband.

Clear the Air

*"And when you stand praying, if you hold
anything against anyone, forgive him."*
MARK 11:25 NIV

*H*ave you ever tried to pray when you were mad at your
husband? Chances are your prayers were difficult at
best. The animosity you felt hung over you like a toxic cloud,
hindering your communion with God. You couldn't offer up a
decent prayer until you had cleared the air.

God knows your every thought. He can tell if you're
harboring ill feelings toward your husband. He sees your anger
and the reason for it. And He knows that if left unaddressed,
such feelings can lead to resentment and bitterness. He wants
your marriage to be healthy and happy. That's why you find it
hard to pray with anger in your heart. God wants you to confess
your injured feelings to your husband so that they can heal.

And make sure to never go to bed angry at your spouse. If
any ill feelings have accumulated throughout the day, air them
before you turn out the lights. Doing so will make your nightly
prayers sweetly fragrant to God and your sleep much more
restful.

*Dear heavenly Father, I realize that prayer is the key to a successful
relationship with both You and my husband. Help me to live in such
a way that my petitions to heaven will always be heard. Amen.*

*Pray, Pray,
and Pray Again*

Day
117

*Keep on asking and it will be given you; keep on seeking and you will find;
keep on knocking [reverently] and [the door] will be opened to you.*
MATTHEW 7:7 AMP

*H*ave you been praying for God to revive the love between you and your husband or to heal your marriage? Have you been praying for a new job, new home, or new attitude?

In our society, where instant gratification seems the norm, sometimes we tend to give up praying about something if we don't get a response right away. But that's not what God would have us do.

Our good Father wants us to ask and keep on asking. That means we should pray, pray, and pray again. Then we are to seek and keep on seeking, actively looking for His answer, combining our endeavors with our prayers. And finally, we are to knock and keep on knocking respectfully, of course, until God opens the door.

If we want something badly enough and if we are working within His will, our good Father is more than willing to give us our heart's desire, to help us find answers, and to open all the doors. But we cannot faint or lose heart. We must be like the widow before the judge, persistent in our requests (Luke 18:1-5).

So, ladies, don't give up! For the woman who keeps on asking, seeking, and knocking will receive and find her heart's desire as door after door opens before her (Matthew 7:8). Alleluia, amen!

God, I come to You again, asking, seeking, and knocking. Hear my prayer!

God's Own

Never again will you be called "The Forsaken City"
or "The Desolate Land." Your new name will be "The City
of God's Delight" and "The Bride of God," for the LORD
delights in you and will claim you as his bride.
ISAIAH 62:4 NLT

*I*n the Old Testament, God is portrayed as Israel's husband. Yet because His people turned away from Him time after time, they were known as the Desolate Land, forsaken by God because of their refusal to follow Him, to be in fellowship with Him, to love Him and delight in Him.

Many marriages are desolate, barren, unfulfilled, for the same reasons. The husband and wife drift apart as they get busy with their own pursuits—work, children, house upkeep, hobbies. They don't have time to talk, to do things together, to enjoy each other. The children grow up and leave home, and wives find they are married to a stranger—the man they married is not the same after many years of neglect.

But we are to follow God's example as He patiently wooed His wayward bride back to Him, as He still is doing today. He loves us with an everlasting love, even when we are unlovable. He claims us as His own and is jealous when we follow after others. He delights in us because He loves us.

Lord, help me love my husband as You love me, unconditionally,
exclusively, boldly. May I delight in him, enjoying the unity
You planned for a man and his wife. Amen.

The Blame Game

*Our fathers have sinned, and are not;
and we have borne their iniquities.*
LAMENTATIONS 5:7 KJV

*I*n this mourning song, Jeremiah tells the sad story of his country's misery. Under attack by Babylon, the superpower of the day, the Jews suffer economic disaster and famine. Enemies raid the countryside, torturing, raping, and killing Judah's inhabitants, who blame their forefathers' sin for the terrible conditions they and their children endure.

As the song continues, however, God's people realize their personal responsibility: "Woe unto us, that we have sinned!" (Lamentations 5:16 KJV). This brief sentence lights a candle in their darkness. They admit their wrongdoing, and they acknowledge God: "Thou, O LORD, remainest for ever; thy throne from generation to generation" (Lamentations 5:19 KJV). Their circumstances do not change, but God's truth swings their universe back into place.

As married couples, we inherit the legacy of our parents, grandparents, and even generations back. Some forebearers may have loved Christ and left us spiritual treasures, but their imperfections still affect us and our families. Other ancestors bequeathed to us heavy physical, emotional, and spiritual damage.

Like Jeremiah's people, we can fixate on family failures and try to hold them responsible for our struggles. Or we can admit our own sins and look to God, freeing ourselves and our children from the blame game forever.

*Lord Jesus, thank You for Your grace, more powerful
than any sin in my family line—past, present, or future. Amen.*

Good Fences Make Good Marriages

*Be self-controlled and alert. Your enemy the devil prowls around like a
roaring lion looking for someone to devour.*
1 PETER 5:8 NIV

There are protective boundaries, or fences, that surround
our homes which are meant to keep weeds, rodents, and
unwelcome visitors out of our lives and our loved ones and
treasures safe and protected inside. We, as wives, also need to
build solid fences around our marriages to protect them and
secure them from the influences and distractions of the outside
world.

The fence of a good marriage is supported by the basic
principles of respect, encouragement, time alone, and protection.
Respect involves active listening and hearing what your partner
has to say and supporting him both publically and privately.
Encouragement involves compliments, support, praise, and
productive prodding. Time alone allows you to celebrate your
marriage, have fun together, and enjoy each other. Protection
establishes boundaries and safety nets that you need for your
relationship. Solid fences guard good marriages.

*Father, help me build a solid boundary around my marriage to protect it from
the world. Help me to always be on guard against the things that the enemy
tries to use to get into my marriage and separate my husband and me. Amen.*

Who's the Boss?

*But if any of you lacks wisdom, let him ask of God,
who gives to all generously and without reproach,
and it will be given to him.*
JAMES 1:5 NASB

Like it or not, we wives are creatures under authority. If we are Christians, we have sworn allegiance to Jesus Christ, and if we believe the Bible as the inerrant word of God, we also must swear allegiance to our husbands.

If a king ruled a country with subjects who were continually offering unwanted advice, criticizing his decisions, and undermining his orders, his rule would be both short and unhappy. Similarly, a boat with two rowers pulling in opposite directions lies dead in the water, at the mercy of wind and waves and in danger of running aground.

Marriage works the same way. Your husband did not put himself in the position of leadership; God did. This does not mean we can't offer respectful advice about crucial decisions, but it does mean that our husbands are the ones who should make the final decisions. Our job is to support them and trust God to direct them.

The best thing we can do is to let go of the rudder and lift our husbands up to the Lord in prayer, asking for wisdom and discernment on their behalf. Besides, has anyone ever truly regretted being obedient to God?

Dear Father, I pray You would strengthen my husband and give him wisdom as he leads. Give me the grace to follow willingly. Amen.

Treasures of Love

He chose us in Him before the foundation of the world,
that we would be holy and blameless before Him.
In love He predestined us to adoption as sons through Jesus
Christ to Himself, according to the kind intention of His will.
EPHESIANS 1:4–5 NASB

*G*od sees us the way we seldom see ourselves—holy, pure, and blameless. It seems impossible. Did He forget the day we impatiently shifted back and forth in line, sending mental daggers to the person ahead who moved too slowly? Or all the times we complain and fret when our plans do not unfold in the way we hope?

We start our day with good intentions. But in our rush to achieve and be, we aim, fall short, and miss the mark, not seeing that who we are has already been named. We have already been claimed. And because of Christ's loving sacrifice, we are free to see ourselves as we really are—chosen and beloved.

Picked out of refuse of our failures, we are restored and covered in a blanket of His grace. Set apart for a glorious purpose, we are bestowed with the jewels of His love. It is not He who forgets, but rather we who need to remember. We are His living treasure here on earth.

Like the way light pours through a diamond, His light reflects best through the love we offer to others, especially to our husbands. We are not to be hidden away for safekeeping, for only in use do the jewels of compassion, kindness, gentleness, and patience (Colossians 3:12) sparkle brightly against a dark and colorless world.

Father, help me to reflect Your love through my words and
deeds so that when others see me, they really see You. Amen.

A Rejoicing Relationship

Let thy fountain be blessed: and rejoice with the wife of thy youth.
PROVERBS 5:18 KJV

*I*s marriage a joy to you and your husband? Did you know that God commanded that it should be?

Proverbs 5:18 doesn't mean that if you got married when you were older, you can't enjoy life with your spouse, but it does encourage marital partners to be faithful to each other and blessed in their physical relationship. God made a marital union for joy, sexually and in other ways.

A wise couple spends time together, not only doing chores and making plans but delighting in each other physically and mentally. Sharing fun and two lively senses of humor will ease a marriage through the challenges it faces.

Have you had time to be alone with your husband? If not, the strains of marital life may begin to get the best of you. Take time for a date night or afternoon. Enjoy a nice romantic dinner, quick takeout in the park, or share the beauties of nature on an afternoon walk. Whatever you do, rejoice together in the relationship God gave you.

Then your fountain can be blessed and you may reconnect with each other in a new way.

Lord, thank You for the blessing of our relationship.
Help us keep it running strongly and watering each other's thirsty hearts.

Establish a New Beat

And Adam called his wife's name Eve;
because she was the mother of all living.
GENESIS 3:20 KJV

*A*dam called his wife *Eve* or "life-giver."

While we don't share Eve's distinction as being the mother of all living, we wives do share her calling as life-givers. It is our job to bring life to the home.

We do this, of course, by giving children physical life. But more important than that is the emotional and spiritual life we create and maintain in the home every day.

As life-givers, we become the heart of the home. The beat we establish will become the pulse of the house. If we have a cheerful countenance and a positive outlook, the rest of the household will tend to be cheerful and positive. If we smile, our family members will smile. If we laugh, so will they.

On the other hand, if our lives resonate with criticism and despair, we will quickly take away the life of the household. Its members will become critical, selfish, and despondent.

If your household isn't the way you'd like it to be, look in a mirror and repent. Ask God to give you a good jolt and establish a new heartbeat.

Let His life pulse through yours as you give new life to your family.

Father, I don't truly understand the power I have in my
house to control the attitudes and actions of my family. Renew my
joy so that I can impart Your love to my household. Amen.

*Don't use foul or abusive language. Let everything
you say be good and helpful, so that your words will
be an encouragement to those who hear them.*
EPHESIANS 4:29 NLT

Larissa winced as her husband Mike spewed venom at the
driver who had cut him off in traffic. She bit her lip as she
glanced over her shoulder at their two adolescent children in the
backseat, who were silently taking it all in.

Road rage is becoming a lamentable part of the American
driving experience. It's frightening to witness the dark side of
those we love bursting forth when they're hunched behind a
wheel. It's even more alarming when the wrath that fills our car
erupts from our own deep recesses. What are we teaching our
children? What would Jesus think if He were a passenger?

Larissa waited for a peaceful moment at home to raise her
concerns with Mike. As a believer, Mike agreed that God was
not glorified by volatile highway behavior, so they committed to
prioritizing better driving attitudes. They decided that when one
of them began showing symptoms of growing annoyance, the
other would quietly hum "This little light of mine, I'm gonna let
it shine. . ." or initiate a participatory game like 100 Questions
with the kids.

The plan worked! Larissa and Mike began diverting road
rage into pleasant family memories.

Make it a point to curb your road rage. By being calm in the
midst of whatever highway hazards you face, you'll be setting an
example for all your passengers.

*Master of the tempest, help us master our tempers
and relinquish even our ugliest habits to You. Amen.*

*The World's First
GPS System*

*Then the angel of God, who had been traveling in front of Israel's army,
withdrew and went behind them. The pillar of cloud also moved from in
front and stood behind them, coming between the armies of Egypt and Israel.
Throughout the night the cloud brought darkness to the one side and light to
the other side; so neither went near the other all night long.*
EXODUS 14:19–20 NIV

The world's first known GPS system was the pillar of cloud by day and fire by night that led the Israelites through the Sinai Peninsula. Imagine how comforting it was for the Israelites to follow that pillar on their trek. Better than a road map! It was a visible symbol—concrete evidence—of the presence of God.

Imagine if we had that holy pillar outside our front door to help us with big decisions: *Lord, should we take that job and move to another state? Or should we just stay put?*

We do have that holy pillar outside our homes. Inside, too. The Bible! Searching God's Word is like choosing to follow a map in a new country. He shows us where we need to end up and how we need to get there. Like God's people crossing the barren Sinai desert, the Bible teaches us to listen for God's directions, whether it's "Stop!" or "Camp here tonight" or "Quick, get a move on!" or "Time to rest." God's voice in our ear is the only map we need.

*Lord God, Your Word is better than a holy pillar.
In my daily life may I sense Your nearness.*

In God's Presence

> *Glory and honour are in his presence;*
> *strength and gladness are in his place.*
> 1 CHRONICLES 16:27 KJV

$\mathcal{I}$t is impossible for us with our imperfect minds to grasp the greatness of God. It is simply beyond our comprehension. However, God's Word gives us some really amazing insight into His character.

You know, in the Old Testament very few people were allowed into God's presence in the Holy of Holies because God is just that—holy. Now, because of Christ's blood, that veil separating the Holy Place from the Holy of Holies has been torn in two. Jesus is our High Priest, and because of that we have access to the Father. This doesn't make God less holy. It just means that because of Christ's blood those barriers have been removed.

In God's presence are glory, honor, strength, gladness, and a host of other wonderful characteristics. Our God is truly awesome. We can see that in creation, at Calvary, at the Garden tomb, and in our own lives.

Yes, God wants very much to be involved in our lives. He wants to be included in every aspect of our marriages, families, careers, and so forth. Great God that He is, He still cares for each of us individually. How about it? Will *you* let Him have the primary place in your home?

It's hard to understand why a great God like You would want to invest
so much in a sinner like me, but I'm so thankful that You do, Lord.

*Trusting Him
Enough to Wait*

*Now the LORD was gracious to Sarah as he had said,
and the Lord did for Sarah what he had promised.*
GENESIS 21:1 NIV

When God promised Abraham that he would have many descendents, it must have seemed too good to be true. (See Genesis 15.) Sarah must have thought that it *was* too good to be true, because rather than waiting on God, she decided to take matters into her own hands. To ensure the continuation of the family line, she gave Abraham her maidservant, Hagar. Unfortunately, her plan backfired and caused a great deal of pain for Sarah, Hagar, and Abraham and Hagar's son, Ishmael. Later, when she was blessed with her own son, Isaac, Sarah must have wondered why she didn't simply wait for God's plan to be fulfilled. His plan was *so* much better than hers.

Have you ever prayed for something and then told God how to get it for you? "Lord, we really need this miracle, and honestly, it would be easiest if you would just follow my simple three-step plan. . . ." The problem with this approach is that it ceases to be a miracle when we take matters into our own hands.

What are you waiting for today? Perhaps you are in a marriage that needs to be healed. Maybe you have a financial need or a physical problem. Whether your need is physical, spiritual, or emotional, entrust it to God. Relax and let Him handle it for you. The results will be better than you could ever dream.

*Father, when I need a miracle, I confess that at times it's tempting
for me to take matters into my own hands. Please help me to trust You,
to wait on You, and to rest secure in the knowledge that Your
plans are better than I could ever ask or imagine. Amen.*

Living Joyfully

Day
129

Live joyfully with the wife whom thou lovest.
ECCLESIASTES 9:9 ASV

What a wonderful admonition for a husband to live joyfully with his wife. Newlyweds are eager to start their lives together and often picture only the wonderful times they will share. As hardships come and go, we can lose that glow that surrounded us at first. We begin to struggle just to get through the day.

As wives, we have a responsibility to make our homes places of comfort, a places our husbands can come to relax after a hard day of work. Instead, we often hit them with a list of problems or censures as soon as they walk in the door. How are they to be joyful then? Let us try to meet them with smiles on our faces, thankful for them, no matter the situation. We can ask God to make us thankful and pleasant to live with.

Because of life's disappointments, we can lose our pleasure in God's company, too. We must work to regain that closeness so that we will be at peace and not causing contention. When we find joy in God, we are more apt to find joy in our husbands. With time and prayer we begin to look forward to time with God and our husbands. Imagine how joyful our homes will be then.

Thank You, Lord, for Your patience with me.
Please teach me to be joyful because You love me. Amen.

Reflections

*You are precious to me.
You are honored, and I love you.*
Isaiah 43:4 nlt

*B*renda stood before the bathroom mirror, her fingers clutching a mass of hip flesh. Humph. Pinch an inch? I think this might be *three* inches. She sighed heavily and, with shoulders bent in discouragement, walked out of the bathroom and away from her reflection.

The world would have us believe that we need to be skinny, 5'8" tall, blond, blue-eyed, and amply endowed in the bosom to have any self-worth. But that's not the truth.

No matter what we look like on the outside, in God's eyes, we are precious. He says so. It's written down. Not only are we precious, but we are honored. And He loves us!

That's not to say we should neglect our appearance. After all, our bodies are God's temples. They need to be exercised, well fed, and well slept. But our confidence and self-worth should not depend on how the world sees us, just on how God sees us precious, honored, and loved. It doesn't get any better than that.

So the next time you're discouraged with your appearance, check your reflection in God's mirror. You'll be picture-perfect!

Lord, my body may not be perfect, but Your love for me is! I am so precious in Your sight that you sent Your one and only Son to die for me. My heart, Lord, is overwhelmed. Thank You for loving me so very much just as I am!

Bear with each other and forgive whatever grievances
you may have against one another. Forgive as the Lord forgave you.
Colossians 3:13 NIV

*S*ometimes in our best attempt to live as one, we bump
into each other and cause some kind of injury instead. It is
inevitable. Live in marriage long enough and conflicts will arise.
Often we stumble unknowingly and trip over hurtful words or
deeds not done and fall into conflict with the one we love most.

It is a paradox to believe that replaying our hurts will give
our wound the air it needs, because it is in the retelling that
keeps us stuck. The word *resentment* comes from a root word
meaning to "re-feel." Thus, reliving our injuries only brings more
hurt feelings to us.

The only remedy for resentment is true forgiveness. True
forgiveness is God's idea and an extension of His love for
us, His wayward creation. It is a love that offers us complete
restoration with Him. Forgiveness is a sacred practice rooted
first in accepting His love and grace and thereby extending it to
our husbands. Through this we learn that peace comes after we
lay down our hurts at the cross and receive His power to forgive
those who have hurt us.

True forgiveness is a mystery that unfolds whenever we
lay down our records of wrongdoing and frees those we have
imprisoned by our pain, including ourselves.

Father, thank You for showing us the road to reconciliation
and the path toward peace. Help me show my husband
the love and grace You have bestowed to me. Amen.

Little White Lies

We are part of the same body.
Stop lying and start telling each other the truth.
EPHESIANS 4:25 CEV

A little white lie isn't so bad, is it? What about when it helps to avoid a problem in a relationship?

A woman recently explained that she felt that her husband was too controlling with money. So instead of making an honest accounting of what she spent on shopping trips, she hid receipts and padded the truth with tales of sales and special deals in order to avoid an argument. That can't be too bad, can it?

In truth, though, the reason that we lie is often for self-protection. We make the excuse that we're saving someone else from hurt, but really we're being selfish and just want to protect ourselves from embarrassment or fault.

Through the covenant of marriage, two become one. One flesh, one body. Lies, even small, white lies, create separation of the union that God established. Honor God by honoring that covenant and be truthful in all things, even when it causes you discomfort. It is selfless and God-honoring to be truthful—no matter what.

Father, I want to honor You by being truthful in all things. Help me to remember that it is selfish of me to lie to my husband, and give me the strength to tell the truth even when it causes me discomfort. Amen.

Mrs. Manners

Be courteous.
1 PETER 3:8 KJV

Today's world is often rude. It seems as if most people are totally consumed with their own concerns, barely giving thought to those around them. The simple courtesies that decades ago were an everyday part of life have long been forgotten. Yet we, as Christian wives, have a responsibility to exercise good manners in our own homes.

After a difficult day, you may be stressed out, exhausted, and want to be left alone. That makes it tempting to take out your frustrations on the one you love most as soon as he walks in the door. But acting on that impulse will only cause friction between you and your husband. Your home should be a refuge from the world. The last thing your spouse needs, after dealing with his own frustrations, is to endure a grumpy wife.

Home may be a place to "let your hair down" and just be yourself, but you don't have to cast off your manners, as well. Don't take unfair advantage of your husband. No matter how rotten you feel, he deserves to be treated courteously. Taking his feelings into consideration will go a long way in getting him to be thoughtful of yours.

*Dear Father, help me to make my home an
oasis from the rudeness of the world. Amen.*

Beauty Is Fleeting

*Charm is deceptive, and beauty is fleeting;
but a woman who fears the LORD is to be praised.*
PROVERBS 31:30 NIV

*L*et's face it. The aging process begins the moment we take our first breath. It's undeniable. We may color our gray or undergo plastic surgery, but we will never again look as we did in our twenties—something society tries to convince us is a problem. Accept the fact that beauty is fleeting. Years of gravitational pull eventually take its toll. Our physical bodies were not created to live forever. Someday we will return to the dust from which we were made.

Do not be distraught. Be encouraged! The Lord reminds us that the spiritual aspect of the aging process is far more important than our physical bodies. Our physical life is for a season. Our spiritual life is forever!

Choose to age gracefully by concentrating on the spiritual aspect of your being. Live in awe and respect for the Lord. Realize that your relationship with Him is the most important thing in this life. Then you will be able to laugh at your wrinkles while embracing your grandchildren. Your inner beauty will shine forth by the transforming power of the Holy Spirit. You will truly become more beautiful with each passing day!

*Dear Lord, my physical beauty may not last forever,
but my relationship with You will. So help me focus on that! Amen.*

On the Winning Side

*For the earth shall be filled with the knowledge
of the glory of the LORD, as the waters cover the sea.*
HABAKKUK 2:14 KJV

*L*eah scanned the newspaper before work—and then
wondered why on earth she had bothered. Just once, she'd
love to read an upbeat story! Wars, dictators, disasters, disease.
Even the gardening page contained dire warnings about killer bees.

Leah slapped the paper shut. Life seemed complicated
enough without importing trouble. She and her husband, Drew,
clashed more often than they clicked. Leah wanted a child; he
insisted they shouldn't.

"There's no such thing as job security anymore." Drew shook
his head. "Besides, do we really want to bring a child into this
rotten world?"

Habakkuk, the Jewish prophet, also lived during dangerous
times, with powerful, cruel Babylon threatening his country. Still,
God's people refused to renounce their idols. How Habakkuk
longed for his nation to return to the Lord! Someday, the
prophet predicted, God's magnificent power will overwhelm the
earth like a mighty ocean. Waves of truth, justice, and grace will
roll over Judah, Israel, Babylon, and all mankind.

God will not allow violence and injustice to continue forever.
With the resurrection of Jesus, He began the great invasion of
grace that wars against evil. Leah, Drew, and we can trust in
Christ as the conflict continues, knowing that God will prove the
overwhelming winner in the end.

*Almighty Father, when evil surrounds my family and me,
help us run into Your arms.
Amen.*

Winning Arguments
God's Way

*Do not be bitter or angry or mad. Never shout angrily
or say things to hurt others. Never do anything evil.*
EPHESIANS 4:31 NCV

Conflict resolution is a major challenge in a marriage where
everyone ultimately wants to be right. It's important to first
develop tools to help avoid conflict and then, when arguments
happen, to help get through them without doing damage.

During a disagreement, it's vital to avoid criticism and blame.
Phrase your needs or concerns as a request, not an accusation.
Listen. Don't interrupt or spend the time your husband is talking
thinking of what you're going to say next. Nothing fuels an
argument more than when someone thinks he isnít being heard.
Next, try to focus on the things in your discussion that you agree
on until the heat passes.

If you want to change your husband, change yourself first.
If you win the argument by getting what you want but in the
process damage your relationship by hurting trust and respect,
have you really won?

And as in all things, pray. It's the best way to refocus your
heart and mind onto the ways of God.

*Father, please forgive me for putting my agenda first so often. Help me to
honor You by respecting my husband. Aid me in holding my tongue, putting
aside my need to be right, and making peace and unity the goal. Amen.*

Spiritual Mortar

*Like a city whose walls are broken down
is a man who lacks self-control.*
PROVERBS 25:28 NIV

As wives, do we protect our spouses and ourselves from the effect of out-of-control feelings? Or do we think we can freely engage in harmful, unbridled emotions? If our anger and bitterness often fly out of control and attack our unsuspecting spouses, we must beware.

Experiencing and expressing negative emotions is normal, but that doesn't mean we use our loved ones as emotional punching bags. If we punish our spouses, we risk damaged households or even divorces.

But there's good news: Self-control is part of the fruit of the Spirit. As we grow in faith, God enables us to put uncontrolled emotions behind us and use our feelings to a better purpose. We don't stuff them into a box that explodes on us later, but through spiritual growth we effectively deal with sensitive issues that could harm our marriages.

Let's build the walls of marriage with the mortar of self-control. God has given us bricks of love to be put together with this fruit of His Spirit. But bricks alone, even those composed of love, will never build a strong wall.

How is this, your most personal building project, going?

*Lord, help me build my marriage with love and self-control.
May Your Spirit guide my heart in loving emotions
and actions that glorify You.*

Glory Be!

*For a man indeed ought not to cover his head,
forasmuch as he is the image and glory of God:
but the woman is the glory of the man.*
1 CORINTHIANS 11:7 KJV

Glory is one of those words in the Bible we don't think much about. We think we know what it means, so we don't dwell on it.

But then we come to 1 Corinthians 11:7 and are stumped. The man is the "glory of God, but the woman is the glory of the man." What does this mean, and how are we to live it out?

Glory has many definitions, but at its heart it carries the idea of splendor, praiseworthiness, and honor.

Man in his God-given manliness reflects the nature of God and brings honor to Him. Jesus was the ultimate example of this as He reflected and honored His Father.

But women are different. Having been created for man, we become their glory. As Jesus brought honor and praise to the Father, so we are to bring honor and praise to our husbands.

In practice, this means a wife should order her life according to her husband's wishes; she should defer decisions until after consulting him, and she should dress and act in ways that uphold his reputation.

Modern women may balk at this, but it is to God's glory that we so honor our husbands. Let us a glory be!

Father, help me honor my husband, knowing that as I do, my glory will grow inside, because the king's daughter is all glorious within. Amen.

Unconditional Love

*Do you think anyone is going to be able to drive a wedge
between us and Christ's love for us? There is no way! Not trouble,
not hard times. . .not even the worst sins listed in Scripture.*
ROMANS 8:35 MSG

All of us crave unconditional love. From our parents, from
our children, from our siblings and friends—but for us
women, we especially desire to experience it with our husbands.
However, for many of us, unconditional love is elusive.

We are commanded in scripture to love God with all that
we have and our neighbors as ourselves. Even if that love is not
returned. Our neighbors *include* our husbands. In 1 Corinthians
13:4–7, the challenge is given for us to love with perseverance,
selflessness, and humility. Unconditional love means we love
without keeping a record of his sins; we put up with anything,
looking for the best and not giving up.

George Matheson, a preacher in the Church of Scotland, was
completely blind at the age of twenty. When the woman who
had promised to marry him learned that he was going blind, she
broke their engagement. Years later, on the evening of his sister's
marriage, he was left alone. George wrote these words after an
experience known only to him that caused him severe mental
suffering:

> *O Love that will not let me go,
> I rest my weary soul in Thee.*

While George never knew the love of a wife, he rested in the
unconditional love of His Savior. Let us do the same.

*Jesus, thank You for Your love that never fails.
Help me love my husband as You have loved me. Amen.*

Dreaming Together

*The heart of her husband trusts in her,
and he will have no lack of gain. She does him
good and not evil all the days of her life.*
PROVERBS 31:11–12 NASB

Your wedding day was probably full of excitement, hope, and great expectations. Many marriages fade because of unmet expectations and disappointment. God gave man a wife to help him fulfill their God-given potential. You are now a couple with exponential possibilities.

If your husband isn't living up to your expectations and dreams for life, don't look to him to change; take it to the Dream Giver. God knows your husband's heart, and He knows what He created Him to be. He knows what the two of you can accomplish together.

If you feel like your husband isn't on your side, take God's side. Let go of the urge to push your husband for what you want and instead love him patiently, letting God take the lead.

It's hard to wait for your dreams to be realized, but when you talk to God about them, He'll bring them about in a way you never imagined, and you'll be surprised when you find you and your husband going in the same direction, down the same path, sharing the dream that God has for your lives—together!

Lord, help me to be patient and wait on You. Show me how to talk to my husband about the things You've put in his heart and mine. Amen.

*" 'Obey me, and I will be your God and you will
be my people. Walk in all the ways I command you,
that it may go well with you.' "*
JEREMIAH 7:23 NIV

One of the wonderful things about reading history is that we are able to see mistakes that have been made in the past and strive to avoid making them again. The command above is taken from a passage in which God is speaking through His prophet, Jeremiah. God is essentially asking the Israelites, Remember when I told you to obey Me? Yeah, you didn't listen to Me, did you? God is angry with His people, and He threatens to destroy the temple (which He does in Jeremiah's lifetime).

When the Israelites heard these words from Jeremiah's mouth, God was angry and hurt by their unfaithfulness. We, on the other hand, have the ability to read these words with the intention of obeying. We have seen the historical result of those who do not live the way God instructs. Now, as we look back on this history of God's people, we can choose to obey God's Word and to be His people. Our Bibles are full of examples of the ways God wants us to live and act. Delving into God's Word and applying it to our lives is what He wants for each one of us.

*Dear Lord, I want to please You with the way I live. Give me the discipline
to read Your Word and the desire to apply what I read to my life. Amen.*

Show Your Love

*My little children, let us not love in word,
neither in tongue; but in deed and in truth.*
1 JOHN 3:18 KJV

You've heard over and over from your childhood that actions speak louder than words. It's so true that it's almost a cliché, but it's a biblical concept nonetheless. It's also common sense. Another way to say it is "Put your hands and feet where your mouth is."

You know how you feel if someone tells you over and over again that he will do something and he continually fails to come through. Love is like that. You can tell your husband day after day that you love him, but if you never show him, your words are meaningless. It's true that he needs to hear those three little but powerful words, but you have to back them up with attitude and action.

You know this is what you want from him. Can you truly do any less? When he tries to do something nice for you, don't criticize his efforts even if it's not what you had in mind. When he shows you affection in public, don't pull away in embarrassment. That just sends a very negative message to him and everyone around you.

Find special ways to show your husband that you love him. But more importantly, show him you love him just by the way you treat him throughout your daily activities. It will bring more joy to your marriage.

*Jesus, You showed Your love by laying down Your life for me.
With Your help I will show love through my actions.*

Attitude of the Heart: Forgiveness

Jesus said, "Father, forgive them,
for they do not know what they are doing."
LUKE 23:34 NIV

*V*anessa was distraught, as her marriage seemed to be dissolving into divorce. How could her husband hurt her like this? How could he cheat on her?

No one could blame Vanessa if she could not forgive her husband. No one, that is, except God. As our Lord, God incarnate, laid on the cross, He voiced miraculous words and attitude of the heart: "Father, forgive them. . . ." God modeled forgiveness for us in giving us Jesus who, as our Lord, without sin, died for us while we were still sinners (Romans 5:8). Jesus did not forgive us *after* we came to Him but *while* we were still sinning.

God calls each of us to forgive our husbands even when they have not repented and continue to sin (Romans 12:14–21). God also calls us to pray for our husbands. God can transform our marriages when we have His attitude of forgiveness.

God knows we are not able to forgive the hurt and pain in our marriage without His supernatural power. Jesus said, "Whatever you ask for in prayer, believe that you have received it, and it will be yours" (Mark 11:24 NIV). When we ask Him, God promises to give us the ability through the power of the Holy Spirit to have this attitude of the heart—forgiveness.

Lord, I don't have the ability to forgive, but I desire to
follow Your model of forgiveness and forgive my husband.
Give me the attitude of Your heart of forgiveness.

Yes, I Did That

*When pride comes, then comes disgrace,
but with humility comes wisdom.*
PROVERBS 11:2 NIV

*K*ate was late again, and her husband was angry. Kate's chronic lateness was starting to affect her marriage, but unfortunately, any time her husband brought it up, Kate got defensive and blamed him or someone else for her inability to arrive on time. Their discussions on the topic always ended in a stalemate—to be swept under the carpet until the next episode.

After running late several times in a row, Kate finally ran out of excuses. One day she simply decided to forgo the explanations and admit she was wrong. "I'm sorry I was late again, honey. I am selfish with my time and haven't respected your time either. Could you please forgive me?" The change in her husband's response was dramatic. When Kate finally let go of her pride, she and her husband were able to have a productive conversation.

When your spouse or someone else in your life confronts you with a shortcoming, how do you respond? Do you find yourself becoming defensive? Does your pride ever get in the way? Pride can keep us from admitting we are wrong, and it can prevent us from effectively resolving conflict. Ask the Lord to reveal areas of pride in your life so that you can do your part to live wisely and in harmony with others.

*Father, I know pride is not pleasing to You. Please expose
the areas of my life that are controlled by pride, and teach me a spirit
of wisdom and humility so that I might serve You better. Amen.*

Nobility

A wife of noble character who can find?
She is worth far more than rubies.
PROVERBS 31:10 NIV

*P*rincess mania. It seems that every young girl dreams of being a princess wearing a glittering crown of jewels. We are captivated by the story of Cinderella. Fairy-tale romances tug at our heartstrings. Rubies, diamonds, emeralds—we're drawn to precious stones that glitter and sparkle.

We may be attracted to all that glitters, but the Lord sees diamonds in the rough. He sought us and bought us with His precious blood. We are now daughters of the King. He perceives our inner character from afar. In God's eyes, a wife of noble character is worth far more than rubies! Noble character denotes greatness and dignity. Yet as daughters of the King, our temperament should reflect His. Jesus did not flaunt His position or power when He walked on earth. Instead, He humbly served others.

A wife of noble character serves the members of her family. Meeting their needs is of utmost importance. She is industrious and productive. Providing for those less fortunate is a priority. Her interests are focused on others instead of simply creating a comfortable environment for herself. As a daughter of the King, she views her position as a privilege and responsibility, not something to lord over others. Are you a wife of noble character?

Dear Lord, help me become a wife of noble character.
Teach me what that means. Amen.

His and His Alone

I am my beloved's.
SONG OF SOLOMON 7:10 KJV

*A*ntoine de Saint-Exupery said in his book *The Little
Prince that "you become responsible, forever, for what you
have tamed." When you choose to relinquish your freedom and
embrace the bonds of marriage, your husband becomes forever
responsible for you. He must care for you, the one he has tamed,
and for better or worse, you belong to him.

You are not an object to be manipulated but a woman to be
cherished! You are your beloved's. He staked his claim to your
heart and declared before the God of heaven to love you until
death. And you made the same promise to love him in return.
Such vows are not to be taken lightly.

Show your husband you are completely his. Be discreet and
chaste, saving your affections for the man you married. Dress to
impress your husband, not others who might be looking on. Give
yourself to him completely. In doing so, you will prove your trust
and adoration and leave no doubt in his mind that he is truly
your beloved.

*Heavenly Father, help me to fully realize the commitment that
I made to my husband on the day of our marriage. May I forever
prove to him through my actions that I am his and his alone. Amen.*

Lead Me Not into Temptation

Day
147

Marriage is to be held in honor among all.
HEBREWS 13:4 NASB

Jessica returned to her cubicle after the staff meeting to find a bag of her favorite vending machine chips on her desk. Yesterday it had been a tiny box of chocolates and the day before, a cup of hot tea fixed just the way she liked it.

Jessica's eyes darted across the workroom to the source of the unsolicited gifts. Phillip, the new copy editor, nodded and smiled. As Jessica automatically nodded in return, uneasiness clouded her heart.

Innocuous items, she'd told herself. Innocent expressions of friendship among coworkers. Or. . .was there something more?

With her eight-year marriage experiencing a rocky patch, Jessica knew that she was vulnerable to the attentions of other men. But she also knew that the Lord had brought her husband into her life and joined them together by vows in His omnipotent name. God expected her to honor those vows, her solemn promise to fight for her marriage and work out problems that would inevitably arise.

Taking a deep breath, Jessica crossed the floor and placed the chips on Phillip's desk. "Thank you for your thoughtfulness, Phillip, but I can't accept any other gifts. I appreciate your friendship as a work associate, but I feel it wouldn't honor my marriage—or God—for me to accept the generosity of another man."

Ever-loving Lord, give me strength to honor my marriage
as the sacred relationship You created it to be. Amen.

God's Wonder Woman

Now Deborah, a prophetess, the wife of Lapidoth,
was judging Israel at that time.
JUDGES 4:4 NKJV

*P*rophetess. Judge. Wife. Mother. All these describe
Deborah, a remarkable woman who answered God's
leadership call and governed Israel for sixty years. In an era
when women did not learn to read, let alone interpret the
Law, Deborah held court every day under a palm tree. Her
countrymen arrived from near and far to entrust their disputes
to Deborah's godly insights. We don't know Lapidoth's reaction,
but during Old Testament times, a woman could not act without
her husband's consent. So by God's grace, Deborah managed her
home at the same time she managed the nation.

During the early years of Deborah's tenure, Israel struggled
with unstable spiritual and political conditions. Many
worshipped idols; as a result, God could not bless them. For
twenty years, Jabin, the cruel Canaanite king, and his general,
Sisera, made constant raids on their villages. Then God spoke
through Deborah, summoning Barak to lead an army against
Sisera's forces. Barak refused to go to war without Deborah, so
she traveled far from home to experience the same dangers he
and his soldiers faced. God led them to victory and disposed of
Sisera through Jael, another woman. Deborah's praise welled
up in a warlike song of triumph that reminded the Israelites to
worship their powerful, wonderful God.

God has equipped each of us with the ability to perform the
duties to which He has called us. Are you letting Him work His
way in your life?

Father, I often limit the possibilities You envision for me.
Help me to dream Your dreams. Amen.

Practicing to Sin

*"For out of the overflow of the
heart the mouth speaks."*
MATTHEW 12:34 NIV

A week after their blowup, she couldn't even remember
the comment that had set her off. But that morning, her
husband's words had stung. All day, bitterness grew in her soul as
their conversation replayed in her head, prompting her to think
up things to say to let him know how wrong he was.

She knew she ought to forgive him, but the words that came
out of her mouth the minute he got home from work were the
very same words that had been running through her head since
the morning. They slipped out as easily as if she'd been practicing
them all day long—which, in fact, she had.

An actress rehearses her lines so that when she's standing in
front of the audience on opening night, she gets her part right.
No matter how nervous she is or what else might go wrong on
stage, what comes out of her mouth will be what she's practiced.
We are the same. The thousands of separate thoughts we think
every day are the seeds from which our speech grows. If we want
to please God with our lips, we need to please Him with our
hearts and our thoughts first.

*Dear God, may the thoughts in my heart and the words
that come out of my mouth be pleasing in Your sight. Amen.*

The Compare Snare

Do not want anything that belongs to someone else.
Don't want anyone's house, wife or husband,
slaves, oxen, donkeys or anything else.
EXODUS 20:17 CEV

Connie and Sarah took their daughters on a trip together to celebrate the girls' birthdays. On this trip, the green-eyed monster seemed to come along, uninvited, to join Connie. Sarah's husband had tucked love notes in her suitcase. Connie's husband didn't even call her. Sarah's daughter loved the theater and museums they went to; Connie's daughter was bored and just wanted to shop.

By the trip's end, Connie felt consumed with envy. She couldn't even remember anything good about her husband! Only his shortcomings. And her daughter's faults loomed large compared to those of Sarah's daughter. Connie returned home angry and disappointed.

Women have a tendency to compete with each other: the size of our husband's paychecks, the grandeur of our homes, the accomplishments of our kids. There's a reason that coveting appears in the Ten Commandments. God is concerned with what fills our minds. He wants us to take envy seriously; if unchecked, it can trip us up, sending us right into sin's lure.

When we have a tendency to compare ourselves with other women, we need to check ourselves, confess those sinful (yes, sinful!) thoughts, and love our husbands and children for who they are—*not* who we think they should be.

Lord, it is so easy to let envy snuff out gratitude.
Put a check on my spirit when I start to envy. Make me a
woman whose confidence rests in knowing my value to You.

Pick Your Battles

*Don't have anything to do with foolish and
stupid arguments, because you know they produce quarrels.*
2 TIMOTHY 2:23 NIV

*H*ave you gotten into a foolish argument with your spouse and regretted the words almost as soon as they left your mouth? If not, you probably haven't been married long. The temptation to disagree over even the most frivolous issues comes to everyone. Paul advised young pastor Timothy not to get into such disputes with his congregation. Since congregations are made up of people, many of whom are married, that becomes good family advice, too.

Quarrels over foolish topics can be quick to appear, but they may also have long-lasting negative effects on your marriage. So don't waste time debating unimportant issues that are unlikely to positively influence your love for each other. Instead, carefully pick your battles with your spouse. What color he paints his workroom isn't likely to affect your marriage (you probably don't have to go into that room often), but the color of your spiritual life will. So let him paint those walls as he likes. Just make sure you hash out the idea of buying that four-bedroom, three-full-baths house with a two-car garage that doesn't fit into your present budget.

Don't be afraid to disagree on important issues, but let those stupid ones pass you by. Agree to disagree in love when nothing else will work.

Lord, help us to disagree with gentleness and to pick our battles carefully.

Day 152

Burden-Bearing

*The heartfelt counsel of a friend is
as sweet as perfume and incense.*
PROVERBS 27:9 NLT

Janet's friends and family often came to her for advice. She always seemed to have just the right words to say. Lately though, she was feeling overwhelmed because it seemed like everyone needed her at once. Besides, she had her own problems and responsibilities. What she really wanted was some time away—from her loved ones *and* their problems.

Caring for others, listening to them, and offering wise counsel is biblical. God created us to live in community, and we are instructed to bear one another's burdens. But there is often a fine line between bearing others' burdens and bearing *responsibility* for their burdens. It drains us and, more importantly, it can keep them from seeking answers directly from God.

It's essential to remember that our job is to point others to Christ, not become a substitute for Him. Allowing our friends unlimited access to our advice and counsel is one way this can happen. Sometimes the wisest words of advice we can offer are "Tell it to Jesus."

*Father, help me to wisely discern the difference between
bearing others' burdens and taking responsibility for their problems.
Help me to point others to You. Amen.*

Fruitful Wives

Day
153

*Thy wife shall be as a fruitful vine by the sides
of thine house: thy children like olive plants
round about thy table.*
PSALM 128:3 KJV

In Psalm 128, God makes several promises to the man who
fears the Lord and walks in His ways. This man will be blessed
with a happy life. He will have a job that will enable him to eat. He
will have many children. And he will have a fruitful wife.

How do wives become fruitful? Apparently, it is not
something we do in and of ourselves. Psalm 128:4 says, "Thus
shall the man be blessed. . ." (KJV). This implies that God will
cause all these promises to become reality for the faithful man.
God will make us fruitful.

As fruitful vines in the houses of faithful men, we require
the nourishment of love (Ephesians 5:29), the fertilizer of
praise (Proverbs 31:28), and sometimes the pruning of reproof
(Proverbs 27:6). Truly God-fearing husbands will give us
everything we need to grow, even when we don't like it.

But what about the woman whose husband doesn't fear
God? She also requires love, praise, and, at times, reproof. And,
like Abigail, she must remain faithful. As she fulfills her duties
toward her husband and behaves in a godly manner, God will
bring fruit in her life. And that fruit may include her husband's
salvation.

No matter what your situation, praise God for His Son of Jesus
Christ, for working in your lives, for blessing your home. And pray
that as you abide in Jesus, you will bear much eternal fruit.

*Father, thank You for being in my life. Help me to grow
in Your Spirit and bear eternal fruit. In Your name, amen.*

Word of Mouth

*In Joppa there was a disciple named Tabitha. . .
who was always doing good and helping the poor.*
ACTS 9:36 NIV

*H*ave you ever had your husband brag about you? His words of praise can be embarrassing and uplifting at the same time. While we are ill at ease, knowing that what we've accomplished has been by the grace of God, we are also gratified to know that our husband is delighted with our efforts.

Although we aren't to seek out confirmation from others, we still need to make sure our actions find our husband's approval. Without that, we will have strife in our marriage that shouldn't be there. We need to listen to what our husbands are saying about us to others.

At the same time, we should pray about God's desire for our lives. Would He say, "Well done, good and faithful servant" (Matthew 25:23 NIV)?

Each time we take on a task, we must consider what both God and our husband would say. Our actions reflect back on them, and we would not want to cast shadows instead of light.

Doing good can be rewarding, but our actions must be for the right reason. Let us ask ourselves, "Is this what God wants me to do? Would my husband approve?" If the answer is yes, then we can step out in faith, confident of pleasing those who mean the most.

*Lord, so often I want to do everything I'm asked to do.
Help me to weigh those choices I make. Amen.*

Resting in Hope

Day
155

I wait for the LORD, my soul waits,
and in his word I put my hope.
PSALM 130:5 NIV

The old adage "If you always expect the worst, you will never be disappointed" had been drilled into April's head since childhood. But now, as a new believer, she knew that this worldly view was not God's truth. Yet she was having difficulty training her mind and heart to hope and expect good things.

One night, unable to sleep, April left her husband and their warm bed, grabbed her bedside Bible, and headed downstairs to her favorite living room chair. She switched on the lamp, opened her Bible, and turned to the psalms, reading aloud the verses she had previously highlighted and bookmarked: "You have granted him the desire of his heart and have not withheld the request of his lips" (Psalm 21:2 NIV); "They cried to you and were saved; in you they trusted and were not disappointed" (Psalm 22:5 NIV); and then, finally, her favorite, "Find rest, O my soul, in God alone; my hope comes from him" (Psalm 62:5 NIV). As she closed her Bible and then her eyes, she began to pray, asking God to renew her mind, to help her trust in Him, and to give her an expectant hope.

Several minutes later, April crawled back into bed and gave her husband a light kiss before settling into the deep slumber that comes with trusting and resting in the hope of God's Word.

Lord, renew my mind and spirit. Help me to trust in You, to have great
expectations, and to rest easy in the hope and truth of Your Word.

Faith Booster

*Therefore by Him let us continually offer the
sacrifice of praise to God, that is, the fruit of our lips,
giving thanks to His name.*
HEBREWS 13:15 NKJV

*D*on't we just love it when people say thank you after we've done something for them? For some reason, it makes us more willing to perform some other duty, maybe an even greater task than the one we've already provided.

On the flip side, we consider it somewhat rude, even a bit disheartening, when we don't get that simple thank-you for our efforts whether that person is our spouse, our child, a neighbor, or a stranger on the street.

Imagine God not getting a thank-you for all He's done for us. Imagine His disappointment when we neglect to say those two simple words.

Remember when Jesus healed the ten lepers and only one, a Samaritan, returned, and with a loud voice glorified God, and fell down on his face at His feet, giving Him thanks (Luke 17:15-16 NKJV)? What was Jesus response? 'But where are the nine? Were there not any found who returned to give glory to God except this foreigner?' (Luke 17:17-18 NKJV).

Be like that good Samaritan: 'Consider what great things [the Lord] has done for you' (1 Samuel 12:24 NKJV) and give Him thanks. When you do, you will not only be pleasing God but also boosting your faith as you remember all the ways He has answered your prayers in the past. Such assurance of His hand in your life cannot help but fill you with peace.

So go ahead make God's day. Thank Him, and then bask in that peace that surpasses all understanding (Philippians 4:6-7 NKJV).

*Dear God, there are so many things You have done for me.
So here I am, falling down at Your feet to shout, THANK YOU!*

A Day in the Life

*So be careful how you live. Don't live like fools,
but like those who are wise. Make the most of every
opportunity in these evil days. Don't act thoughtlessly,
but understand what the Lord wants you to do.*
EPHESIANS 5:15–17 NLT

*M*ost of us feel the same way: busy, busy, busy! Work-at-home wives, work-outside-the-home wives, stay-at-home-with-the-kids wives. . .whatever the case, busyness seems to prevail. Women often say that things would be much easier if they had a wife at home to help them. Their point is that they have to work *and* take care of the home, etc., while their husbands only have to work since they still have a wife to take care of the day-to-day things around the house.

So does that mean that God got it wrong? Was He wrong when He designed men and women to be different and to fulfill different roles in the home? These days, women want it all: a career, a family, a home, church responsibilities, hobbies, etc. It's not necessarily wrong to want all of those things, but maybe it's a little off balance to demand that our husbands live at the same frenetic pace that we impose upon ourselves.

If things seem a bit skewed in your life, perhaps it's time to consider reordering priorities and lightening your load.

*Heavenly Father, please show me what You have for me.
I want to live as You have called me to live, not as how
I contrive to be the best way. Help me to change my focus to Your
will and to want nothing more than that out of my life. Amen.*

Full of Laughter

*A merry heart doeth good like a medicine:
but a broken spirit drieth the bones.*
PROVERBS 17:22 KJV

What type of atmosphere fills your home? Are you and your husband truly able to enjoy being in each other's company? Do you look forward to coming home from wherever it is you have been? Think about it. Your home should be a haven—a retreat from the cares of the world. That doesn't mean you should never discuss your concerns, but you also need to have fun. You really do need to laugh.

Now don't use this to justify mocking your husband's weaknesses or failures. Just realize that finding ways to laugh together is physically healthy—and a lot less expensive than medicine and doctors! Laughter is so healthy for your marriage. If you can have fun with your husband, your marriage will be much happier.

Share funny stories together. Play games that incite laughter. Watch a comedy together. Just acting silly together will draw you closer to one another.

If joy and laughter fill your home, you're on the right track. If you've always taken life completely seriously, it's time to let down your guard and loosen up a bit. Decide to do some genuine laughing. You'll be glad you did.

*Lord, fill our home with joyous laughter,
and let our gladness spread cheer to those around us.*

Looking for Love

*"As the Father has loved me, so have I loved you.
Now remain in my love."*
JOHN 15:9 NIV

*A*ll her life, Tanya had dreamed of being swept off her feet by the man of her dreams. She knew that if she waited long enough and patiently enough, her prince charming would eventually come and give her the love she'd always longed for. When she finally fell in love and married, Tanya prepared herself for the happily ever after.

What Tanya didn't know was that her husband could never love her in the way that she longed for. No husband can. Many couples enter marriage believing that it's the beginning of an effortless happily ever after. They look to one another to fulfill their every need. It doesn't take long for disappointment and disillusionment to set in when spouses fail to meet expectations.

No human being can love us the way God intends for us to be loved. When we look to our spouse to provide that love, we will be disappointed time and time again. Only God can fill the void in our heart. When we learn to allow God's love to seep into our deepest places and fill our deepest needs, our human relationships become transformed. We no longer hold others to high and impossible expectations but are free to receive the love that they can offer us without being selfish and demanding, for God is meeting our deepest love needs.

Father, You are the Lover of my soul. You alone can meet all my needs. Help me to accept Your love so that I can love others with purity and grace. Amen.

Put Prayer First

*And we will receive from him whatever we ask
because we obey him and do the things that please him.*
1 JOHN 3:22 NLT

It's easy to pray for the needs of others and to make requests for our own health and welfare. But it's very difficult to invite God into the marital conflicts that we create ourselves. Not only is it difficult, it's often the last thing on our minds! That's His desire, though. He wants to be a part of even that aspect of our marital relationships.

As human beings, we aren't equipped to lay aside pride and surrender control in all circumstances. Our personal wills and our desire to be right are powerful forces that limit good judgment and get in the way of self-control. But if God, the One who calms the seas and stops the wind, is truly the captain of our lives, we need to cry to Him in the midst of our marital storms. He will help us to surrender all to Him and then guide us safely to shore.

So the next time you find yourself bickering with your husband, remember that God is not the author of confusion but brings peace and harmony to all situations. Go to God in prayer, surrendering your will, asking for His guidance. It will be impossible to resume the bickering after refocusing and turning it over to the Lord.

*Father, I thank You for my husband and for all of the
wonderful things about him. Please help me to be willing
to set aside my pride and to release control to You. Amen.*

Dehydrated

*"Blessed are those who hunger and thirst
for righteousness, for they will be filled."*
MATTHEW 5:6 NIV

*A*re you thirsting for more of God in your life and in your marriage? Or are you feeling a little dehydrated? Many marriages start out strong, but as the years go by and children come along, we forget why we do what we do. We forget our purpose. We forget why we got married in the first place. What was once a marriage full of love and passion is now in daily survival mode.

Take the time today to pray for your marriage. Ask God to stir up your passion for the things of Christ and for your husband. Ask the Lord to remind you about your purpose as His child and as a wife.

Then set aside a day this weekend to reconnect with your husband. Talk about all of the little things that made you fall in love in the first place. Hold hands as you take a walk in the park. Get yourselves back to the basics.

And take time to reconnect to God. Ask forgiveness for getting out of touch with Him and ask Him to fill you up and be the center of your life and marriage again. If you hunger and thirst after God and His righteousness, you will be filled! That's a promise straight from the lips of Jesus.

*Dear Heavenly Father, take control of my life and marriage.
Fill me up with Your love, and allow it to spill over onto my husband.
Help us rekindle our romance. Amen.*

Endless Love

And because iniquity shall abound,
the love of many shall wax cold.
MATTHEW 24:12 KJV

*P*eople fall in and out of love everyday. Starry-eyed couples pledge undying devotion in marriage ceremonies while judges award divorces in courtrooms. How is it possible that two people who adore each other could eventually part ways? How do marriages fall apart? And most importantly, how can you keep it from happening to you?

Marriages rarely crumble overnight. It is generally a slow process that takes years to complete. Most couples don't even realize that it's happening. But gradually their love for one another is replaced by something—or someone—else. There are a host of love killers that prey on marriages. The best way to prevent them from attacking yours is to stay on guard.

Relationships require a lot of maintenance. Your marriage won't survive on the back burner. No matter how hectic life may be, take time for your husband. Don't allow outside commitments to distract you from the person who matters most. Keep the flame of your marriage fanned and you'll never have to worry about your love growing cold.

Dear God, help me to guard against the things that would
try to replace my love for my husband, and bless my marriage
so that it will last for the rest of my life. Amen.

Casting Away Anxiety

*Casting the whole of your care [all your anxieties,
all your worries, all your concerns, once and for all] on Him,
for He cares for you affectionately and cares about you watchfully.*
1 PETER 5:7 AMP

A young bride stands at the window late at night, willing her husband's return from working late. He hasn't called to tell her where he is or what time to expect him home. Any moment now, she's sure the police will be at her door to tell her she's a widow.

Parents sit at the bedside of their child who is sick, unable to comprehend the illness that is sucking the life from her. Or a husband loses his job and is unable to find another quickly. The bills are piling up because there is no money to pay them.

These are extreme examples of circumstances that cause us to be anxious. Yet the little things cause just as much worry as the big things. The Amplified Bible expands on the word *care* in 1 Peter 5:7 by lumping together all our anxieties, all our worries, and all our concerns.

With every anxiety, God calls us to throw everything on Him, to let go of the burden of worry, large or small. The picture here is one of Him gathering them all together into one sack and carrying it on His shoulders. He wants to be our burden-bearer because He is able, because He cares for us affectionately and watchfully.

He knows the burden of anxiety we carry. Roll it off onto His mighty shoulders today.

*Father, give me the strength to let go of this burden of anxiety I carry.
You desire to bear my burden for me because of Your awesome love.
Thank You for carrying my load. Amen.*

Season for Love

My beloved spake, and said unto me,
Rise up, my love, my fair one, and come away.
For, lo, the winter is past, the rain is over and gone.
SONG OF SOLOMON 2:10–11 KJV

Cara never wanted to live through another winter like the past one.

After Christmas, her husband's company reduced his hours. Nathan rarely talked about it. He spent his time on the computer, under his car, and in the basement, working on projects that seemed to go nowhere.

Meanwhile, Cara struggled with job overload. Her bosses loved her work—too much! She worked late and buried herself in the assignments she brought home. Cara tried not to nag Nathan about laundry, dirty dishes, and other tasks. By March, Cara's pounding headaches showed up every day as if she'd made an appointment with them.

Finally, Nathan began to work a full shift again. He resumed singing off-key in the shower. He even smiled at breakfast sometimes. And he began talking about their going away together.

Cara wanted to yell, "Excuse me? Maybe you've noticed that my job problems *haven't* let up?" A romantic getaway—the last thing on her mind! But something inside, like the little purple crocuses in her icy flower bed, turned toward Nathan like the sun. Perhaps they could talk.

Maybe it was the season for love after all.

Lord of love, the world wages war against our marriage. Please help
us cling to You and to each other, celebrating every victory we can. Amen.

The Power to Change

Accept one another, then,
just as Christ accepted you.
ROMANS 15:7 NIV

There is an old saying that men marry women hoping they won't change, while women marry men hoping that they will. Humorous at it may be, it instills a sense of sadness when we realize in our own lives how often it is true.

We usually begin marriage with high hopes and towering expectations, only to experience the pain and disillusion when our hopes come crashing down. And on it goes. We cope by keeping our love locked away and creating a list of conditions: "If only he would do *this* or stop doing *that*, I would accept him completely." It seems so reasonable. Everyone agrees. He needs to do better.

The saddest part of living this way is that conditional acceptance means we only love those who deserve it. Jesus, on the other hand, loves us exactly as we are. He accepts us despite our failings and shortcomings. He has redeemed us and blessed us with gifts of mercy, kindness, gentleness, and patience. These are gifts so powerful that when given to our husbands as an offering to Christ, things do begin to change.

Change is a funny thing. It is always there, breathing underneath the surface of our lives. Our job is simply to love our husbands and put the work of change in God's capable hands. After all, He loves more and sees more than we do.

Father, thank You for accepting me exactly as I am. Help me to accept and love my husband where he is today, trusting that You have a plan. Amen.

The Perfect Architect

*"You hypocrite, first take the log out of your own eye,
and then you will see clearly to take the speck out of your brother's eye."*
MATTHEW 7:5 ESV

How easy is it to see our husband's flaws? If we wanted to, we all could probably make a long list of husband improvements—soon we'd be redesigning his floor plan, repainting the dark places in his life, and adding on a new roof.

But God didn't make us the designers of our spouses' lives, and there's a good reason for it. Hard as it may be to believe, we aren't perfect either. If He made us the architects of our husbands' lives, eventually we'd realize that those brightly painted walls weren't quite plumb, that we'd added too many rooms (or left out an important one), or that the new roof wasn't quite waterproof. Less-than-perfect vision leads to serious errors being made.

But there's good news—our husbands don't get to design our lives, either. Though spouses can make suggestions and give wise advice, they can't take the place of God. He's the designer who is never mistaken in the plan.

Let's let God become the architect of our lives. Then we'll be blessed in our marriages—and able to see without that log getting in our way.

*Lord, we want You as our life designer.
Show us where—and when—we need to change.*

Becoming Love

*May the God who gives endurance and encouragement
give you a spirit of unity among yourselves as you follow Christ Jesus.*
ROMANS 15:5 NIV

*I*n today's culture, we are led to believe that true love is something we find through an instantaneous connection with another person. And while some measure of that may be true, authentic love is that which is created and sustained by God. That is the love that withstands many tests and weathers every storm.

We do not begin our marriages fully equipped to handle all that life will hurl at us. It comes with time. Just like a runner who faces a marathon, we cannot tread upon the sacred ground of love without the training that living each day together provides. There are days we make great strides and others when we trip over the detritus of life. Eventually, though, we learn the art of jumping over the obstacles we sense are there.

Staying in the race has a lot to do with breathing and good shoes, but the secret to our stamina lies in keeping our eyes on the lead runner ahead. Jesus, who already conquered death and finished the race, has come back amid our sweat and tears to show us the way.

It takes a lifetime of marriage to learn the secret of true love. Love is found not in the beginning of our expectations but in the end of our becoming love itself.

*Father, You are the Creator of Love. Thank You for giving us the strength
to endure the journey and the light for showing us the way. Amen.*

Pleasing God or
Pleasing Self

*Obviously, I'm not trying to win the approval of people, but of God.
If pleasing people were my goal, I would not be Christ's servant.*
GALATIANS 1:10 NLT

A Christian camp director read the following statement,
burning it into the minds of his listeners: "Only two
choices on the shelf, pleasing God or pleasing self."

While this statement should sum up all our relationships, it
especially applies in marriage. There is no room for selfishness in
a marriage.

In Galatians 1:10, Paul states that his goal is to please God.
And the proof he gives is that he wouldn't be serving Christ as he
did if he were seeking to please others or himself. He could have
done without the aggravations, the misunderstandings, and the
persecutions he experienced. Yet he accepted them because he
no longer mattered—only by choosing to please God instead of
others or himself was he fulfilled and content.

Most of us wives fall into the trap of people-pleasing. But
it seems that the harder we try to please others, the less we are
fulfilled.

When we choose to put our focus on pleasing God, it doesn't
matter what people say about us. Only in pleasing God, being
obedient to His commands and guidelines for life, especially in
our marriage relationships, do we truly feel fulfilled and content.

*Father, I long to hear the words, "Well done, My good and faithful servant."
Help me choose to please You in all things today, for only then am I satisfied.
Amen.*

*The next day John saw Jesus coming toward him and said,
"Look, the Lamb of God, who takes away the sin of the world!"*
JOHN 1:29 NIV

These words of John, spoken soon after Jesus' baptism in the Jordan River, contain the essence of the Bible in a nutshell. Though the Bible was written by different men from different countries, in different languages, over a span of thousands of years, it has a singular focus: Jesus. The books of history, law, and prophecy in the Old Testament point ahead to Jesus' coming; the Gospels and epistles of the New Testament point back to His ministry on earth and ahead to His heavenly reign. Essentially, the Bible is like a big neon arrow shining in the darkness, pointing to Jesus, saying as John did, "Look, the Lamb of God!"

The Bible may be our road map to heaven, but if we don't read it, we may lose the way. The world flashes many bright and enticing things before our eyes. Detours, shortcuts, potholes, and pitfalls in the form of missed opportunities, wrong choices, and sinful relationships all threaten to derail our spiritual journey.

The world will try to pull our eyes away from Jesus. Staying faithful to reading and meditating on God's Word will keep our eyes focused where they should be, on the Author and Perfecter of our faith (Hebrews 12:2).

*Dear Father, Your Word is a lamp to my feet and a light to my path.
Help me read Your Word daily and keep my eyes fixed on Jesus. Amen.*

The Master Designer

*Two are better than one, because they
have a good reward for their labor.
For if they fall, one will lift up his companion.*
ECCLESIASTES 4:9–10 NKJV

It usually does not take long to wonder what God was thinking when He designed a man and a woman, such uniquely different people, to bond together in marriage. We don't always see our differences at first, but they are there, just lying under the surface, waiting to be exposed. We may feel disillusioned when faced with the fact that our husbands don't think like we do or react to situations the way we would. And often we may conclude that they are not just different, they're wrong.

It is comforting to know that God has a marvelous plan when He joins a man and a woman in marriage. Conventional wisdom says we are complete as we are but, in truth, we are no more than a breathing puzzle with some of our pieces missing. His plan is slowly revealed like a picture quietly coming into view when we let Him start fitting our different pieces together.

The choice that is laid out before us is this—do we complete each other or compete with each other? Do we bang away and clash against each other, hoping that one side will change, or do we search for God's perspective and make the necessary shift so that His design is revealed? In time, we will see that our marriage was designed to be His masterpiece here on earth.

*Father, thank You for using our entire beings, even our differences,
to fulfill Your purpose for our marriage. Amen.*

Flying off the Handle

A gentle response defuses anger,
but a sharp tongue kindles a temper-fire.
PROVERBS 15:1 MSG

The "love is patient, love is kind" passage in Paul's letter to the Corinthians (1 Corinthians 13:4) is one of the world's most well-known descriptions of love. After giving the positive attributes of love, Paul flips the coin to explain what love is *not*: It is not rude or easily angered.

The Greek word for "easily angered" is *paroxyn*. In different Bible versions, it is translated to mean greatly distressed, easily angered, irritable. Bottom line, Paul was saying that love means we don't fly off the handle to our husbands and children.

When we snap at those we love, what happens? Our actions create emotional and physical distance. People scatter! They escape to another room until we cool off. Or they might respond by getting even and snapping back. Irritability can quickly escalate into anger. Little things turn into big things, and big things turn into bad things.

We all have frustrating days that put us close to the edge. So what's a better way to handle irritability? Instead of expecting our family to excuse bad behavior after it happens, ask for some allowance. Be candid, before you snap. "I've had a horrible day and I'm not feeling very patient" is a much healthier response than flying off the handle.

Try it! There's nothing to lose and everything to gain: real love.

Lord, put a bit in my mouth!
Pull on the reins so that I stop before I snap.

Sheep and Shepherd

I will be like a shepherd looking for his scattered flock.
I will find my sheep and rescue them from all the places where
they were scattered on that dark and cloudy day.
EZEKIEL 34:12 NLT

We've probably read passages about the shepherd and his flock before now. Throughout the Bible, shepherd imagery is prevalent. In many cases, the shepherd leads his flock and the sheep follow him trustingly. In Ezekiel, God describes Himself as a shepherd looking for his lost flock. The sheep to which God refers are not following their Shepherd in a nice straight line, but rather, they are scattered. Whether driven away by fear of the weather or if they have simply wandered off through inattention, these sheep have ended up in dangerous places from which the Shepherd must rescue them.

This image is a wonderful complement to the image of the shepherd leading his flock. This image assures us that if we somehow get distracted by carelessness or fear, God will come looking for us. We are not completely lost and abandoned if we somehow wander away. Even when we find ourselves in dangerous places, we can have the confidence that our Shepherd will rescue us from all danger, bringing us back to the fold, and eventually leading us to good pastures and to rest.

Dear Lord, thank You for being my Shepherd. Thank You for not
only leading me in safe paths but for rescuing me when I go astray.
I'm so thankful You care so much about me. Amen.

Chosen Words

*May the words of my mouth and the meditation of my
heart be pleasing to you, O LORD, my rock and my redeemer.*
PSALM 19:14 NLT

Kaye couldn't sleep. She was too busy beating herself up about what she'd said to her husband earlier in the day. She'd been stewing about his lack of help around the house, but instead of having a rational conversation about it, she'd exploded in anger and said hurtful things when he forgot to take out the trash. Now it was too late to undo the damage from her careless talk.

The children's song "Oh, Be Careful Little Eyes, What You See" says "Be careful little mouth what you say." Guarding our tongues requires more than merely censoring our words. It's impossible to speak the right words if we're not thinking the right thoughts. The things we think about everyday will eventually come out in our conversations. Those thoughts can emerge in words that can hurt others or encourage them, words that lift them up or tear them down. Since this process begins in our minds, it is essential for us to filter our thoughts through God's Word so that the words *we* speak will glorify Him.

*Lord, help me to be mindful of the connection between my thoughts and my
words. Teach me to meditate on those things that are pleasing to You.*

Faceless,
Faithful Helpers

And Noah went in, and his sons, and his wife, and his sons'
wives with him, into the ark, because of the waters of the flood.
GENESIS 7:7 KJV

*F*our of the most intriguing women in the Bible—Noah's
wife and his three daughters-in-law—are never referenced
by name. We know nothing about these nameless wives.

Or do we?

We know that the sons' wives were responsible for
repopulating the earth after the flood. They were truly daughters
of Eve, having become the mothers of all the living.

But what about Mrs. Noah?

We never see Mrs. Noah nagging Noah for spending a
century building a boat in the backyard. She wasn't like Mrs. Job,
who kicked her husband when he was down. And she wasn't like
Mrs. Lot, who didn't stay by her man through a crisis.

Mrs. Noah must have been a woman of faith. She was, after
all, one of only eight people God saved out of the flood. Noah
found grace in the eyes of the Lord, and so did she.

Are we like Mrs. Noah? Are we content to be faceless, faithful
helpers to our husbands when there's no glory in it for us?

It takes faith to help a husband accomplish his mission,
especially when our support is overlooked by the world. But this
is our calling, and in it we will be blessed.

Father, I look for that day when my children and husband
will arise up and call me blessed. But for now, let me be faithful
and content as I help my husband achieve his goals. Amen.

Never Quit

When my spirit was overwhelmed within me,
You knew my path.
PSALM 142:3 NASB

*D*aniel and Victoria knew they'd heard from God. They packed up their children and moved out of state, away from friends and family, for Victoria to begin a new career. They felt that Daniel would get a job right away, but when his job search stretched from week to months, they began to ask themselves if they'd missed hearing from God.

They tried to encourage one another but began to lose hope. Desperately they cried out to God as their savings dwindled. Feeling as if they had failed God and each other, a door finally opened—and it was a job beyond Daniel's wildest dreams.

When things don't work out like we expected, we often question ourselves and God. The devil would have you believe you missed God—especially if you truly believed it was God's plan and you acted on it by faith. He wins if he can get you to doubt your ability to hear God for your life.

Hold fast to what you believe. Stand firm, trusting that God will not forsake you but will carry you through the most difficult times. Never give up on your dream—and never doubt your faith to hear God's truth for your life.

God, I know the Bible is true and full of wisdom for my life.
Help me to grow and understand what I read and apply it to my life. Amen.

A Constant Dripping

A quarrelsome wife is like a constant dripping.
PROVERBS 19:13 NIV

What do barking dogs, dripping faucets, and honking horns have in common? They can be annoying and exasperating. Driving us to the brink of insanity, we yearn for a break, a reprieve, from the incessant noise. Yet the aggravation continues. Like the Energizer Bunny, it keeps going and going! We may not realize it, but husbands perceive quarrelsome wives in the same way—a constant dripping.

A quarrelsome wife is argumentative, disagreeable, or belligerent. Arguing becomes a sport at which she wants to excel. She relishes the role of playing the devil's advocate and expressing opposite opinions. Seldom is her tongue held. Rarely are her views kept to herself. Her husband cannot escape her constant chatter. *Drip. Drip. Drip.*

Evaluate yourself. Would your husband consider you a quarrelsome wife? Honestly assess your words and responses. Ask the Lord to reveal your heart. Perhaps we have become immune and gotten used to our constant dripping. Unfortunately, our husbands never will. Instead, they will avoid conversation. They will distance themselves. They will seek peaceful surroundings.

Let's desire to attract our husbands, not to repel them. Turn off the faucet!

Dear Lord, reveal to me whether my husband perceives me as a constant dripping. If so, change me. Amen.

Yes, Dear

Wives, submit yourselves unto your own husbands,
as it is fit in the Lord.
COLOSSIANS 3:18 KJV

Submission is a negative word in our society. Centuries of abuse and oppression toward women have made the concept of submitting to a man a thing of scorn. But when the Bible's principles are applied as God intended, the result is always one of peace and happiness.

The Word of God commands you to submit to your husband. This doesn't mean that you are on the same level as the doormat. You are not inferior to your spouse, nor are you less intelligent. But your place as a wife is not a dominant one. Women who pride themselves on "wearing the pants" in the family are not only out of order with God but causing the other members of their family to be out of order, as well.

Let your husband be the head of his home. Don't insist that your way is the best way—it may not be. Give him the liberty of fulfilling his God-given role. You need not fear that you are somehow less of a woman because you are not the boss. Rather, the opposite is true. You are more of a woman because you are fulfilling God's plan for you.

Dear Father, help me to obey Your Word by being the submissive
wife that You have commanded me to be. Amen.

Sealed Hearts

*Set me as a seal upon thy heart, as a seal upon thine arm:
for love is strong as death; jealousy is cruel as Sheol;
the flashes thereof are flashes of fire, a very flame of Jehovah.*
SONG OF SOLOMON 8:6 ASV

The wife couldn't keep from laughing at the stories her husband's coworker shared. She was sure her husband would be pleased that she fit in so well into his world. She didn't expect the jealousy he displayed on the way home.

So often we meet men who are easy to interact with at work, church, or socially. As wives we must be careful. Jealousy is a powerful emotion, and we should be aware of how easy it is to encourage another man and to incite feelings of envy in our husbands. Our spouse should always know that he is the only one for us. We are to be sealed to him in a relationship where we are cleaved together as one. No matter how platonic we may see the relationship with another man, our husband will see it through different eyes. He may lose confidence in our love.

God, too, is a jealous God. He wants our total devotion. We should be careful not to indulge in practices that are against biblical teachings. We need to let God know that He is the only One for us. Our hearts are sealed for Him and for His purpose.

*God, please protect my heart. Keep me from hurting
my husband and from hurting You. Amen.*

The house of the wicked will be destroyed,
but the tent of the upright will flourish.
PROVERBS 14:11 ESV

ave you felt tempted to become angry when you've seen
a neighbor, friend, or coworker receive a better home
than yours, high-flying vacations, or many nicer things? Don't
sweat it. That neighbor may have a "house" compared to your
"tent," and while you have the basics, she may get all the goodies
life seems to offer. But in God's eyes, you may still be the one
who flourishes while she heads off towards destruction.

If you have a faithful husband who loves you well, don't covet
a man who makes the big bucks. Because all the things Daddy
Warbucks could give you wouldn't match up to the love you have
with your husband today. Chances are that wealthy man spends
so much time making the money that you'd never be together.
And couples who spend little time with each other usually see
more of the divorce courts than the tennis courts.

Don't fall for Satan's lie that things are better than God. It's
so old it has whiskers, but there's no truth in it.

Lord, I have to admit I've been tempted, when I see what others have.
Keep me faithful to You and content in my tent.

A Good Thing

*Whoso findeth a wife findeth a good thing,
and obtaineth favour of the LORD.*
PROVERBS 18:22 KJV

What's so great about being a wife? You may wonder that sometimes, when you're up to your eyeballs in household chores and dying for a night out. But the Bible itself speaks highly of your role in the home and calls you a good thing!

God's crowning creation was man. But even this superior being, made in the image of God Himself, was not complete without the woman. And, like Eve, you are the only one who can fill the void in your husband's life.

God created woman to complement man. . .to bring out the best in him. Your husband is a better, stronger person because of you. You bring stability and structure to his life. You give him purpose and direction. He would be lost without you!

So be the best wife you can be. Strive to fulfill his needs and desires. Realize the importance of your God-given role. You're not just a housekeeper, cook, laundress, and errand runner. You're a *wife*, and the Bible calls you a good thing.

*Dear Father, help me to understand how important it is to be a good wife.
Let me complement my husband and bring out the best in him,
as You bring out the best in me. Amen.*

Anxiety and God-Worship

"If you decide for God, living a life of God-worship, it follows that you don't fuss about what's on the table at mealtimes or whether the clothes in your closet are in fashion."
MATTHEW 6:25 MSG

*J*esus knows how to get to the heart of any problem. In the Sermon on the Mount He touched on a number of topics, but He especially focused on things that cause anxiety. He says that the cure for anxiety is deciding to live a life of God-worship. When our thoughts are totally focused on God, we won't fuss about what we're going to eat or whether we're dressed in the latest fashions.

As wives and perhaps mothers, we tend to worry about the everyday necessities of life. And it's easy to blame our husbands when these needs are jeopardized. Food and clothing are basic needs, but at times it seems that women are more concerned with these issues than men, probably because of our nurturing natures. We need to be careful that we don't put more emphasis on the necessities than God does.

If we decide for God, we must trust that He will provide exactly what we need. While it may not be gourmet food or haute couture, we can be content, knowing that many times He gives us our wants, as well. Trust God to provide; rest in His love. And thank Him for every provision. God loves to receive our worship for what we take for granted.

*Father, thank You for providing all that we need,
many times even more than we ask for. You are good. Amen.*

Recipe

*Finally, my friends, keep your minds on whatever is true, pure,
right, holy, friendly, and proper. Don't ever stop thinking about
what is truly worthwhile and worthy of praise.*
PHILIPPIANS 4:8 CEV

A cookie recipe calls for specific ingredients. Most of us
have learned the hard way that, if we want our cookies
to be enjoyable, we had better make sure that we have all the
ingredients on hand and that we add them each in the right
amount at the right time. Leaving out just one thing or with
inaccurate measuring can have a devastating effect on an
otherwise delectable dessert.

The same is true for our marriages. God has written a recipe
for us to follow, and any little deviations from that recipe will
have devastating effects on our marriages. Look at the verse
above. What if purity were left out of a marriage—or how about
basic friendliness? A godly marriage cannot do without any of
the things that God has ordained for it. All the ingredients that
God has included in His recipe are vital for our marriages. Take
a moment to consider which areas in your marriage need some
remeasuring. The results will be well worth the effort!

*Jesus, thank You for the perfect recipe for a healthy and satisfying marriage.
Help me to recognize the areas in my marriage that need some attention.
I want my marriage to be pleasing to You. Amen.*

Light for a
Dark Journey

And I will bring the blind by a way that they knew not;
I will lead them in paths that they have not known:
I will make darkness light before them, and crooked things straight.
These things will I do unto them, and not forsake them.
ISAIAH 42:16 KJV

A blind person depends on unchanging organization in her home to help her navigate through life. No one can shift a piece of furniture. Every pan or dish must find its given place in a cabinet after washing. Matching clothes must be grouped together, or the blind person may walk out the door wearing a color combination never conceived in the civilized world!

Given such dependence on everyday consistency, why would God take a blind person down unfamiliar paths where she might fall? And while most of us possess physical sight, we may often find ourselves in dark circumstances where we feel ignorant, confused, even helpless. Does God enjoy our struggles? Does He laugh when we stumble?

No. Isaiah tells us that God promises to do the impossible for His blind, stressed people: He will give light to those who don't even know what it is. He will straighten our paths in ways we could never envision. Just as a faithful friend guides a blind person through a dangerous intersection in a strange city, God will help us deal with the unknown. He never leaves us alone.

Lord Jesus, my humanity blinds me to Your possibilities.
Please hold my hand and lead me along Your way. Amen.

Love Never Fails

*[Love] beareth all things, believeth all things,
hopeth all things, endureth all things.*
1 CORINTHIANS 13:7 KJV

*M*any wedding ceremonies include the reading of the Love Chapter (1 Corinthians 13). When the text is read and we are staring into the sparkling eyes of our betrothed, we imagine a wonderful life ahead with the man of our dreams.

Then the days begin to roll by and, inevitably, we begin to realize that the man we married is perhaps not, um, perfect. We begin to discover some things we never really knew about him before, like the fact that he doesn't fold the face towel before putting it back on the rack. Instead, he leaves it balled up on the bathroom counter. He leaves his dishes in the sink instead of taking a few extra seconds to put them in the dishwasher. It's November and he still hasn't taken the air conditioners out of the windows. And he leaves his fingernail clippings strewn at the bottom of the just-cleaned bathroom sink. What happened to the prince we married?

He's still there. It's just that we've realized he's only human. Now is our chance to live out God's Word by bearing, believing, hoping, and enduring *all* things. God wants us to love each other in spite of our faults. Because that's how He loves us. He is constantly forgiving us and enduring our shortcomings.

Although we now more clearly see our husband's faults, we love him in spite of them. In doing so, our marriage, faith, and love for each other will grow ever stronger and deeper. For love never fails!

Lord, help me to love my husband as You love me.

Legacy of Love

*But from everlasting to everlasting the LORD's love
is with those who fear him, and his righteousness
with their children's children.*
PSALM 103:17 NIV

*W*ill your marriage be a legacy for your children and
all those you love? Verses Psalm 103:15–18 begin by
reminding us that our days on earth are few. The love of God is
the only thing that matters on this earth. It is so important to
keep this in mind when it comes to marriage. Do others look at
your marriage and see a love that is blessed by God? Do you have
a marriage upon which they can model their own relationships?

Psalm 103:17 tells us that God's love is with those who fear
Him and obey Him. And His righteousness will be with our
"children's children"! Don't you want that for your family?

Even though we all go through difficult times in marriage,
there isn't a relationship that can't be restored by our loving
Father and turned into a testimony of His amazing grace!
Sometimes the difficult relationships turn into an even greater
legacy because of how God has been glorified through our
weaknesses.

Lift your marriage up to God today. Share with Him your
desire to leave a legacy for your loved ones. And He will work
wonders in your lives.

*Dear Father, please turn our marriage into a legacy of love that honors You
and shows the truth of Your love and grace to others. In Jesus' name, amen.*

Real Freedom

*Now the Lord is the Spirit, and where
the Spirit of the Lord is, there is freedom.*
2 CORINTHIANS 3:17 ESV

Over two hundred years ago, our forefathers freed our
nation. But that wasn't the end of the story. With effort and
sacrifice, they and their countrymen had to build a nation.

Free-nation building isn't all that comes with a price. When
it comes to romance, the world claims that real freedom is being
single, playing the field. But no one mentions the price of such
"freedom": singleness easily becomes very lonely, and what the
world describes as blissful sexual independence causes much
sorrow as it becomes license, instead of real, costly freedom.

Scripture teaches us that married people who follow God's
Word have the real freedom—they've been freed by the Spirit to
develop a single deep relationship. Christian husbands and wives
focus on loving the other deeply and uniquely. As each works to
build a godly relationship, a real, lifelong romance is developed.
As our revolutionary forefathers recognized in their nation
building, the blessings far outweigh any cost.

As we build our marriages, what will God's freedom require
of us? Are we willing to take costly actions that store up future
blessings? Or instead will we opt for "freedom" shortcuts that
leave us empty?

*Lord, help us to rejoice in Your Spirit's freedom and
make wise choices that use Your liberty wisely.*

And God saw every thing that he had made, and, behold, it was very good.
And the evening and the morning were the sixth day.
GENESIS 1:31 KJV

Their honeymoon was amazing, straight out of the final pages of a romance novel. They walked hand in hand along white sand beaches, and each sunset was more glorious than the last. He thought she was the sweetest woman in the world; she knew no man had ever been so handsome, strong, and tender.

When they came home, however, things started to fall apart. The pipes in their new apartment leaked. Her cat made him sneeze. His car needed new tires. She complained. He slammed doors. The golden glow of their honeymoon faded into something more like fluorescent lighting, and all their quirks, wrinkles, and flaws were clearly visible. The question on both their minds was, "What now?"

This happened to God, too. He made a beautiful world, but "it was very good" lasted such a short time. Adam and Eve sinned and found themselves standing at the gates of Eden, their perfect world gone forever. But this didn't catch God off guard. Instead of rejecting us, He loved us even more spectacularly: He sent His only Son to die to save us.

So what do you do when your knight in shining armor turns out to snore and leave dirty socks everywhere but the laundry hamper, and, well, be human? Rejoice! Now you get to love like God loves.

Dear God, thank You for loving me despite my sin.
Help me to love my husband like You love me. Amen.

A Good Plan

And be ye kind one to another, tenderhearted,
forgiving one another, even as God for Christ's sake hath forgiven you.
EPHESIANS 4:32 KJV

*E*phesians 4:32 seems to be a verse we teach and apply only to children. We say, "Be nice to Katie. Share your dress-up clothes," or "Help Evan pick up the toys."

As we grow into adulthood, we sometimes leave the commands of this verse behind. We act like the words are there to use as a magic formula when kids aren't getting along. It really would be a good plan to take these words of wisdom into our marriages, though. If we can't behave in a kind, forgiving way toward our own husbands, how will we be able to properly treat others?

So when your husband is a little busier than usual, go ahead and wash the car for him. Love him even when he is filled with all manner of stress. Forgive him when he forgets that he promised you a date and schedules a tee-time with his buddies.

This certainly doesn't let him off the hook, but Paul is speaking to individuals here. You are not responsible for how your husband acts; you are responsible for how you react (and how you act in the first place). Read Ephesians 4:31, as well. It admonishes us to put away all the negative attitudes that are so easy to acquire; then verse 32 shows us how to replace those bad attitudes with good. It's a plan that works—even for adults.

Lord, teach me to be kind and forgiving—to be more like You.

The Greatest Virtue

LORD, my heart is not haughty, nor mine eyes lofty:
neither do I exercise myself in great matters, or in things too high for me.
PSALM 131:1 KJV

We cannot be the reverent, submissive wives God calls us to be if we spend our days filling our minds with great ideas and imaginations that have no root in reality.

While it's not bad to dream or to have a vision to accomplish something great for God, God warns us about our imagination. Our lofty imaginations are often evil. In fact, Paul says they exalt themselves "against the knowledge of God" (2 Corinthians 10:5 KJV).

If we are to know Him and understand what He wants for our lives, we must have humility. We must let go of great thoughts, of the "what ifs" and "if onlys." We must not waste precious time, wondering how life might have been different. We should not pride ourselves on our ability to think great thoughts or make great plans.

Rather, we must learn to quiet ourselves before the Lord, to be as little children—simple, honest, and direct. While we can and should study His Word, we must take it at face value, without pretense.

Keep your eyes on His Word and He will lift you up in His good time.

Father, I spend more of my time wildly thinking about Your plans for me
than reading about what You plan for me. Let me be sober-minded. I want
to take You at Your word and not impose my imaginations on Your truth.
Teach me true humility. Amen.

Your Reputation

A good name is rather to be chosen than great riches,
and loving favour rather than silver or gold.
PROVERBS 22:1 KJV

*I*t is probable that if most wives were honest, we'd have to admit that we'd like ourselves or our husbands to have jobs that give us financial comfort and security. That means different things to different women, but we just aren't programmed to prefer poverty over pleasure.

There's nothing wrong with financial security as long as it is earned honestly and acknowledged as a blessing from God. There's something even more valuable than money and things, though, and that's a good reputation. We can have that without wealth.

Ask yourself, "What kind of wife am I? How do I treat others? Do I faithfully serve the Lord? Am I honest? Responsible? Am I a good neighbor?" There are many other questions you could probably think of. After you answer them— honestly—check the Word of God to see if you meet up to His standards. If you do, others will see the Lord in you, and yours will be a good reputation. What a desirable asset! There might be times when people won't understand you, but your name is good in God's eyes. What a joy to know that you please the Lord.

It is my desire, O God, to be pleasing in Your eyes.
Strengthen me to do those things that would make my home truly good.

Zip It

*Where there are many words, transgression is unavoidable,
but he who restrains his lips is wise.*
PROVERBS 10:19 NASB

*L*isa walked into the kitchen with a bag of groceries as her husband, Mark, was discussing their recent camping trip with their neighbor Aaron.

". . .and then the golden retriever took off after that rabbit like his tail was on fire—"

"Mark," Lisa interrupted, "you're telling it wrong. It was an Irish setter. And he was chasing a raccoon, not a rabbit."

Mark's face lost a fraction of its animation as he resumed his story. "Yeah, okay—the dog chased the raccoon right into our campsite and turned over the grill that was full of food—"

"Steaks, to be precise," Lisa added, unloading groceries onto the table. "And you forgot the part about the trash can."

Lisa became aware of strained silence as she stocked the refrigerator. She turned to see Mark's face flushed with embarrassment and Aaron shuffling toward the door.

"Oh, honey, I'm sorry," Lisa said.

"I know I don't tell stories as well as you, but I'd like to finish my own sentences. When you jump in like that, it makes me feel dumb and, well. . .disrespected."

Lisa knew that respect was the number one need of husbands, and she resolved to allow Mark to express himself without her assistance in the future.

Be wise. Use lip restraints.

Lord of the locked lip, help us remember that respecting our husbands sometimes means wisely restraining our tongues. Amen.

Walk the Talk

*Wives, in the same way be submissive to your
husbands so that, if any of them do not believe the word,
they may be won over without words by the behavior of their wives,
when they see the purity and reverence of your lives.*
1 PETER 3:1–2 NIV

*A*ctions certainly speak louder than words. Christian
wives married to unbelievers face unique challenges. Our
husbands are scrutinizing our walk more carefully than our talk.
We may say we love them, yet do we demonstrate unconditional
love? Or do we nag and chastise them instead? Our behavior
should match what we profess to believe.

We must draw close to the Lord and love Him foremost.
As we grow in our relationship with Him, we learn about His
character. The Holy Spirit transforms our hearts to reflect His
heart. We come to understand how to love our husbands as the
Lord loves us.

We cannot change our husbands. The Holy Spirit calls and
draws hearts to Himself. Yet, as wives, we can either hinder or
help that process. Concentrate on being a living testimony of
God's truth, and leave the results to Him. Walk the talk. Keep
your eyes on the Lord, knowing that He has His eyes on your
marriage. Trust the Lord and continue to follow Him in all your
ways. May the Lord use you to win over your husband.

*Dear Lord, may my walk match my talk. Use me in my husband's life
so that he will come into a personal relationship with You. Amen.*

Stem the Flow

*A quarrelsome wife is as annoying as constant
dripping on a rainy day.*
PROVERBS 27:15 NLT

*D*rip. Drip. Drip.

"Jimbo, will you please take a look at that leaking toilet
when you get a chance? Thanks, honey!"

Drip. Drip. Drip.

"Jimmy, the toilet is still dripping. Could you please get to it
before company comes tomorrow?"

Drip. Drip. Drip.

"Jim, my mother is going to think Junior's aim is off if you
don't get that puddle off the floor before they get here."

Drip. Drip. Drip.

"JAMES ALAN MULROONY, we could have floated to
China with all the water pouring onto that bathroom floor! If
you don't get in there and fix it right now, I'm calling a plumber!"

In our zeal to run our homes like a smooth-sailing vessel, we
may inadvertently drive our first mate to the point of mutiny. Or,
worse, into deserting the ship altogether.

We must ask ourselves: Is it really worth it? Is my nagging
going to accomplish my goal of honoring God by honoring my
marriage partner? Or will it just drive a wedge between us and
erode the intimacy of our relationship?

Wise wives use creativity and wit to accomplish the end
result of husbands willingly swabbing the deck or hoisting
the sails. After all, we do want to end up on the same boat at
journey's end.

*Give me patience, Father, to resist nagging and wisdom
in how to best approach my husband. Amen.*

Sincere Love

*Love must be sincere.
Hate what is evil; cling to what is good.*
ROMANS 12:9 NIV

*L*ove isn't always the vibrant excitement we have when we first get married. Trials come, and love can ebb. If we aren't careful, love can become more of a dim memory or even something long forgotten. Without work, the vibrancy we once had with our spouse can become nonexistent, leaving us to wonder why we are still together when we no longer love one another.

That's when we have to ask the question, "How do I love my husband? As a lover? As a friend? As an enemy?" As Christians, we are called to love no matter what. We may not believe that we love our husband as a lover, but we are called to still love him. With Christ's help, that will be enough to reawaken spousal love, if we're willing to try. Love is not an emotion that should be allowed to ebb and flow but an action that we choose to do.

Jesus loved us when we were sinners. Before we knew Him and had been changed, He loved us enough to die for us. What a beautiful example of sacrificial action love. As wives and as followers of Christ, we, too, can learn to have a sacrificial love in our marriages. When our feelings for our spouse begin to fade, we can remember the way Jesus gave His all for us and follow in His footsteps.

Jesus, thank You for showing me how to love my husband. Amen.

A Difficult Marriage

David said to Abigail, "Praise be to the LORD,
the God of Israel, who has sent you today to meet me.
May you be blessed for your good judgment."
1 SAMUEL 25:32–33 NIV

While David was hiding from Saul in the desert, he and his men took on odd jobs—such as protecting shepherds and their flocks from pillage. Nabal, a wealthy property owner, was one of those men whose sheep were protected by David. When asked for remuneration, Nabal refused. David erupted! He planned to kill Nabal, but Abigail—Nabal's wife—quickly intervened and saved the day.

Scripture says that "A kindhearted woman gains respect, but ruthless men gain only wealth" (Proverbs 11:16 NIV). Abigail was highly respected by everyone, including David. Nabal, a ruthless man, enjoyed his wealth for a short while, but God paid Nabal back for his arrogance and greed.

We don't know if Abigail was a wise woman before she married Nabal. Maybe she was. Or maybe she developed those virtues in the midst—or because of—her difficult marriage.

What we do know is that Abigail did not let Nabal influence or affect her adversely. Her relationship with God fortified her to endure a difficult marriage.

We have the same resource in God to face the challenges in our marriage that Abigail did. Even better! We have the indwelling of the Holy Spirit to comfort and counsel us.

Lord, You know every difficulty and disappointment
that I face in my marriage. Give me Your wisdom to
know what to do and grace to trust You for the outcome.

Light

*You are my lamp, O LORD;
the LORD turns my darkness into light.*
2 SAMUEL 22:29 NIV

The Bible begins with light. Genesis 1:3 tells us, "And God said, 'Let there be light,' and there was light" (NIV). It also ends with light. Revelation 22:5 says, "There will be no more night. They will not need the light of a lamp or the light of the sun, for the Lord God will give them light" (NIV). Unfortunately, there's a lot of darkness in between. War. Murder. Pain. Loss. Scripture certainly doesn't candy-coat the difficulties of life; however, even in the midst of the darkness there are glorious glimpses of His marvelous light. David's sin is forgiven and he becomes a man after God's own heart. Paul is transformed from a murderer of Christians to a passionate evangelist. Peter denied Christ, but that wasn't his destiny—instead he defends Christ to the death. God has the amazing ability to turn even our darkest situations into personal and spiritual victories.

Perhaps you are facing a dark situation right now. Maybe you've suffered loss, a moral failure, or missed a chance to defend your faith. If so, you're not alone—you have a lot of company. When it seems that you're surrounded by darkness, remember that light is both your foundation and your future. Release the situation to God's marvelous light and know that He is able to transform it into something more than you could ever dream.

*God, you are Light. In you there is no darkness at all.
Thank You for the truth that Your light illumines even my blackest night.*

Humble Servants

*Do not merely look out for your own personal interests,
but also for the interests of others.*
PHILIPPIANS 2:4 NASB

Rachel indignantly cried out, "I have rights! I will not be a doormat!" Lori lovingly explained the life of Christ.

The Lord Jesus was the Word made flesh (John 1:14). Philippians 2:6–8 explains that during Jesus' time on earth, He did not exploit the fact that He was God. Rather, Jesus took the form of a humble servant by being born as a human and daily following the will of God, to the point of dying on the cross for our sins.

Christ came not to be served, but to serve (Mark 10:45). Jesus desires for us to have this same mind-set of being a humble servant (Philippians 2:5). As we look to Christ as the perfect example, we can be humble servants to our husbands. It does not mean that we are doormats or give up our rights, but we are willing to lay down our lives for the interests of our husband. We are choosing to put God first, our husbands next, and ourselves last. We can intentionally, willingly, and eagerly look for ways to minister to our husbands by meeting their needs and interests (1 Peter 5:2).

Christ placed our need for a Savior, forgiveness, and redemption above all else and died on the cross for us. Therefore, not through obligation as wives but through Christ in us, we can strive to be humble servants to our husbands.

*Lord, as I look to You, enable me to be a humble servant to my husband.
To place his interests above my own.*

"Simple" Gifts?

And whosoever shall give to drink unto one of these
little ones a cup of cold water only in the name of a disciple,
verily I say unto you, he shall in no wise lose his reward.
MATTHEW 10:42 KJV

*M*arianne lifted her toddler to the park's drinking
fountain and felt her back muscles protest. *When had
Landon grown so heavy?* She huffed and puffed, trying to hold
him level with the flow of water. Landon, however, was in no
hurry. He lapped a little and then decided it was more fun to
splash water on Mommy.

Marianne, her new capris now wet and sloppy, fought
irritation as she plopped her son down and told him to go pick
dandelions. Landon zoomed around the playground like one of
his favorite race cars. Marianne collapsed onto a bench. How
could one small task wear her out?

Jesus, during His day-in, day-out ministry, found that even
straightforward efforts to preach the Good News and heal
hurting people resulted in complications. His family questioned
His sanity. His hometown rejected Him. The Pharisees argued
about the legality of His healing on the Sabbath and tried to
intimidate Him. And needy people pursued Him night and day,
begging for attention.

When wives and mothers bear the weariness of 24-7 love and
service, Jesus knows exactly how we feel. And He will reward us.

Lord, sometimes I think I cannot take one more step—
yet I know by Your love and power that I can. Amen.

A Place of Your Own

*For this cause shall a man leave his father
and mother, and cleave to his wife.*
MARK 10:7 KJV

When young men and women begin their search for a
mate, they are usually looking for someone like their
parents. If the home they grew up in was a happy one, they often
try to emulate that environment. But trying to make your home
like the one you were raised in can lead to disappointment and
dysfunction.

If your mother-in-law faithfully served nightly dinners of
meat and potatoes, your husband may expect the same of you.
If your father insisted on changing the oil in his car, you'll likely
assume that your man should do the same. Simple assumptions
like these can lead to big problems.

God commanded that a man leave his father and mother
when he marries so that he and his new wife can build their own
home together. Your lives have already been influenced by your
upbringing, and from time to time you may hear your mother's
words flow from your own lips. But it is important to remember
that the place you are creating with your husband is *your own*.
Glean the good from your parents' marriages, but make sure you
leave plenty of room to blaze your own path.

*Heavenly Father, help me to work with my husband to build a functional,
happy home that is a mirror of who we are, not who our parents are. Amen.*

Armed and Ready

*Take everything the Master has set out for you,
well-made weapons. . . . Put them to use so you will be
able to stand up to everything the Devil throws your way. . . .
This is for keeps, a life-or-death fight to the finish.*
EPHESIANS 6:11–12 MSG

We don't want to think of marriage as a battleground. But unless we do, we won't fight to keep our marriages intact. Satan would love nothing more than to destroy the institution of marriage, because when even one fails, God doesn't get the glory. And the picture of Christ and His bride, the church, is marred.

God equips each of His children with the armor needed for the battle. He has uniquely gifted each of us with strengths to complement our spouses. Because of that, each marriage is unique and, as a result, has its own weaknesses and battles that must be fought in the spiritual realm before we see the results in the physical realm.

Put on the armor. Stand firm against everything Satan and his demons would throw at you. Be prepared to pray earnestly as you work to maintain a marriage that glorifies God. And know that it is a fight to the finish, one that doesn't end this side of heaven. It takes courage to persevere in the face of spiritual opposition. But God can equip you to take on all challengers.

*Father, thank You for equipping me for the battle not only in
my marriage but also in every other area of life. Give me
courage to stand firm as I fight for righteousness and truth. Amen.*

The Power of Prayer

*For the eyes of the Lord are on the righteous and his
ears are attentive to their prayer, but the face
of the Lord is against those who do evil.*
1 PETER 3:12 NIV

The Bible tells us that when two or more are gathered together in Jesus' name, He is right there with us (Matthew 18:20)! God's Word also tells us that the prayers of the righteous are "powerful and effective" (James 5:16). Are you praying with others on a regular basis? If you are living a godly life, your prayers have power, and when two of you are praying together. . . there is even more power!

Most of us lead very busy lives, and we're lucky if we can squeeze in our own private prayer time, let alone finding the time to pray with others. But we need to do whatever we can to *make* time to pray with others—whether in person, over the phone, by texting, or via the Internet.

Prayer ushers us into the presence of God. Prayer allows us to hear and echo the needs of others. Prayer changes things. Prayer is crucial to a growing marriage, a burgeoning family, and your very life!

*Father, I come here now, in Your name, to praise You,
to know You more, and to lift my concerns up to You. Help me make
prayer a priority in my marriage, my family, my life. Amen.*

Eliminate Distractions

*But the Holy Spirit produces this kind of fruit in our lives:
love, joy, peace, patience, kindness, goodness, faithfulness,
gentleness, and self-control. There is no law against these things!*
GALATIANS 5:22–23 NLT

*A*nna was tired of fighting. Marriage wasn't what she'd imagined it would be. Before the wedding, Peter's focus had been on her—what she wanted, what she needed. They were less than a year into their marriage and the fire of passion seemed to be smoldering. She wanted to go back to who they had been—who they were together before life became a jungle of schedules, bills, commitments to work and school—but it never seemed as if they had a moment together. *And the few moments we do get together, we spend our energy fighting about how we never make time for each other,* she thought.

Anna rummaged through the fridge and began preparing dinner—something she hadn't taken time to do in a while. Peter loved it when she cooked. Tonight she wouldn't let anything steal her focus. She was going to give time to her marriage, and nothing was going to distract her.

Where do you put your energy? Are you focused on the right things for a healthy marriage? Take a good look at the distractions that have come between you and a successful relationship with your husband. Set aside time to really focus on your relationship with him.

*Heavenly Father, my marriage is important to You and to me.
Show me how to make it a top priority. Amen.*

Pleasant Boundaries

Lord, you have assigned me my portion and my cup;
you have made my lot secure. The boundary lines have fallen
for me in pleasant places; surely I have a delightful inheritance.
PSALM 16:5–6 NIV

*G*ranted, they didn't have much notice, but when the angels of God told Lot and his family to leave Sodom, they weren't kidding. There was no time to spare. The instructions were clear: Pack up, leave, don't look back. But Lot's wife couldn't do it. The temptation to look back on all she had left behind was too great. She paid for her disobedience with her life.

Obeying God's commands is difficult when we focus on what we're giving up. His guidelines for living a holy life can seem restrictive and unfair when we think about all we're leaving behind. However, when we look back, we miss what's ahead.

God's boundaries may sometimes seem restrictive, but the truth is, He put them into place because He has our best interest in mind. For example, innocent friendships with the opposite sex can quickly turn into disaster. Because of this, many couples find that it is best to restrict these one-on-one relationships. This can be frustrating, especially when we value these friendships and have no ill intent. However, when we only look at what we're missing out on, it's difficult to see what lies ahead. But you can trust your heavenly Father. His boundaries provide security and protection, and your future holds great promise and reward.

Father, thank You for the boundaries You have placed around my life.
Help me to focus on what I'm gaining rather than what
I'm leaving behind when I choose to obey You.

Ceaseless Prayers

*For God is my witness. . .that without ceasing
I make mention of you always in my prayers.*
ROMANS 1:9 KJV

*P*aul didn't take a vacation from praying for his distant
Roman church family. Should we fail to pray for our spouses?
Prayer is one of the most important things we do as Christians.
Should we leave our most beloved out of this spiritual loop?

We need not lock ourselves in a room and spend the whole
day praying about our marriage. But we need to make such
prayers a daily priority.

Perhaps mornings are too busy for you to engage in long
prayers for your husband. But on your commute to work or while
washing the dishes, you can lift your husband up to God. When
he comes to your mind at the office or in the grocery store,
you can pray a quick blessing on him. When you do get some
minutes for some quality quiet time, make sure you don't spend
so much time praying for other people's needs that you forget to
lift your husband up to God.

Wives who pray fervently for their husbands rediscover
improved marital communication. By asking him how you can
pray for him, you suddenly understand him more clearly. And if
he's a believer as well, he'll ask how he can pray for you, which
will open his eyes to your needs and cares. As the Spirit works
in your life, you'll feel God's oil on the rough parts of your
relationship.

So don't forget to pray!

*Lord, I lift my husband up to You right now. Bless him today. Open
his eyes to Your presence. Together may we look to You and serve You well.*

God's Picket Fence

The name of the LORD is a strong tower;
the righteous runs to it and is safe.
PROVERBS 18:10 NASB

It's a dangerous world out there. Drunk drivers, heart attacks, rabid dogs, cancer, unemployment, terrorism, E. coli... The list goes on. It is easy to use a lot of energy thinking about all the bad things that could happen, as if our mental vigilance will somehow ward them off. But the Bible is very clear in commanding us not to worry. Jesus says it in unmistakably direct language: " 'Do not worry'" (Matthew 6:31). We should be very wary about disobeying a direct command from Jesus!

At its root, worry shows our lack of trust in both God's love and His power. The Bible is as clear about God's promises of protection for those who love Him as it is about the injunction not to worry. In fact, one necessarily follows the other: We shouldn't worry *because* God is taking care of us. The Bible says that we can rejoice; we can spend our days singing praise to God, knowing that His protection is all around us.

We don't always have fences around our houses, and even if we did, they couldn't protect our families from everything. But what we do have is a promise from God that He stands eternal sentry over those who love Him.

Dear Lord, I praise You for Your immense power,
Your love, and Your faithfulness. Forgive me for worrying
and help me trust in Your promises. Amen.

The Rock of Perfect Peace

The Lord God is an everlasting Rock.
ISAIAH 26:4 AMP

*F*rancine couldn't believe it. He'd done it again. With one thoughtless comment, Angelo had ruined her day. And then he'd gone off to work, leaving her thoughts scattered and her confidence shattered.

Slowly she went about her daily tasks, yet her heart was heavy. All she kept hearing in her mind were Angelo's words. She'd known that he was under a lot of pressure at work, and with the cost of food, gas, you name it, he was very worried about their finances. She knew he probably hadn't even thought before he'd spoken, but the words had still come out, leaving her wounded and raw.

Finally, unable to fight it on her own anymore, Francine ran to her Bible and began leafing through its pages, looking for a soothing word to replace the disturbing echo in her head. And there in Isaiah 26:3, she found gold: You will keep him in perfect peace, whose mind is stayed on You, because he trusts in You (NKJV). Grabbing an index card, Francine wrote down the verse and spent the rest of her busy day trying to memorize Isaiah's words, to keep her mind on God and His faithfulness.

That night, Angelo came home quiet and reserved. Francine greeted him with an understanding yet shy smile. For a few seconds they stared at each other then embraced.

"Sorry," he whispered in her ear.

Francine silently prayed, *Thank You, God, for Your words of perfect peace.*

God, in You alone I find peace and refuge, strength and constancy.
Stay with me throughout my day as I keep my eyes and mind on You.

Pure Love

*Now the end of the commandment is charity out of a
pure heart, and of a good conscience, and of faith unfeigned.*
1 TIMOTHY 1:5 KJV

The timer began to buzz, and Diana peeked into the oven. *Perfect!* The chicken had just the right golden color; the twice-baked potatoes looked fabulous. The Caesar salad, sweet tea, and raspberry cheesecake waited in the refrigerator.

Diana glanced at the clock. *Still a few minutes before Tony gets home,* she thought. Quickly she wiped off the counter then ran a brush through her hair. She smiled when she heard the garage door open. With her new business taking off as well as her various other engagements, it wasn't often that she had an opportunity to spend time on an elaborate meal. She looked up and smiled expectantly as her husband walked through the door.

"Something smells terrific." Tony grinned as he hugged Diana. "What's the occasion?"

"Just that God has allowed me to be married to the most wonderful man in the world." As she returned his hug, Diana knew it was true.

No one is perfect. But when our lives are centered on our relationship with the Lord Jesus, our faith will sustain and encourage us each day of our married lives. As our love for God deepens, our love for our husbands will become more sincere. It's a beautiful thing.

*Lord Jesus, Your love is pure and perfect. As my faith in You deepens,
let my love for my husband grow stronger.*

Receiving the Undeserved

"But the Lord our God is merciful and forgiving,
even though we have rebelled against him."
DANIEL 9:9 NLT

*R*ebellion is a word one comes across in many different contexts. One reads of historical rebellion, of literary rebellion, even of rebellious teenagers. Regardless of the context, rebellion—the flagrant defiance of the authority in charge—is often seriously punished. Rarely does one come across a case where outright rebellion is treated with mercy and forgiveness.

In his prayer to God, Daniel admits that he and his people have rebelled against God and His word. Punishment is the obvious recompense for such behavior. But Daniel doesn't talk about punishment; he speaks instead about the incredible mercy and forgiveness of God.

As Christians today, we remain a people of unclean hearts, rebellious and disobedient toward God. And yet, despite our rebellion, we serve a God who loves and cares for us, a God who desires reconciliation above all else, a God who sent his Son to die on the cross so that our sins could be washed away once and for all. Instead of punishment, we are graced with God's mercy and forgiveness. Praise God for His infinite love!

Dear Lord, although I sometimes rebel against You, You continually show me forgiveness and mercy. Thank You for loving me so. Teach me to obey Your Word today and every day. Help me live to please You. Amen.

The First and
Last Word

Day
209

O God, You are my God; early will I seek You. . . .
When I remember You on my bed, I meditate on You in the night watches.
Because You have been my help, therefore in the shadow of Your wings I will
rejoice. My soul follows close behind You; Your right hand upholds me.
PSALM 63:1, 6–8 NKJV

Nothing starts a day out better than spending some
moments in God's Word. Our perspective shifts,
becoming His, not ours. We notice the wonder of His creation,
seeing His hand in each leaf of the tree, each feather on the bird,
each hair on our husband's head, and, in so doing, we are moved
to praise Him for His glorious works.

As the day progresses, we turn to feel Him beside us,
surrounding us, supporting us. We occasionally send up desperate
prayers and are then strengthened as we feel His reassuring hand
upon our shoulder. At times, we hear Him whisper and stop what
we're doing to listen. And then, in God's power, we step out of
our comfort zone to heed His direction.

When the day is done and we are about to close our eyes, we
open His book to hear the last word of the day. As we focus on
the Light, the world fades away, losing its strength, its hold over
us, and we are renewed in His wisdom, falling asleep in the quiet
comfort of His ever-loving, everlasting arms.

Lord, be my help, my guide, my strength as
I seek the light of Your Word—day and night.

Unattainable Expectations

*For no sooner has the sun risen with a burning heat
than it withers the grass; its flower falls, and its beautiful appearance
perishes. So the rich man also will fade away in his pursuits.*
JAMES 1:11 NKJV

A spotless house, a manicured lawn, clean cars, fancy dinner parties—unreachable expectations and illusions of the perfect family. We think that our home reflects our success, so we work frantically in pursuit of the unattainable, and our expectations of others are unreasonable. When preparing for a dinner party, for example, we want so badly for the event to be perfect that we spend hours barking orders and complaining to our husbands and then get angry when they give up in frustration. Funny, though—when the doorbell rings, the smile comes back and it's as if everything were perfect. Except to our husbands, that is, who feel beaten down.

It's no wonder that men sometimes give up trying to help. They see things differently and have different expectations for the home. Yes, it's good for them to respect the needs and wants that we have for our homes, but it's also necessary for us to let go and not impose our expectations so rigidly that we break the spirit of unity in the marriage.

*Oh, Lord, forgive me for the times I have imposed unrealistic
expectations upon my husband. Help me to lighten up and place his
feelings and needs far above the value that I alone place on appearances.
Help me to order my priorities. Amen.*

Pilgrim Mothers

And Abram took Sarai his wife, and Lot his brother's son,
and all their substance that they had gathered, and the souls that
they had gotten in Haran; and they went forth to go into the
land of Canaan; and into the land of Canaan they came.
GENESIS 12:5 KJV

*A*s God has providentially intervened in history, men have been moved all over the world. While we often remember them, we sometimes forget the wives who went along.

God told Noah to get in the ark. His wife got in, too.

God called Abram out of Ur. Sarai "packed up the tent."

God called Moses from Midian. Zipporah followed.

And so it was when the Separatists left Holland and headed to the new world. They didn't go as individuals—they went as families. Fathers, mothers, and children piled into the Mayflower and set sail into the unknown.

Those pioneering Pilgrim mothers went out in faith, trusting their husbands and God to lead them to safety. They endured hardship to forge a new life and, in so doing, became examples for generations to follow.

Like them, we, too, must be willing to follow our husbands, trusting that God's direction for them is His direction for us, as well.

May we be daughters of Sarah and have a trusting, submissive, yet pioneering faith (1 Peter 3:5–7).

Father, I thank You for the way You lead in the affairs of men—
and their wives. Thank You for the Separatists' wives who risked their
lives to advance the faith. Let me be a pioneering wife, willing
to follow my husband wherever You lead him. Amen.

Live and Learn

*This one thing I do, forgetting those things which are behind,
and reaching forth unto those things which are before.*
PHILIPPIANS 3:13 KJV

You can probably remember the first time you ruined dinner. Doubtless you were a newlywed with high hopes of pleasing your husband and flushed with failure when smoke began pouring from the oven. Regardless of what you ended up eating that night, chances are you learned from your mistake and chalked it up to experience.

Since then, you've made numerous errors in your marriage, some more serious than others, and your husband has made his share, as well. The truth is that no marriage is perfect, and as long as you're learning from them, mistakes are actually healthy!

Experience is the best teacher in any case and especially in marriage. Reading every book ever written by experts on relationships can't teach you what simple failure can. Mistakes are embarrassing and often painful and can send you spiraling into depression. But the wealth of knowledge gained from them will make you a better wife.

Don't despair over your goofs and gaffes. Learn from them and keep that knowledge handy. You never know when you'll need it next.

*Dear God, help me to learn from my failures so that I do not repeat them,
and help me to share the wisdom I gain with others who may need it. Amen.*

Spotless Windows

*Those who are wise shall shine like the brightness
of the firmament, and those who turn many to
righteousness like the stars forever and ever.*
DANIEL 12:3 NKJV

*H*ave you ever washed a glass door or picture window and thought you had it clean, but when the sun hit it the next day, there were spots everywhere? You have to get out the cleanser again and try to wipe away the streaks and spots, wanting to leave the window clear and sparkling so the light can pass through unhindered.

Harsh words, misunderstood actions, and other hurts can mar our marriages. We push away the anger and hurt, thinking this will leave everything like new. Yet underneath, the wounds are still there, festering and ugly. A simple cleaning in our own power isn't what we need to make our marriages glow.

Only with God's light can we see the blemishes for what they are. He can help clean them up and make our lives together new. God wants to be able to shine through us and through our marriages. To do our part, we must allow Him to show us areas where we harbor bad attitudes or hurts. When those are brought to light and dealt with, then we can truly radiate God's love.

Thank You, Lord, for showing me the changes I need to make and for helping me to do the deep cleaning that allows You to shine. Amen.

The Mysterious Visitor

For it came to pass, when the flame went up toward heaven from off the altar, that the angel of the LORD ascended in the flame of the altar. And Manoah and his wife looked on it, and fell on their faces to the ground.
JUDGES 13:20 KJV

*M*anoah and his wife could not have children. Although we don't know her name, the angel of the Lord knew this woman's address. He appeared before her, predicted her baby's birth, and told her to follow strict dietary regulations since her son would serve God as a Nazarite, one set apart for God.

Overwhelmed at her news, Manoah prayed, "Lord, please send the man again. Tell us how to raise this child!"

Once more, the angel appeared to Manoah's wife. She introduced her husband to the awesome being, who now repeated his earlier instructions. Manoah presented him a meal, but the angel urged him to offer it to God. No wonder the couple nearly fainted when the angel rose to heaven in the sacrificial flame!

"We've seen God! We're going to die!" Manoah moaned.

His down-to-earth wife didn't buy it. No God would not have accepted their offering or promised them a baby if He were angry. Her faith was confirmed when Samson was born and became a mighty judge of Israel.

Like Manoah's wife, we may play essential but behind-the-scenes roles in helping our spouses understand and follow Christ wherever He leads.

Lord, thank You for my marriage. Let my influence always steer us toward Your plan and purpose. Amen.

Wise Investments

*What you receive from me is more valuable
than even the finest gold or the purest silver.*
PROVERBS 8:19 CEV

*M*elanie had a tough decision. Her husband, Alex, had
been offered a work promotion.

"If I accept the position, I'll make a lot more money because
I'll be spending more time out in the field," Alex said. "That would
mean evenings away from home—and many weekends, too."

"But what about the kids' soccer matches and school events?"
Melanie wondered. "You'd miss them?"

"I'm afraid so. With the traveling, our monthly camping trips
will have to be curtailed, too. But we'd be able to afford a bigger
house, a nicer car, and even some help for you with the cooking
and housework. Wouldn't you like that?"

"Of course I would, but not at the expense of an absent
husband and father." Melanie weighed the options in her mind.
Which was more important to her—investing in the lives of her
family or in the stock market?

"The way I see it, Alex, God has already made us wealthy.
Maybe not with *stuff* money can buy, but it'll all burn one day
anyway. We're rich with a healthy, happy, loving family. And
that's more valuable than the finest gold or purest silver."

*Heavenly Father, help us focus on our wealth
of love instead of our love of wealth. Amen.*

True Beauty

*Don't be concerned about the outward beauty that
depends on jewelry, or beautiful clothes, or hair arrangement.
Be beautiful inside, in your hearts, with the lasting charm
of a gentle and quiet spirit which is so precious to God.*
1 PETER 3:3–4 TLB

Slipping the diamond ring on our finger, we exclaim,
"Diamonds are a girl's best friend!" We enjoy perusing
glamour magazines, keeping up with the latest fashion trends.
Spending the morning at a nail or hair salon can make our day.
There is nothing wrong with looking our best—but we can cross
the line when we become more concerned about our outward
appearance than our inward beauty.

True beauty resides within our hearts. Clothing fashions
come and go. Hairstyles change. Yet a beautiful heart is eternally
radiant. It is more brilliant than any diamond. It is more stylish
than any fashion. It is precious to God.

What does a beautiful heart look like? It is molded and
shaped after God's own heart. A beautiful heart loves others
unconditionally. Compassion and grace freely flow out of it.
Forgiveness is ever-present. It is gentle and kind, putting the
interests of others first. Do you desire lasting charm and beauty
that never fades? Give attention to your heart. Adorn it with
God's attributes. Dress it in eternal style. True beauty is a heart
that radiates God's love.

*Dear Lord, I desire true beauty.
Fashion my heart after Yours. Amen.*

Words of Love

*If I speak in the tongues of men and of angels,
but have not love, I am only a resounding gong or a clanging cymbal.*
1 CORINTHIANS 13:1 NIV

"The nagging wife" is such a cliché, and it generates a lot of hard feelings. Most women don't think they nag their husbands, and their defense is something like, "Well, if he would just do things right, I wouldn't have to nag!" Oops, that kind of defeats the defense, doesn't it?

Nagging is often borne out of fear—fear that things won't get done, fear that someone will see the messy house, fear that the garbage won't make it to the curb in time, etc. But men report that when they feel nagged, they stop listening. Women report that no matter how many times they say something, they feel ignored. It's a vicious cycle.

First Corinthians 13:1 tells us that unloving speech is about as effective as the ringing of a bell—it means nothing. It becomes an incessant, annoying noise that falls on deaf ears. Speech filled with love and grace communicates God's love and is edifying to all. Accomplish things God's way and reap the rewards of His blessing.

*Father, please help me to control my tongue.
Give me words of grace and love to speak to my husband.
Help me to be an example of Your love through the things I say. Amen.*

One Purpose

Make my joy complete by being of the same mind,
maintaining the same love, united in spirit, intent on one purpose.
PHILIPPIANS 2:2 NASB

*D*oes this verse remind you of your marriage? If just thinking about that verse makes you squirm, it sounds like you may have a lot of work to do. If you are confident that your marriage is going well. . .then congratulations! However, you still have work to do to keep it that way!

Every marriage seems to go through a dry spell when you wonder if either of you *ever* had the same goals and purpose in life. So it's important to take stock of your marriage and sit down with your spouse to go over your purpose. Schedule a date night, a weekend, or even just a few hours of uninterrupted time at home. If you have children, wait until the kids are in bed. Then each of you should come to the table with questions about what you think is important. Don't be afraid to ask your spouse the hard questions like "Do you feel like I am meeting your needs?" "Do you feel loved and respected by me?" "What are your personal goals for life and for our marriage?"

These conversations may be difficult, but they will most definitely help you get your marriage back to "one purpose." Block out time at least once a year to take stock and grow together as one.

Dear Lord, help us to be united in spirit as we talk about our purpose.
Show us how to align our goals with Your plan for our lives. Amen.

A Master Builder

Every wise woman buildeth her house.
PROVERBS 14:1 KJV

What does your dream home look like? Is it a log cabin in the woods? A mansion in the country? A beachfront condo? Whatever it is, it takes skill to build. And while you may hire a contractor and construction crew to erect the physical structure, you are the actual builder of your home.

The most important part of any building is the foundation, and there is no surer foundation than Christ. He must be at the center of your family life. It is His wisdom that makes a home strong, His love that holds the bricks and mortar together. Once He is established as the groundwork for your structure, you can successfully add the walls, roof, and all of the interior details.

Your home should be a refuge from the world. A place that reflects who you are. It should feel warm and welcoming, tranquil and content. If it doesn't, then perhaps it's time to take a second look at your building materials. Don't settle for less than the best.

Remember that the home you are erecting now will become a heritage for generations to come. Dream big, dream bright, and with the right tools and a sure foundation, that dream will become a reality.

Dear Father, help me to be a wise builder.
To make my home a peaceful habitation that will stand
the tests of time and remain long after I am gone. Amen.

Getting Even

*Starting a quarrel is like breaching a dam;
so drop the matter before a dispute breaks out.*
PROVERBS 17:14 NIV

When a fire breaks out in the walls of a house, it can be hard to put out. It can spread, unseen, within the walls and pop out in another place. Masked anger in a marriage can have the same affect as a fire within a wall. When anger isn't expressed directly and appropriately, it will emerge in other ways. Usually those ways are completely unrelated to the source of our anger. For example, a husband forgets an anniversary. Rather than tell him how disappointed she is, his wife quietly goes out and blows the week's budget. That's called "passive aggressive anger." We women seem to have a knack for it.

Passive aggressive anger can wreck havoc on a relationship. Scripture tells us that it is easier to avoid strife than to contain it. Like trying to hold back water, anger seeps out and overpowers.

More marriages are hurt by people who leak anger without confronting what's really going on. A healthy relationship requires open and honest discussion about our feelings before they get out of control and cause irreparable damage.

Father, thank You for loving me enough to point out trouble areas. Teach me to stop stuffing my feelings under the rug but to speak out with objectivity and honesty. Help me face my own shortcomings, to deal with them quickly so that I can experience the joy that comes from receiving forgiveness.

The Reward Is Coming

Her children arise up, and call her blessed;
her husband also, and he praiseth her.
PROVERBS 31:28 KJV

Perhaps the worst part of the curse God levied on Mother Eve was that she would desire to rule over her husband—as she had when she gave Adam the fruit—but he would rule over her.

In the beginning, Adam and Eve were true coregents amid the Garden of Eden. Although she was his helper, scripture does not show us that Adam dominated her.

All that changed in the Fall. Once sin entered, a struggle for power within marriage ensued. Man was declared the head, and woman was to revere, honor, and obey him. The wife is to "do him good and not evil all the days of his life" (Proverbs 31:12 KJV). She is to help him fulfill his mission so he will be a leader in the community.

While we in our flesh may tend to fight this new order, as we submit to it we will find sustaining grace. As we apply ourselves to helping our husbands, we will eventually reap the reward. Any children we may have will someday arise and bless us, as will our husband. One day our works will also be praised in the community.

By remaining diligent in your calling as a helpmeet to your husband and a faithful daughter of God, this glorious day may come sooner than you think.

Lord Jesus, I want to do my husband good all the days of his life. Help me in this endeavor. And thank You for entrusting me with this sacred duty. Amen.

Raised Scars

*And as we have borne the image of the man of dust,
we shall also bear the image of the heavenly Man.*
1 CORINTHIANS 15:49 NKJV

As wives, daughters, mothers, and friends, we all bear scars from painful experiences. Some scars are visible, like the ones from childhood spills or the marks from an appendectomy, cesarian section, or some other surgery. Then there are the scars that are less visible. The wounds on our hearts when our husband speaks a cross word, a loved one has died, or a cherished relationship has been severed.

Yes, we all bear scars. But with Jesus in our hearts, we, although wounded, still have the victory. We have been born anew, into the life of Christ. Nothing in this world can ever truly harm us, for the Great Healer lives within. Amid the wounds and suffering of this world, we can access His peace, His life, His power.

Yes, like Jesus after the Resurrection on that long-ago Easter morn, we still bear the scars of this world, in our hands, our feet, our sides. They are proof of the pain we have endured. But because our Champion rose again with His wounds disfiguring but not disabling we are more than enabled to live mighty lives in Christ.

Don't let the scars you bear disable you. Instead, experience the peace, strength, healing, and victory you have in Christ. Then rise anew in His power!

*Dear God, You know my scars inside and out. Although the wounds
have healed, the scars remain. But Your Son has given me power, victory,
and strength over the pain of this world. In Him I have peace.
Thank You for giving us Your Son and raising Him again!*

An Attractive Man

His mouth is most sweet: yea, he is altogether lovely.
This is my beloved, and this is my friend, O daughters of Jerusalem.
SONG OF SOLOMON 5:16 KJV

Think back to some of the boys you had crushes on when you were in high school. How did you describe them when you were with your friends? If you're honest, you'd have to admit that you found them attractive, smart, fun, athletic, or any combination of the above and with possible additions to the list.

Now consider how you would describe your husband. Are you proud of him? Solomon's wife was obviously quite smitten with him. It doesn't mean he was perfect. Just read his life story and you'll find the numerous mistakes he made. The imperfections are not what his wife focused on, however. She was more interested in his positive traits.

Is your husband perfect? Of course not! He's human just like you are. If you concentrate on all his good points rather than complaining about his weaknesses, you will have a stronger marriage. That doesn't mean you inflate his ego, but you can certainly compliment him. You like to be told you look nice. Don't you think he does, too? Don't even consider whining about him to others. Instead, love and encourage him. Be proud of the man in your life.

Jesus, I am proud that I will be Your bride one day.
Let me be just as proud of the earthly husband You have given me.

Clay Jars

> *We are like clay jars in which this treasure is stored.*
> *The real power comes from God and not from us. We often suffer,*
> *but we are never crushed. . . . In times of trouble God is with us.*
> 2 CORINTHIANS 4:7–9 CEV

Even with good counsel before marriage, many couples think love will gloss over any problems and be the glue that holds everything together. But that glue is imperfect and only masks the inherent weaknesses of two flawed people in a marriage.

Clay jars are only as strong as the potter who molds them and the fire that removes the impurities and strengthens the elements. If the potter hasn't been careful to punch out the bubbles of weakness, the pot is weakened in the firing. Then the vessel may be repaired with imperfect glue.

We are all flawed, earthen vessels of clay, and marriage tends to highlight the weaknesses in each other rather than maintaining the strengths. Blessed are the men and women who learn early in their marriage that the real power to hold their union together comes from God.

God, the Master Potter, knows exactly what to do to expose the weaknesses and strengthen each vessel. He never leaves us to work out our problems alone, nor does He repair our cracks with imperfect glue. We may suffer, but God is ready to do what is necessary to make us useful vessels once again.

> *Father, thank You for the refining fire that*
> *purifies me as well as my marriage. Amen.*

Rejoice and Mourn

Rejoice with those who rejoice;
mourn with those who mourn.
ROMANS 12:15 NIV

*E*mpathy comes easy for most women. We rescue the needy and comfort the hurting. Whether nursing a loved one back to health or preparing a meal for a sick neighbor, our hearts instinctively reach out to others in their hour of need. Mourning with those who mourn seems natural. Why is it more difficult to rejoice with those who rejoice?

Ponder the following scenarios: Your best friend's son got accepted to Harvard while your son will be attending the local junior college. A coworker received the promotion you had anticipated. Your sister found out she's expecting her third child while you have faced years of infertility. Sometimes our hearts are prevented from embracing another's happiness. Why?

When we encounter difficulty rejoicing with those who rejoice, we must examine the underlying attitude of our heart. Envy and jealousy have reared their ugly heads. We have trouble rejoicing because inwardly we desire the blessing ourselves. Confess your attitude to the Lord. Ask for forgiveness. Trust that the Lord will provide just what you need. Don't be jealous of what the Lord bestows upon another. Remember that He lavishes blessings upon you, as well. And when your day of rejoicing comes, you will want others to share in your joy. Start today by rejoicing with them!

Dear Lord, forgive me when envy prevents me from rejoicing.
May I learn to truly rejoice from my heart. Amen.

Abundant Leftovers

*Then he took the seven loaves and the fish,
and when he had given thanks, he broke them and gave
them to the disciples, and they in turn to the people.*
MATTHEW 15:36 NIV

*A*ll day long it had been one demand after another. Her mother-in-law was sick and needed groceries; she had to run off two hundred copies of Sunday's bulletin; the car needed an oil change; the neighbor's little boy came over, wanting to play Go Fish—again. Then her husband came home from work and announced that his boss, three coworkers, and all their wives were coming for dinner at 7 o'clock. She stood in front of the open refrigerator, despairing.

The disciples had despaired, too, and they had a few more than eight people to feed; they had a crowd of four thousand! But Jesus simply asked them to give Him what they *did* have and offered it up with thanksgiving to God. Then came the miracle that we still read about today with awe.

We can be run ragged with giving; we can feel like we have nothing left to offer those around us. But Jesus offers us, if we ask, the abundant resources of His power and love. Notice, though, how the giving of thanks came *before* the miracle. Thank God for giving you the grace to give to those in need around you, and watch Him rain down blessings. Even the *leftovers* will be more abundant than we can imagine.

*Dear Father, help me cry out to You when I feel like I have
nothing left to give. Thank You for how You will answer. Amen.*

Look Before You Leap

*It is not good for a person to be without knowledge,
and he who hurries his footsteps errs.*
PROVERBS 19:2 NASB

*J*anice was furious. Her husband was almost an hour late for
dinner and hadn't even called. *How typical,* Janice thought.
Rick can be so inconsiderate. All he thinks about is himself. After
checking the roast for the third time, Janice was ready to throw
the whole thing in the garbage when Rick rushed in the door.

"Sorry I didn't call, honey. . . . I just came upon a car accident,
and I needed to wait with one of the victims until help arrived."
As Janice tried to salvage what was left of the roast, she found
herself wishing that she hadn't thought the worst of her husband,
who was actually a pretty good guy.

We've all been guilty of jumping to conclusions before we
have all the information. We make judgments and decisions
based on what we *think* might have happened or what we have
seen happen in the past. Assumptions like these can get us into
trouble because often there is more to the story.

Proverbs 19:2 reminds us that it is wise to avoid making
judgments before we have all the information. Ask questions; be
patient. It may keep you from having to apologize later.

> *Lord, help me to wait until I have all the information
> before I make judgments and decisions—and to offer
> others grace when they don't meet my expectations.*

The Right Focus

*Let us run with patience the race that is set before us,
looking unto Jesus the author and finisher of our faith.*
HEBREWS 12:1–2 KJV

*U*nused to the fast pace of freeway travel, the wife tensed every time a car cut in front of them or the traffic did the unexpected. Her husband's going from high speed to sudden stops for no apparent reason and then zooming ahead again had her nerves frazzled. She wanted to tell her husband to slow down, but she knew that would impede traffic and make the situation worse. She knew he was a responsible driver, yet the urge to tell him how to drive better was almost overpowering.

Knowing she had to trust, the wife began to watch her husband's strong hands as he drove. She kept her focus there, talking with him, praying for their safety. Before long, she realized she'd relaxed. The driving conditions hadn't changed, but her focal point had.

Sometimes in life, trials hit us from every side. We find ourselves tense and disoriented, wanting to take control even when we know God is there watching out for us. The race we are running becomes more than we can bear as we see obstacles we hadn't counted on in front of us. This is when we must take a deep breath and focus on Jesus. By changing our outlook from the stumbling blocks to Jesus, we will begin to relax and allow Him to handle the adversities.

*Thank You, Lord, for the way You look out for
me so that all I have to do is look to You. Amen.*

Marital Mirror

*An excellent wife is the crown of her husband,
but she who brings shame is like rottenness in his bones.*
PROVERBS 12:4 ESV

Anna never spoke a bad word about her husband. You didn't have to know her long before you understood that there was much love in this couple's relationship. Though most of her coworkers had never met Jason, they admired him deeply.

If your friends and coworkers held your words up as a mirror to your marriage, what would they see? A bitter relationship or a warm one? Doubt or devotion to God?

Never doubt that the way we portray our spouses will be noticed by others—and they'll come to conclusions about our husbands based on our words. Those words might even affect whether or not someone offers our husbands positions of authority in the community, professional field, or, if he's a believer, church. After all, we live with them, and others will believe we know what we're talking about.

Husbands don't have to be perfect to be appreciated, and they deeply need our support. Will our words bring honor or shame? Are we crowns or painful bones?

Have we appreciated our husbands today? Let's share good news with others and let them know what special fellows we've married.

*Lord, thank You for my husband. You put our lives together—
help me to honor him and You together.*

Give Thanks for Him?

*I thank my God, making mention of thee always
in my prayers, hearing of thy love and faith, which thou
hast toward the Lord Jesus, and toward all saints.*
PHILEMON 1:4–5 KJV

The women's Bible study group studied scriptures, shared needs, and prayed for each others' children. They cheered each other on during the Christmas rush, survived teen driving, and fought the devil and bigger dress sizes with every step of their spiritual journey together.

One day, they decided to emphasize giving thanks. Crystal's suggestion quieted the group as if they had been muzzled: "Let's thank God for our husbands."

Silence. They often prayed for grace to endure their guys' inability to function on a normal level. But give *thanks* for them?

Crystal persisted. "Last night Brad killed a big hairy spider in my closet." She shuddered. "Brad couldn't find a can of chicken noodle soup in the kitchen if he fell over it. He never drops his socks into the hamper. But if it weren't for Brad, I would never sleep in that house again."

The others recalled wildlife their husbands had expelled, drains they had unplugged after a long day's work, and imaginary burglars they had routed at 2 a.m. Plus the fact their husbands had been faithful in more ways than one.

The women bowed their heads and gave thanks.

*Lord Jesus, my husband endures many pressures in this life.
Help me give thanks for his faithfulness. Amen.*

A High Calling

To be discreet, chaste, keepers at home. . .
TITUS 2:5 KJV

Society places a lot of demands on today's women. The pressure to have a successful career while trying to balance a home and family leaves many wives feeling stretched to the limit. With so many responsibilities cluttering our plates, it's easy to get our priorities out of order. But the Bible clearly indicates that one of women's highest callings is to be keepers at home.

The job of keeping house is often misrepresented as a menial chore. But managing a household is no easy task. The keeper of the home must be a master planner and budgeter. She must possess culinary skills and excel in interior design. She is organized and disciplined, a hard worker who takes pride in the fruits of her labor.

A well-kept home is a blessing to others and a glory to God. It is a place of comfort and peace, of hospitality and welcome. As a keeper of the home, you have answered a high calling and are fulfilling a beautiful role.

*Dear Father, in this hectic world that I live in, help me
to keep my priorities in order. Give me a strong desire to keep my
house in order so that I may be a blessing to my family. Amen.*

Who Do You Run To?

Immediately, when the entire crowd saw Him,
they were amazed and began running up to greet Him.
MARK 9:15 NASB

After Jesus transfiguration, He came down the mountain. As soon as the people saw Him, they ran to greet Him. When Jesus asked what was happening, a man spoke up, telling Jesus how His disciples were having trouble healing his son, a boy who was seized by a mute spirit.

After giving Jesus an update on his boy's condition, the father said, If You can do anything, take pity on us and help us! (Mark 9:22 NASB).

Jesus responded with, If You can? All things are possible to him who believes (Mark 9:23 NASB).

The boy's father cried out, I do believe; help my unbelief (Mark 9:24 NASB).

When the crowd began to gather around, Jesus rebuked the boy's unclean spirit and he was healed.

What do you do when you're having trouble at home? Who do *you* run to? Are you running to Jesus, pleading for Him to help you? Do you know that if you only believe, *anything* is possible? Are you confirming that belief to Jesus and asking Him for more?

Run to Jesus. Tell Him all. Cry out for more faith. And watch the miracles commence!

Jesus, I run to You today, amazement in my eyes, my heart in my hand,
my troubles on my shoulders. Help me, Lord! Take pity upon me!
I do believe in You! Help my unbelief! Show me a miracle!

Picture Window

*But the path of the righteous is like the light of dawn,
which shines brighter and brighter until full day.*
PROVERBS 4:18 ESV

Have you ever looked at a classic stained-glass window at night? You don't see much. Though the leading around each form may give an outline of the subject, you can't see the bright colors that make such windows so appealing in the daylight.

When the sun rises colors begin to appear, and as bright sunlight shines through the panes of glass, a beautiful picture appears, portraying biblical characters, parables—most often Jesus.

Our lives are like those windows. Before we know Jesus, our window is dark. But when we come to know Him, His light shines in us and a spiritual picture appears—faintly, perhaps, at first, but with much potential for brightness. As we grow in Him, His light brightens, and our testimonies shine forth with increasing beauty.

Can our husbands testify to the light shining through our lives? Do the robes of Jesus shine whitely, or has sin muddied the picture, blocking His light from our witness? As Jesus influences our marriages, our paths shine first in the power of dawn sunshine then ever increasing, till a more-than-noonday brightness enlivens all the colors of our picture window.

*Lord, help me to live in Your brightness and reflect that light in my life.
May my husband and others clearly see my testimony of faith.*

The Simple Truth

*"You are truly my disciples if you remain faithful
to my teachings. And you will know the truth,
and the truth will set you free."*
JOHN 8:31–32 NLT

The best evidence we can offer the world that Jesus is active in our lives is to obey His teachings of love and forgiveness. Outside of that, few words are usually needed. Words simply add to the noise in a world overpopulated with opinion columns and Internet blogs, while our actions as Christians speak volumes.

There is a blessing that comes when we answer harsh words with kindness or demonstrate patience in otherwise unreasonable situations. The world may not understand, but it is not the world we serve. We serve a Savior and Redeemer who guides us and helps us by performing these miracles of grace through us, if we allow Him.

By this collaboration of spirit, we begin to see things the way God sees them. Decisions about our schedules become clearer as God shows us what really matters and what doesn't. We begin to see the simple truth that our husbands need our love and acceptance more than our advice. And, in time, we begin to hear a voice whisper timeless and sacred truths over the din of our own busy lives.

*Father, as Your ways become my ways, I see the blessing of
Your truth in my life. Thank You for showing me the way to a simpler
and more fulfilling life when I walk in obedience to You. Amen.*

Speaking Truth

*"My mouth speaks what is true,
for my lips detest wickedness."*
PROVERBS 8:7 NIV

*M*ary sighed as she hung up the phone. It was her
mom—for the third time that day. "Your sister says I'm
too involved in your lives," her mother had announced. "*You* don't
think that's true, do you?"

Mary hesitated. Her sister was right, but Mary couldn't bear
to tell her mother what she actually thought. Instead she said,
"Mom, I think you just care very much about us, that's all." As
the words left her mouth, Mary felt her face redden. Once again
she'd copped out and missed another opportunity to have an
honest conversation with her mom. The truth was, her mother's
constant meddling was really starting to take its toll on their
relationship.

Telling the truth is often accompanied by consequences.
When we are truthful with others, it can sometimes mean
hurting their feelings or changing the relationship. But the Bible
is clear—when we fail to speak the truth in love, we are failing
to live authentic lives and ultimately can do real damage to
ourselves and others.

Is there someone in your life with whom you are having
difficulty telling the truth? What steps can you take today to be
more truthful?

*Lord, teach me how to speak truth in love,
even when I am unsure of the outcome. Amen.*

When He Just Doesn't Get It

Then said Elkanah her husband to her, Hannah,
why weepest thou? and why eatest thou not? and why is
thy heart grieved? am not I better to thee than ten sons?
1 SAMUEL 1:8 KJV

*D*o you ever get the feeling that your husband just doesn't
"get it"? That no matter how clear you are or how specific
your body language is, he just doesn't understand?

Take heart. This problem has been with us for a long time. So
long, in fact, that it's detailed in the Old Testament.

Picture Hannah. The Lord had shut her womb, and she
was in grief and bitterness over her barrenness. Her sorrow was
compounded by the other woman in the household, Peninnah,
Elkanah's other wife.

If any wife had a good reason to cry, it was Hannah.

Enter Elkanah, the typical husband, with his typical-
husband question: "Why are you crying?"

We might want to say, "Don't you know?" or "You ought to
know—it's your fault!" But Hannah was wise. She apparently said
nothing. Instead, she went to the temple to pray and weep before
the Lord.

Instead of taking her frustrations out on her husband,
Hannah placed her expectations in the Lord—and God blessed
it. Her prayer was answered.

The next time your husband doesn't understand, keep your
peace and pray. Because God always "gets it"—and He always
gets it right.

Dear Lord, I shouldn't demand so much of my husband. I know he
doesn't think like a woman and sometimes doesn't understand. But You do.
Remind me that all my expectations must be in You alone. Amen.

Love of Money

For the love of money is a root of all sorts of evil,
and some by longing for it have wandered away from
the faith and pierced themselves with many griefs.
1 TIMOTHY 6:10 NASB

*R*osalyn and her husband found the home of their dreams. They did everything they knew to get enough money to buy the home. . .borrowing more money than they could afford and working longer hours.

The Lord warns us that the love of money is the root of all kinds of evil. In pursuit of making more money, we may choose to neglect the most important priorities in our lives. We get deeper into debt, take on huge credit card payments, and exceed our budget. Or we may begin to allow ourselves to neglect time with God, reading and studying the Bible, praying, corporate worship, serving those in need, spending time with our families, or making poor decisions that lack integrity and ethics.

We cannot take anything with us when we die (1 Timothy 6:7; 1 John 2:17). God tells us to be "free from the love of money, being content with what [we] have" (Hebrews 13:5 NASB) because there is great gain in godliness combined with contentment (1 Timothy 6:6 NASB).

Prayerfully determine your financial priorities. Distinguish between needs and wants, trusting that our heavenly Provider will not forsake you (Hebrews 13:5).

Provider Lord, I surrender our financial priorities to You and
ask that You would align them with Your will for us as a family.

Mrs. Pilate

While court was still in session, Pilate's wife sent
him a message: "Don't get mixed up in judging this
noble man. I've just been through a long and troubled
night because of a dream about him."
MATTHEW 27:19 MSG

As Jesus stood before Pilate the governor to be tried as a criminal, Pilate's wife interrupted court proceedings to send her husband a warning. But Pilate didn't listen to his wife, didn't heed a message that probably originated from God, and he washed his hands of this case. "He had Jesus whipped, and then handed over for crucifixion" (Matthew 27:26 MSG).

The phrase "I wash my hands of this" has been linked to Pilate since. It indicates that one absolves himself or herself from the outcome of an event. Ironically, Pilate couldn't really wash his hands of Christ's death. He was just as guilty as His accusers.

Jesus' silence before Pilate was haunting. Mrs. Pilate, though, was a mouthpiece for God. Whether she had a full understanding of God or a dim pagan-filtered one, she sensed there was a divine component to Jesus. She was right to speak up!

Wrong is wrong. It takes courage and prayer, but we need to speak forth when others, including our husbands, are moving in the wrong direction.

If only Pilate had listened to his wife's warning! What a missed opportunity, for all eternity, for that man.

Lord, nothing misses Your attention, especially the receptivity of our hearts.
Help me to do whatever is in my power to stop wrong behavior.
Give me courage to act well.

Mirrors of Light

*"Arise, shine; for your light has come,
and the glory of the LORD has risen upon you."*
ISAIAH 60:1 NASB

God said, "Light be," and light came into existence on the earth. Light appeared from the lips of God so that He could see all He was about to create—and His creation could see Him.

When you gave your heart to God, His light came on inside your heart. Christianity lives from the inside out. When your heart is right, then your actions truly portray the influence that God and His Word have in your life.

Your life should then begin to reflect the character and nature of the One who created you, opposing all darkness. You are a reflection of His light to everyone around you. From within you, shine upon the lives of others and become a light to the world.

As you point others to God, to His light—His goodness, mercy, and love—your light shines, repelling darkness and bringing comfort to everyone God brings across your path.

How encouraging to know that your life can brighten the whole room. You have the power to open the door of someone's heart for the Holy Spirit to speak to them about his or her own salvation. Don't miss a moment to let your life shine!

*Jesus, show me what I can do and say to
let my light shine brightly. Amen.*

Weakness

But he said to me, "My grace is sufficient for you,
for my power is made perfect in weakness."
2 CORINTHIANS 12:9 NIV

Second Corinthians 12:9 brings to mind the words of the
song "Jesus Loves Me":

> *Jesus loves me, this I know,*
> *For the Bible tells me so.*
> *Little ones to Him belong,*
> *They are weak but He is strong.*
> *Yes, Jesus loves me!*

What does this have to do with marriage? Well, there are
times in every marriage when weakness rears its ugly head and
we must rely solely on the strength of God. Maybe your spouse
did something inexcusable and you aren't strong enough to
forgive. Or maybe you're the one who sinned and you aren't
strong enough to confess to your spouse. Whatever the issues,
remember that everyone struggles with weakness! We struggle
because we are sinners saved only by the grace of God. We are
weak, but *He* is strong!

Sometimes weakness can be devastating to a marriage. But
Jesus loves you, regardless of your weakness, and He is there to
provide His strength at all times. Ask Him for the strength to do
the right thing. His grace is enough to cover your weakness, and
He is glorified in the process!

> *Dear Father, please be my strength during this time of weakness.*
> *I am so thankful for Your love and grace. Help me to be loving*
> *and gracious to my spouse. In Jesus' name, amen.*

Just Say Thank You

> *"If you then, being evil, know how to give good gifts
> to your children, how much more will your Father who
> is in heaven give what is good to those who ask Him!"*
> MATTHEW 7:11 NASB

*S*he could always tell what was coming. It began with a certain tilt of the head, eyes rolled in disgust, lips curled into a sarcastic smile, and the words, "My husband." She cringed when she heard these young wives speak such bitter, unkind words about the men whose rings they wore, the men they had promised to love and respect. They had no idea what they were really saying.

Marriage was God's idea, not ours, and our husbands are gifts from Him. When we speak disparagingly about our husbands, it's as if we are saying to God, "What is *this*? It's the wrong size! I don't like the color. It's not what I would have picked out. Why didn't You just get me a gift certificate?"

God has given each wife her particular husband for a reason. He knows what we need better than we do. In all things, even this, He is conforming us to the image of Christ.

A husband is the only gift with a true lifetime warranty! Enjoy the gift, and remember to thank the Giver.

*Dear gracious heavenly Father, thank You so much for my husband.
Help me to treat him as a precious gift from You. Amen.*

Come Away, My Love

Arise, my love, my fair one, and come away. . . .
Let me see thy countenance, let me hear thy voice.
SONG OF SOLOMON 2:13–14 KJV

To celebrate their anniversary, Karen and Bill planned a short and inexpensive getaway weekend to their favorite bed-and-breakfast at a popular seaside resort. When asked why they always went back to the same place, Karen responded, "Because we've been there so many times before, we can just relax, walk in and out of shops, or simply stroll on the beach."

Then Karen smiled and said, "What's really nice is just spending time lounging in our room, reading a book or watching TV, with no telephone ringing and no dog or kids climbing into bed between us. It's just Bill and me. Alone. Together."

With a world getting busier every day, we can sometimes take our husbands for granted, which can turn a close relationship into one filled with barriers of kids, careers, extended family obligations, church functions, and other responsibilities.

Don't let the busyness of this world keep you from focusing in on the beloved in your life. Leave e-mail behind, turn the cell phones off, and get away for a day, a weekend, or a week somewhere far from the responsibilities of home, work, and family.

Make it a point to regularly rise up, come away, and explore your love anew.

Lord, my husband and I need time alone. Give us wisdom
in planning a getaway far from the busyness of this world.
Help my beloved and I find a way to come away, together.

Vows of Grace

*I will betroth thee unto me in righteousness, and in judgment,
and in lovingkindness, and in mercies. I will even betroth
thee unto me in faithfulness: and thou shalt know the LORD.*
HOSEA 2:19–20 KJV

osea the prophet suffered as his wife, Gomer, pursued
other lovers. His sad story reflected God's anguish when
Israel followed other gods.

During Hosea's era, no self-respecting man tolerated
marriage to an adulteress. Hosea, however, determined to bring
Gomer home. When he found her, Gomer had seen terrible days,
possibly even slavery. He paid for her, but by law, he possessed
the right to put Gomer to death for her sin. Instead, Hosea
confronted his wife and demanded the respect he deserved. He
promised total faithfulness to her, as if she merited his love.

Like Hosea, God endured betrayal by His people Israel. He
still experiences the hurt of unrequited love when we forget Him
and pursue money, status, or pleasure as if they will give us what
we need. God could look elsewhere for worshippers—but He
loves us too much to give up on us.

Hosea's and Gomer's struggles demonstrate that no marriage
is beyond repair if both spouses forgive and recommit. And the
story brings us face-to-face with the God of second chances who
would rather suffer death than live without us.

*Jesus, it takes only a moment for my heart to wander away from You—
and from the man You have given me. Help me turn
from evil and cling to Your will. Amen.*

True Joy

*Yet I will rejoice in the LORD,
I will joy in the God of my salvation.*
HABAKKUK 3:18 KJV

*H*ave you ever wanted your husband to do a job a certain way, sure that would be the perfect way? Yet when he tries to please you by doing it the way you ask, you find that you aren't really as pleased as you thought you would be? Most wives have been in a situation where they've changed their mind and wanted that task done differently.

In times like this we want to say, "If only he would do this, I would be happy." This is not God's design for marriage. Our husband isn't there to ensure our happiness. He has many God-given purposes in marriage, but seeing to our happiness is not one of them. We won't be at peace as long as we look to our spouse for fulfillment.

Our true source of hope and joy comes in knowing the Lord. He is the One who won't leave us or forsake us. God is always there. He understands our hurts from the inside out. Only God can truly empathize with our loneliness or disillusionment with life. God sees our heart and knows our intent. This is something our husband can never fully do. When we learn to look to God for our joy, then we will be happy in our marriage, too.

*Thank You, Jesus, for bringing me true joy. Help me to release my
husband from unrealistic expectations and only look to You. Amen.*

Deep Waters

"When you go through deep waters, I will be with you.
When you go through rivers of difficulty, you will not drown.
When you walk through the fire of oppression, you will not be burned up."
ISAIAH 43:2 NLT

A godly, vibrant marriage is a blessing. And we rejoice when we are in harmony with our husbands. But in any marriage, we need to expect and be prepared for deep waters, rivers of difficulty, and fires of oppression. God promises that He will not allow us to drown in the rapids or to be burned in the fire.

Sometimes the deep water may be that we're not working as a single unit, especially when one or both spouses decides to go his or her own way, leaving God out of the marriage. Many will find themselves in a raging fire of oppression when they lose a child or other loved one. Financial problems can turn into a flooded river of difficulty. How we choose to go through the trials of life as a couple will have a great effect on our marriages.

No matter what the problem or trial we face, we can know that God doesn't ever leave us to walk through it alone. He promises to restore all we lose—or think we lose—in these trials because we are precious in His sight (Isaiah 43:4).

Father, may I remember in the middle of trial that You love me.
When You have refined me in the fire and tempered me
in the deep water, I will come forth as gold. Amen.

Day
246

*One Plus One
Equals One*

*And they twain shall be one flesh:
so then they are no more twain, but one flesh.*
MARK 10:8 KJV

*I*t seems to defy every math principle you've been taught since kindergarten, but if you've been married for any length of time you know it's true. You and your husband were once two separate individuals, but now you are one flesh. This isn't referring to just your sexual oneness, either, although that certainly plays a role. Look at Mark 10:8 in its entirety. It is referring to the grafting of two lives. It's a beautiful union that can really only be experienced by husband and wife. It's true that a set of friends might enjoy some bonding moments, and family ties are strong, too, but it's not the same as the oneness shared by husband and wife.

God did this on purpose when He created male and female and then ordained marriage. He intended for the union between husband and wife to be sacred. Just as it hurts to have a bone broken or a limb removed, so does a broken or severed marriage cause pain. Remember: Just as our physical bodies need care, so do our marriages. Your doctor gives you advice and prescriptions so that you can maintain good health. Your Great Physician also gives directions for a healthy marriage and offers healing for one that is hurting. Study His prescriptions carefully and be sure to apply them.

*Father, the oneness I share with my husband is beautiful.
Help us to follow Your orders to keep our marriage healthy.*

In the multitude of counselors there is safety.
PROVERBS 11:14 NKJV

There's nothing like getting married to prove to a person that they don't know much about the opposite sex. Husbands and wives differ from one another in many ways, and such diversity can lead to a host of problems. But yours isn't the first relationship to hit a bump in the road. Plenty of other couples have been there and done that and can offer a wealth of experience and wisdom to get you through the tough spots in your relationship.

Marriage is full of mysteries, some more perplexing than others. And while you may not know the answers to the problems you face, chances are that someone older and wiser than you does. There is nothing wrong with seeking guidance from trusted family and friends about the woes you face with your companion.

Not all advice is good advice. Magazine racks are full of glossy publications with tantalizing titles on how to make your marriage sizzle. But the Bible encourages us to seek godly wisdom. If there's a wrinkle in your relationship that you can't seem to smooth out, don't be afraid or ashamed to ask for help. A few healthy tips from the right people can make a world of difference in you marriage.

Dear God, when I don't know what to do about a problem with my spouse,
lead me to the source of advice that will strengthen and help my marriage.
Amen.

Let the Man Sleep!

*I charge you, O ye daughters of Jerusalem, by the roes,
and by the hinds of the field, that ye stir not up,
nor awake my love, till he please.*
Song of Solomon 2:7 kjv

*M*en can be very annoying sleepers.
While wives toss and turn, taking many minutes—
or even hours—to clean out their mental closets before going
to sleep, husbands can shut all the boxes in their heads and be
asleep before hitting the pillow.

This can be a cause for resentment in a marriage. A wife
can become jealous of her husband's ability to sleep. Sometimes
it seems so unfair that she needs rest, but he's the one who is
sleeping.

What's a wife to do?

Hear what the gracious bride of Solomon says: "Stir not up,
nor awake my love, till he please."

Husbands carry a great weight on their shoulders. They work
hard to provide for their families. When they come home, they
want and need time to unwind. For some, that means falling
asleep in the recliner after supper or napping before bedtime.

A gracious, reverent wife will let her husband rest whenever
he pleases, without stirring him up with guilt or criticism.

He works hard for you. Let him sleep!

*Father, I appreciate my husband's hard work for the family, I really do.
But sometimes I am amazed how he can sleep. Give him the rest he needs.
And give me the grace to let him. Amen.*

Time Management

But Jesus answered them,
"My Father is working until now, and I am working."
JOHN 5:17 ESV

*O*ur effectiveness in life is directly proportional to our willingness to work hard and use our time in a manner that is pleasing to the Lord. Women often feel like their job never ends. From morning to night, there are tasks and responsibilities that occupy lots of time yet never get completed. It's defeating to come to the end of a day feeling like the work still isn't done. However, God doesn't judge us based on what's unfinished; He looks at what got accomplished and our attitude through the process.

Jesus never wasted a moment or passed up an opportunity to do what was right. He took breaks, He went to quiet places to pray, and He fed his soul with rest, but He was always ready to do His Father's work. If we feed our souls with the Word, go to our quiet places to pray, and get rest as we let the Holy Spirit minister to us, we will be prepared to tackle our Father's work in our homes and in the world.

Jesus, help me to plan my day in such a way that it pleases You.
Help me to prioritize and manage my time so that I can be an effective
woman who brings honor to my husband and to You. Amen.

Quiet Voices

""Then you will call upon Me and come
and pray to Me, and I will listen to you.'"
JEREMIAH 29:12 NASB

For forty years, Jeremiah, the "reluctant prophet," proclaimed God's message to Judah, a nation that neither saw, heard, nor responded. What was the main gist of Jeremiah's message of hope from God? "Come to me and *I will listen to you.*"

Listening is essential in intimate relationships. God likened the relationship between marriage partners to His relationship with His beloved bride, the church (Ephesians 5:22–33). In other words, our relationship with God models how our relationship should be with our husbands.

But really *hearing* is not always easy. As God demonstrated to another prophet, Elijah, in 1 Kings 19:9–12, we must listen carefully for His still, small voice. It's not in the ferocious wind or mighty earthquake or roaring fire. God's voice is a gentle breeze that we'll miss if we're detoured by loud or blustering distractions.

In the same way, we must specifically listen for the quiet heart-voice of the man we chose to love, help, and honor until death parts us. The vulnerable voice in his deepest recesses is often very different than the showy, confident voice on the surface. But God gave many women an uncanny sixth sense to truly *hear* inner cries from those we love.

Lover of my soul, just as You listen to my inner voice, help me see, hear, and respond to the true, beneath-the-surface voice of my husband. Amen.

Heavenly Treasure

*"But store up for yourselves treasures in heaven,
where moth and rust do not destroy, and where
thieves do not break in and steal."*
MATTHEW 6:20 NIV

You've got ten minutes to leave your home before it is destroyed by fire. What will you take with you? Once you knew your loved ones were safe, you would likely grab the things that remind you of them—photos, heirloom jewelry, a precious family Bible.

A question like "In case of fire, what would you take with you?" has a way of whittling our priorities to the bare essentials. Most of what we own is easily destroyed and just as easily replaced. There are, however, a few things really worth having, and Jesus reminds us that these are things on which we can't put a price tag. Relationships. Eternal life. The assurance that our loved ones will live eternally with Him.

What will you take with you? This isn't a rhetorical question. The practicality of Jesus' words about heavenly treasure remind us that the way we live our lives each and every day should be led by this principle. Invest yourself in the things that matter. Take a look at your calendar and your checkbook. Do these items reflect your desire to store up eternal treasures?

*Lord, You know that it is easy to get distracted by earthly things—
things that will ultimately be worth nothing. Help me to shift my
focus to things that have eternal significance and to invest my
life in those things that will bring eternal dividends.*

Practice, Not Perfect

Share with God's people who are in need.
Practice hospitality.
ROMANS 12:13 NIV

You've had a long day at work. You know that when you go home, you have dishes piled in your sink, loads of laundry to wash, and dust an inch thick on your coffee table. The last thing you can possibly imagine or desire is inviting people into your house for a meal. You are tired, and all you have in your cabinets is a box of macaroni and cheese. How in the world can you expect to practice hospitality with a dirty house, an exhausted body, and one box of mac and cheese?

God knows our limits, and while He will always stretch us if we are willing, He does not demand more of us than we can do with His help. God does not demand that we use our best china, serve seven-course gourmet meals, provide a string quartet for entertainment, and put everyone into beds with silk sheets. Instead, God simply asks us to share what we have, to be generous and warmhearted, and, most of all, to be willing to seek out those who are in need and share God's love with them.

Dear Lord, please open my eyes to the needs of people around me. Teach me to be generous, and help me to practice hospitality. Thank You for Your blessings and the opportunities You will give me to share them with others. Amen.

Offensive Ways

*Search me, O God, and know my heart; test me and
know my anxious thoughts. See if there is any offensive
way in me, and lead me in the way everlasting.*
PSALM 139:23–24 NIV

Worry. Anxiety. Fear. It is easy to become consumed with
anxious thoughts, the "what-ifs" in life. What if my
breast lump turns out to be malignant? What if my husband
gets laid off? What if my friend doesn't forgive me? Our mind
dwells on scenarios that may or may not come to pass. Mental
and emotional energy is expended needlessly because worrying
changes nothing. Instead, we are the ones adversely affected.
The stress generated by worry can cause physical, mental, and
emotional illnesses.

Worry, anxiety, and fear are also spiritual roadblocks. Did
you know that anxious thoughts are offensive to God? Anxiety is
a red flag signaling that we are not trusting God. Fear and faith
cannot coexist. We are either worrying or trusting, anxious or
peaceful.

Come before the Lord. Invite Him to search your heart.
Allow His light to expose any anxious thoughts lurking in the
shadows. Acknowledge and confess your fears. Then trust Him
with those concerns. Ask that His will be done, knowing and
believing that His will is best. Then receive His peace by faith.
Let's desire to live by faith, trusting all your cares to God.

*Dear Lord, search my heart. Forgive my anxious thoughts.
May I trust You instead. Amen.*

A Match Aflame

Beloved, do not be surprised at the fiery ordeal among you,
which comes upon you for your testing, as though
some strange thing were happening to you.
1 PETER 4:12 NASB

It begins as a simple discussion about finances and suddenly, without warning, light and easy talk ignites into a blaze of anger and blame. In a matter of moments, marital bliss tears into flames, and we wonder if a crowd will gather. Siren's cry fades as night crawls into day. Anger has melted into despair. And lying in an exhausted heap of smoke and ash are our dreams—hollow remnants of what we thought we had.

Although it is natural to experience flare-ups in marriage, the impact need not spread to our hearts. The secret lies in giving our voice the air it sometimes needs without feeding embers of fear that smolder under the surface.

When we believe that God has brought us together for His great purpose, then we know our marriage is stronger than the arguments that threaten to pull us apart. God uses friction to erode away our rough edges, the way water meets land and carves new landscapes. His presence is rain in a drought—full of a freshness that even charred and blackened hearts can absorb. And out of the ashes, new dreams rise up in a downpour of God's love.

Father, please help me to include You in all my conversations with my
husband, even in the darkest moments. Help me to not lose faith that
You are working in me and through me for Your glory. Amen.

A Third Partner

May the Lord make your love increase and overflow
for each other and for everyone else, just as ours does for you.
1 THESSALONIANS 3:12 NIV

*I*n our world, love doesn't come easily. We're tempted to seek
a short-term emotional connection that seems beneficial
today but costs us a lot tomorrow. Or we love someone deeply
but lose out to a worldly pleasure, emotional confusion, or death.
A thousand things snatch love from our grasp. Without God,
love is impossible to hold on to.

What would we give to have the overflowing, 1 Thessalonians 3:12 kind of love in our marriages? This love isn't rooted
in our abilities to grasp it but in God's ability to give it. Any real
Christian born of God's Spirit grasps divine love. Its "price" is a
deep relationship with God. As our relationship with Him grows,
His love flows. When we allow His Spirit to work freely in our
lives, we'll rarely have a love problem. Overflowing love will
surround us, helping us in every need. All we need do is reach for
Him.

Such love is not marital love, yet it makes love flow in
marriages, too. With God as our third partner, our marriages
thrive.

What *will* we give for such love?

Lord, I want my husband and me to have this love in our marriage.
Work in our spirits and in our lives so that Your love overflows.
May our hearts always be open to You.

Letting Go

> *"'For this reason a man shall leave his father and
> mother and be joined to his wife, and the two will
> become one flesh'? So they are no longer two, but one flesh.
> What therefore God has joined together, let no man separate."*
> MATTHEW 19:5–6 NASB

The admonition to leave and cleave is given four times throughout the Bible. Four times! It's a warning to be taken seriously, whether a husband and wife live in a parents' home—as they did in ancient days—or whether they move across the country. Families of origin can have a long stretch. Leaving isn't just a physical act. There is a psychological and emotional leaving that undergirds the commitment to a new marriage.

We know that as brides, but someday, if and when we have children, we might forget that as mothers-in-law. If and when that time comes in our life, we need to be willing to let our children go. It's not too soon to start now.

Families that hang on tightly to traditions have a harder time incorporating change. As wives, daughters-in-law, and mothers-in-law, we need to remain flexible. We don't have to do the exact same thing every single holiday. We can include others at our holiday table or adjust traditions to suit a schedule. By embracing change, we are teaching our families to let go. And letting go is part of being a good wife, daughter-in-law, and mother-in-law.

*Lord God, I don't want to ever be a woman who creates a tug-of-war for my
family. Help me to hold on lightly, knowing my loved ones belong to You.*

Grace—
It's Still Amazing

Create in me a clean heart, O God; and renew a right spirit within me.
PSALM 51:10 KJV

*D*o you hold grudges? Sometimes it's really hard to let go of the grief and anger when someone has caused you hurt and pain. And it's often the ones who know you best that can hurt you the most.

You trusted them, perhaps opened up and became transparent, leaving yourself vulnerable. Maybe you've resolved never to do that again. Holding on to offenses, remembering the incident, and experiencing those feelings over and over again can't hurt the person who hurt you—it only hurts *you*.

The greatest gift you can give yourself is to forgive the offender. It's hard to let go, but think of it as not letting go but giving it up—giving it to God. Make a trade-off. Give Him your shame, anger, guilt, and memories of the assault or insult. Then when you're empty, really empty, let Him fill you with His grace! Try it, and you'll find that grace is still amazing every single time you experience it.

Lord, help me to let go of the injuries I've experienced at the hands of others, from the smallest little hurt to the deepest wounds of my heart. Show me how to really let it go and live in Your grace every day! Amen.

The Gift of Marriage

*Every good and perfect gift is from above,
coming down from the Father of the heavenly lights,
who does not change like shifting shadows.*
JAMES 1:17 NIV

*M*arriage is truly a gift from God that should be enjoyed and cherished. After all, it's God's idea, and He wants us to treat this amazing gift as sacred and holy.

Do you view your marriage as a gift? Or is this one gift you wish you still had the receipt for? When we expect marriage to always be happy ever after, we are in for an unpleasant surprise! Yes, marriage is a gift, but it is a gift we have to open and cultivate from day one. We shouldn't expect everything to be perfect after our trip down the aisle.

Marriage is hard—but rewarding—work! The gift of marriage is meant for us to learn many of life's lessons such as love, joy, loss, pain, trust, forgiveness, peace, contentment. . . . These lessons are gifts from the Father, meant for us to experience and learn from during marriage.

So if you are still wishing you could return this gift, ask the Lord to help change your thinking. Take some time to ponder all life's lessons you have learned through your marriage and thank God for them. Thank God for your spouse, too, and ask Him to help you view him as a gift from the Lord.

Father, help us not to settle for a ho-hum marriage. Help me to view my marriage and my husband as a gift from You. In Jesus' name, amen.

Set Apart

*"Before I formed you in the womb I knew you,
before you were born I set you apart."*
JEREMIAH 1:5 NIV

*W*hat an awesome thought! God knew everything about us before we were ever formed in the womb. In fact, Paul tells us in Ephesians 1:4–12 that before the foundation of the world, God chose us and set each of us apart for a specific time and purpose. Even then, He knew and ordained every detail of our lives, including who we would marry.

Think about it: Before the beginning of time, God set us apart to be wives.

Marriage is the first institution God set up during Creation. Eve messed up the perfectness of that relationship when she was deceived by the serpent in the Garden. But marriage still maintains its sanctity in that it is a picture of the church's relationship with Jesus Christ. Make no mistake, marriage takes work!

No marriage is perfect. Some are better than others, but all marriages take work to keep them healthy and functioning within the guidelines of scripture. Knowing that God is aware of the details of our marriage can bring comfort and strength to keep working. It's a blessing to know that God preordained our positions as wives, trusting us to work with our husbands to maintain a marriage that honors Him.

*Father, many times I want to give up trying to make my marriage
one that honors You in every way. In those times, You remind me that
I was set aside to be a wife and You have equipped me for that purpose.
With Your help, my marriage will be healthy. Amen.*

Seek Him with
All Your Heart

Hear my voice when I call, O LORD; be merciful to me and answer me.
My heart says of you, "Seek his face!" Your face, LORD, I will seek.
PSALM 27:7–8 NIV

Her husband was hard to buy for. He had enough tools to start a carpentry shop, a closet full of nice clothes, all the latest fishing gear, and enough unread books to last him the rest of his life. She never knew what to get for him for his birthday or Christmas because he had everything he needed. So for his next birthday, she decided to change her tactics and give him a present right out of the Bible: She decided to seek his heart.

She watched him closely; she asked him subtle questions to find out a few things that she could do differently or do more often to please him. As she quietly began implementing her ideas, she was amazed at the changes, especially in herself. As she sought to know him better and please him more, her love for him grew.

What works in our relationship with our husbands works with God, too! When we seek God's face through prayer and the study of His Word, we will understand Him better, and as we understand Him better and seek to please Him with our lives, we will love Him better.

Dear God, thank You for modeling sacrificial love through Jesus. Help me to change to please both You and my husband. I know I will be blessed. Amen.

No Place Like Home

*She looketh well to the ways of her household,
and eateth not the bread of idleness.*
PROVERBS 31:27 KJV

Taking care of a home is a lot of work, and no one can manage yours better than you!

You know where everything is. You know how much food to prepare to feed your family. You know when to start dinner to make sure it's served at the appropriate time. You're the queen of clean, a whiz at obliterating stubborn stains. You're a bargain hunter, getting the most for your money. When something needs doing, you roll up your sleeves and get to work. Your home is your pride and joy, and it shows!

If you have a lovely home, you know that it didn't get that way by chance. It took a lot of effort, and a great deal of that effort came from you. Give yourself a pat on the back. You have created a place of comfort and beauty that blesses your entire family. With your labor and skill, there truly is no place like home!

Dear heavenly Father, thank You for my home and family. Help me to always cherish it and to care for it as You would have me to. Amen.

Spiritual Health Tips

> But ye, beloved, building up yourselves on your most holy faith,
> praying in the Holy Ghost, keep yourselves in the love of God,
> looking for the mercy of our Lord Jesus Christ unto eternal life.
> JUDE 1:20–21 KJV

*W*e lives spend untold time and energy nurturing other people—a lifelong commitment to Jesus' command to love our neighbors as ourselves. Sometimes, however, we're so busy working, planning, celebrating, comforting, listening, and chauffeuring that we forget to invest in our own spiritual health.

Jude calls on Christians to exercise their faith so they will not only survive but also thrive in a culture that does not worship God. Of course, exercise is never easy! We may spend days in endless activity, yet our spiritual muscles grow flabby because we never stretch them beyond the status quo. When we dare to dream God's dreams and follow His direction, we gain the power to accomplish His will.

Jude urges believers to connect with the Holy Spirit in fervent lifestyle prayer and remain close to God, not wandering off to embrace destructive values and habits.

Finally, he encourages his friends to remain upbeat on a major scale: "Expect God's mercy through Jesus Christ to bless you forever!"

When we follow God's regimen for good spiritual health, we can anticipate great things in our own lives and in those we serve.

*Lord Jesus, I don't like change—yet if I'm to grow and help
others develop, I need to welcome it! Transform me, God. Amen.*

Wanting for Nothing

The LORD is my shepherd; I shall not want.
PSALM 23:1 KJV

The wife couldn't help the surge of envy as she listened to her friend talk about the latest date night she'd had with her husband. Other friends chimed in with stories of romantic occasions when they were alone with their husbands. The wife couldn't remember a time when she and her husband had gone somewhere alone—together.

Before wallowing too much in self-pity, we need to remember as wives that our husbands are all different. We can't compare our man to anyone else's. The spouse who makes time for a date night every week may forget special anniversaries and birthdays. We don't know. What we do know is that our husband has strengths of his own. We must look for his unique qualities and not "want" for something else.

With God as our Shepherd, we can trust Him to supply all that we need. We should not want for anything. We must be thankful to God for our husbands just as they are, not as we wish they would be.

In the same way, we must thank God for who He is and what He's done for us. Our love for Him shouldn't come with stipulations and demands. He knows our needs. Let's be content to trust Him to supply all for us so that we don't want.

*Thank You, Lord, for knowing all about
me and caring so well for me. Amen.*

Escape Clause

*"It has been said, 'Anyone who divorces his wife must
give her a certificate of divorce.' But I tell you that anyone who divorces his
wife, except for marital unfaithfulness, causes her to become an adulteress,
and anyone who marries the divorced woman commits adultery."*
MATTHEW 5:31–32 NIV

An escape clause provides reasons that allow for the breaking of a contractual agreement. Unfortunately, marriage has become more of a contract than a covenant. Reasons include phrases like "fell out of love," "heading in different directions," and "needs aren't being met." But love is not a feeling. It's not an emotion or a whim. It's a choice, a decision, a purposed action borne out of resolve, not a response to whether or not your own wants or needs are met.

It's been said that it is easier for a marriage to survive the death of a child than one in which the top is left off of the toothpaste. That's because when facing the death of a child or any other tragedy, it's common for the couple join together and turn to God. Nitpicky things become meaningless.

Don't wait for a tragedy to cause you to join with your husband. Instead, turn to God to heal your marriage of complacency.

*Father, please renew the love I once had for my husband.
Remind me of the reasons that we promised, before You, to love
and support each other no matter what. Make us one. Amen.*

Lift Up God's Name

O Lord, thou art my God; I will exalt thee,
I will praise thy name; for thou hast done wonderful things;
thy counsels of old are faithfulness and truth.
ISAIAH 25:1 KJV

Kendra sat at the kitchen table savoring the last of her coffee and enjoying her morning fellowship with her Savior. The brightness of the sun streaming through the window caught her attention, and she automatically looked toward the east, where the bright orb was just coming over the horizon. She gasped at the scene before her. Bold oranges coupled with rich pink hues and soft blues bathed the country landscape in a flood of cheerful color that only God could have captured.

She wondered for perhaps the millionth time how anyone could doubt the existence of this great Creator. Not only did God paint beautiful pictures in His creation, He also was the Master Potter who was in the process of molding her into a vessel fit for His use.

How thankful Kendra was to have God in her life. He who made her knew her best. He would give her the strength and wisdom to do her best in everything—her marriage, her career, her service to Him. He is truly a faithful and awesome God!

How amazing You are, O God. Your hand in creation
and on my life are continual reminders of Your greatness.

Prisoners of Hope

*"Return to the stronghold, you prisoners of hope.
Even today I declare that I will restore double to you."*
ZECHARIAH 9:12 NKJV

*A*ll marriages face discouraging times. Husbands and wives suffer from stress within and from outside influences. Many times we feel as battered as a ship at sea in the middle of a storm. The strain can tell on a marriage. Bickering or blaming can add to the tension. If we aren't careful, we can become prisoners of negative influences, which could destroy our marriage.

A prisoner is someone held without choice. None of us want to be a prisoner. . .or do we? When we gave our lives to Jesus, we became a captive of a different sort—a captive to the hope we have in Christ. We can't help having this hope, because it comes with our faith in Him. It is a gift, something to cherish and hold on to.

God knows the trials we face in our marriages. He understands the difficulties and is right there with us. What we must remember is that we have His promise, as prisoners of hope, that He will restore double to us when we come through each trial. As we rely on Him to get us through, we can expect our bond to strengthen to the point where we won't be torn apart.

*Jesus, thank You for making me a captive to the hope You bring.
Protect my marriage. Help us to grow strong together. Amen.*

The Spiritually Intimate Marriage

Day
267

Let's see how inventive we can be in encouraging love and helping out, not avoiding worshiping together as some do but spurring each other on, especially as we see the big Day approaching.
HEBREWS 10:24–25 MSG

In order to start a fire, there must be friction and heat. Just like two sticks being rubbed together to start a fire, a married couple can work together to create the fire of a spiritually intimate marriage. But before you can work with your partner to blaze a roaring fire in your marriage, you must keep your own fire stoked through personal prayer time, study, and worship. Maintain your personal intimacy with Jesus so that you can share in that intimacy with your spouse. While we can't build a fire in someone else, we can help spread the heat. If we are active in our prayer lives and are nurturing our own spiritual fires, we will transfer intensity to our spouses.

If your husband is a believer, join together in spiritual habits that will strengthen the bond you have together. Share your needs with each other and pray for one another. Read the scriptures together and discuss biblical truths. Learn from your husband; value him. Attend church together and nurture spiritual growth through a community of believers.

If your husband is not yet a believer, don't let your own fire grow cold. Continue to nurture your spiritual relationship with Jesus, garnering strength from the fellowship of other believers. And pray for him, hoping that someday, through your testimony or that of others, he will be sparked by the divine fire of faith.

Jesus, please show me ways to develop the spiritual unity I desire to have with my husband. Feed the fire of faith in our hearts. Amen.

Pour Out Your Soul

*But Hannah replied, No, my lord, I am a woman
oppressed in spirit. . . . I have poured out my soul before the LORD.*
1 SAMUEL 1:15 NASB

*H*annah of the Bible had major problems. She was having trouble conceiving and, because of that, was antagonized by her husband's other wife, the child-bearing Peninnah.

So what did she do? She poured out her soul to God. Then, after leaving all her cares at her Father's feet, she "went her way and ate, and her face was no longer sad" (1 Samuel 1:18). The next day, she and her family rose up early and worshipped the Lord (1 Samuel 1:19). Soon after, she conceived. The Lord had answered her prayer.

Are we as smart as Hannah? Do we go to the Lord when we are distressed and pour out our hearts before Him? Or do we sit and simmer in the juices of discontentment, sucking up our hurts and sorrows, becoming so weighed down by our woes that we have trouble even rising to our feet?

Got trouble? Get talking. Pour out your heart before the Lord. He is ready and waiting to listen. Give Him the desires of your heart. Leave your troubles at His feet. And then, knowing all is in His hands, worship Him, letting your newly unburdened heart rejoice!

That's the order: Pour, petition, praise! Then watch the Lord shower miracles into your life!

*Lord, I pour out my heart to You, my Father, my God, my Rock,
and my Fortress! Give me hope, strength, and the desires
of my heart. I thank and praise You in Jesus' name!*

The Time Is Near

Day
269

*Blessed is the one who reads the words of this prophecy,
and blessed are those who hear it and take to heart
what is written in it, because the time is near.*
REVELATION 1:3 NIV

It's so easy to get caught up in the here and now. . .especially in marriage! There are bills to pay, work to do, kids to raise, vacations to take. . .any kind of distraction you can think of. Satan tries to keep us so busy that we don't even realize we've gotten our focus off the Lord.

The Bible tells us that we are blessed if we read God's Word and take it to heart because "the time is near"! Are you living each day with that in mind?

There are several essential principles in this verse that we shouldn't miss. First, we need to be reading God's Word each day. Strapped for time? Go to an online Bible site and have scripture e-mailed to you every day! Second, take to heart what you've read. Meditate on a few verses of scripture each day, and ask God to teach you something from them. Ask Him to help you apply His Word to your life. Third, remember that "the time is near!" Live your everyday life like Jesus might be coming back today!

*Jesus, help me to keep my focus on You. Give me the time and
desire to be in Your Word each day. In Your name, amen.*

Intensely Emotional

Jesus wept.
JOHN 11:35 NIV

*S*he was an emotional woman. Many times her passion
for life was expressed with tears. She cried at her mother's
death and her child's hospitalization. But she also shed tears at
her granddaughter's birth and son's graduation. In celebration
or sorrow, she wore her emotions on her sleeve. She embraced
life by intensely feeling every hill and valley. Embarrassed by her
tears as a teen, she finally learned to view her gift of passion as a
blessing from the Lord.

Perhaps you, too, are an emotional woman. Take heart. Jesus
wept. Although this is the shortest verse in the Bible, it speaks
volumes. Jesus had emotions and was not embarrassed to express
them. He cried when his good friend Lazarus died. In the
Garden of Gethsemane, his soul was overwhelmed with sorrow.
We read that His anger was unleashed when he drove the money
changers out of the temple. Jesus cared. He felt intensely. He
was passionate about life because, as the Creator, He knew that
life was not happenstance. Jesus was sent to Earth for the divine
purpose of redeeming fallen man. How could He not care? How
could things not matter? How could He not weep?

We were created in His image. We were created to feel, to
have emotions. Embrace them. Emotions are an expression of
the heart. Don't be afraid to reveal your heart to others. Follow
Jesus' example.

Dear Lord, thank You for creating me with emotions.
May I express them appropriately. Amen.

God's Grip

*"For I hold you by your right hand—I, the LORD your God.
And I say to you, 'Don't be afraid. I am here to help you.'"*
ISAIAH 41:13 NLT

*T*rouble comes into every life: We all lose jobs, have loved ones fall ill, and face spiritual crises. In our marriages, we experience sometimes-heated disagreements, confusion about what life direction we should take, and seemingly unsolvable dilemmas. As long as we are earthbound, unexpected and unwelcome problems remain our lot.

Often, we feel tempted to ask, "Where was God when this happened?"

The answer? He was gripping our right hands, ready to help us through it all.

It's not as if God didn't see ahead to our life-distorting events. No difficulty we face comes as a surprise to Him. The Omniscient One is aware of all that lies in our futures; but charitably, He does not give us warning. He knows we'd only fuss and worry or try to work things out for ourselves and land ourselves in even bigger trouble. Instead He walks hand in hand with even the most challenged believer who reaches out for His comforting grip.

Facing trouble today? Cling to this verse, believe it, and turn your concerns over to the Lord. Don't waste time in fear and worry. Your Lord knows just where the three of you are headed.

Lord, help me cling to Your hand and feel Your tight and loving grip.

Agreement in God

When you got married, if you imagined yourself in a perpetually joyous union, you were disappointed. Loving a spouse isn't always easy. Any two people sharing a marriage have disagreements. But no couple has to suddenly doubt the wisdom of its vows just because the husband and wife don't always share the same views.

The Galatian Christians had a church-wide disagreement. Some thought all the men should be circumcised, as generations of Jews had been; others declared their freedom in Christ. Paul came down heavily on the freedom side. But he reminded the faithful Galatians that God had freed them to serve one another.

Serving in the midst of disagreement may seem an unusual solution, but where marriage is concerned, it's just what God had in mind. Disagreements, whether they are over theology, politics, or where to live, cannot dissolve the covenant of marriage. Two agreed before God—now they need to live that out day by day. Loving each other despite their differences of thought can bring them through the storm.

Remember, spouses are the closest of neighbors. They need to love each other even more than those who share a street or a multiple dwelling. And with His help, they can.

*Lord, even when we disagree, help us to serve
each other and find agreement in You.*

Cleaving

*Therefore shall a man leave his father and his mother,
and shall cleave unto his wife: and they shall be one flesh.*
GENESIS 2:24 KJV

*E*very Christmas, Kim and Jayson fight over where to spend
the holiday. Kim's family insists that they spend Christmas
together, but Jayson doesn't like the way her family celebrates.
Open presents on Christmas Eve? Have turkey instead of ham
on Christmas Day? It never feels like Christmas to him. He'd
rather stay home and start new traditions. . .modeled after the
way *his* family celebrated. In his eyes, the right way.

We all grew up with certain family patterns that we bring
into the marriage. Too often, we cling to those patterns. Like
Jayson and Kim, we aren't making decisions for the good of the
new entity but are holding fast to our past.

Interestingly, holding fast is what the Hebrew word for
"cleave" originally meant. *Dâbaq* means to cling, to be stuck
together, to be united. It is the same word used for gluing two
pieces of paper together. That's a pretty tight seal!

A great many marriages run into trouble on this issue: There
isn't enough "leaving." A husband or wife fail in some way—
physically or emotionally—to really fully leave his or her family
of origin. When we don't give our marriage the precedence it
deserves, we can set it up for some serious problems. We have to
remember we're on the same team.

*Father, are there areas that I am not leaving and cleaving
to my husband? Help me to take this warning seriously
and make choices that are good for my marriage.*

What's Your Fragrance?

*But thank God! He has made us his captives and continues
to lead us along in Christ's triumphal procession. Now he uses
us to spread the knowledge of Christ everywhere, like a sweet
perfume. Our lives are a Christ-like fragrance rising up to God.*
2 CORINTHIANS 2:14–15 NLT

*I*t has been said that the average human being can detect up
to ten thousand different odors. Smells can evoke powerful
images—the smell of mothballs can take us right back to when
we were eight years old and playing in Grandma's attic. The scent
of pine can transport us to the ski vacation we took in college
with friends.

As followers of Christ we have been given a very unique
fragrance. And whether we intend it to or not, our very presence
in the lives of others always leaves a lingering scent. When we
are kind to someone who doesn't deserve it, it smells wonderful.
When we help a person in need, the fragrance lingers long after
we've gone. Paul says that regardless of what we do, our fragrance
should *always* remind people of Christ.

As you go about your business today, what kind of fragrance
will you take with you? Pause for a moment to ask God to help
you be a sweet representative of Christ, leaving His delightful
aroma lingering in the air behind you.

*Father, help me to touch, in some small way, each person I meet today.
Help me to leave behind a fragrance that reminds them of You.*

How to Praise Your Husband

His eyes are as the eyes of doves by the rivers of waters,
washed with milk, and fitly set.
SONG OF SOLOMON 5:12 KJV

The Shulamite woman's descriptions of Solomon's features seem strange to us modern women. We don't understand how eyes like doves, hair like clusters of dates, and an abdomen like "carved ivory inlaid with sapphires" (Song of Solomon 5:14 NKJV) are desirable features. The man sounds like a statue!

But let's not miss this wife's example.

She is showing us how to praise our husbands. With admiration and in great detail, she describes her beloved's features. With each analogy, she builds him up in her own mind and in his.

To be able to create such magnificent word pictures, she has obviously spent much time thinking about him. We, who too often communicate in slang and sound bites, would be hard-pressed to describe our husbands so eloquently. Saying they have "chiseled features" or "washboard abs" sounds like advertising, not praise.

To begin praising her husband, a wise older woman made a list of the things she admired about him. She posted it on the bathroom mirror, adding new items weekly.

Although she said nothing about it, she noticed that after he would read the list, he'd smile, whistle, or walk taller.

If you want your husband to become a better man, start praising him for the man he already is.

As my head, my husband is worthy of praise, as You are worthy of praise,
Lord. Help me to see his good qualities so I can speak about them. Amen.

Different

Fear not; I will do to thee all that thou requirest:
for all the city of my people doth know that thou art a virtuous woman.
RUTH 3:11 KJV

*R*uth was not a nice Jewish girl. She hailed from Moab, Israel's enemy. Ruth had been exposed to idol worship, some of which may have included human sacrifice and fertility rites. When she arrived in Bethlehem with Naomi, her late husband's mother, the townspeople probably shook their heads at the way she dressed.

Yet Boaz, a prominent citizen, did not hesitate to marry Ruth. Why? Because she cared deeply for Naomi, a penniless old woman, and worked hard to provide for her. Ruth not only left her own family and culture behind but also vowed to follow Naomi's God. Boaz—and his entire hometown—soon recognized Ruth's kindness and determination to change.

Like her, many women today face challenges in adjusting to cultural differences. A wife may struggle with her husband's ethnic upbringing or his attitudes toward money, entertainment, and education. His relatives may seem like inhabitants of a different planet.

Though Ruth lived more than three thousand years ago, her example of love and faithfulness is worth imitating. And when we ask for God's help in blessing those we don't understand and who don't understand us, we can be sure He will come to our aid, just as He helped Ruth.

Lord God, it's not easy to adjust to others' needs.
Let the loving fragrance of my life draw them to You. Amen.

God's Will

Rejoice always; pray without ceasing; in everything
give thanks; for this is God's will for you in Christ Jesus.
1 THESSALONIANS 5:16–18 NASB

Sometimes this exhortation from 1 Thessalonians is easy to obey. Your marriage is the best it has ever been, your job is fulfilling, you have great friends, and life is just plain old good. Rejoicing and giving thanks can come pretty naturally then. At other times, however, when life isn't going so great, this command can be tough to follow. How do we rejoice and give thanks in the midst of suffering and trials?

While we sometimes find it difficult to remember, God is in control of all that we do. We are blessed in all circumstances to know and follow God. *"Rejoice always."* Regardless of whether our lives are going well or whether we are experiencing difficulties, God wants us to tell Him about it. *"Pray without ceasing."* We know that in our trials we will grow and in our blessings we draw strength. *"In everything give thanks."* Even when it doesn't feel like it, God has a plan for us that He longs to share. We must acknowledge and praise Him for His involvement in our lives, praying and deepening our relationship with Him. *"For this is God's will for us in Christ Jesus."*

Dear Lord, no matter my circumstances, please teach me to learn to rejoice,
pray, and be thankful. Let me follow after Your will. Amen.

Making Right Choices—
Together

*The LORD will establish you as his holy people, as he promised you on oath, if
you keep the commands of the LORD your God and walk in his ways.*
DEUTERONOMY 28:9 NIV

*M*arriage is the wills of two people coming together to
build a life. The truth is, you were created in God's
image with a will. That means you have the right to choose your
own life—whether or not it's what God desires most for you.

Jesus said, "Not my will, but yours, Father!" He chose to live
God's dream for His life over His own. Each day you decide
what your life looks like. The Spirit of God stands ready to lead
and guide you, but you must choose to follow His lead to reach
the destiny He planned for you and your family.

He has the whole world in His hands, but daily choices
belong to you. Choose to live in His will, making decisions with
your husband based on His direction that comes from a personal
relationship—time spent with Him—in prayer and in His Word.
Jesus knew the path set before Him, and you can, too. Choose
His will—today.

*Heavenly Father, thank You for making a way for me to be Your daughter.
I choose Your dream, Your destiny for my life and that of my family.
Help me to make the right choices as I follow You. Amen.*

Floating in Grace

"Be still, and know that I am God."
PSALM 46:10 NIV

Sometimes we want the answers while we are still thrashing in the waves of our own doubt, but the truth is, we seldom find wisdom until we are still. When tossed about, the horizon may, for the moment, leave our sight. And we are lost. These are the times when we are called to stillness. For many of us, doing *something* seems better than doing *nothing*, but it is easier to see clear to the bottom of our problems after all the ripples have faded.

Silence and stillness are the doorways that welcome our weary hearts in prayer. Prayer can be full of lamenting and asking, but when we realize that deep prayer is more a quieting of the soul, the power of who God is floods into our hearts. He is order amid the chaos, the foundation of all reason, and pure goodness in an unjust world. Through this kind of prayer, loves rushes in and renews us.

God is endless and unaltered love. The God that parted the Red Sea and calmed the storms is the same God that works His grace into our everyday lives. Eternity is on the horizon. All we need to do is look to Him, and we will float in depths where our feet can't touch and walk over anything that threatens to overcome us.

*Father, You calm the storms and heal my doubt. Help me
begin every day in prayer with a calm heart and stillness of mind,
that I may have a better understanding of You. Amen.*

Under Construction

*But if you are always biting and devouring one
another, watch out! Beware of destroying one another.*
GALATIANS 5:15 NLT

"My husband *never* does laundry," Suzanne told the women in her Bible study. "He thinks folded shirts and matched socks just magically appear in his dresser."

"Yeah, my husband is useless, too," Jacquelyn agreed. "Bob wouldn't scrub a toilet if Oprah were coming for dinner."

"Chad is so dense, I have to tell him when I'm mad!"

"Steve is oblivious—he steps over the overflowing trash can like it's invisible!"

As the other women chimed in, Anne sat quietly. Finally, Suzanne noticed her blinking back tears. "What's wrong, Anne?"

"It grieves my heart to hear you criticizing your husbands. I used to do the same. The more I complained, the more my resentment grew. When we were on the brink of divorce, we finally sought help. The counselor said, 'Anne, if you continue using biting words, you'll devour the Larry you married. He'll *become* the lazy good-for-nothing you complain about. You're destroying your intimacy one criticism at a time.'"

Silence descended.

"Praise God, it wasn't too late." Anne wiped away a tear. "The next three years were the best of our marriage. My speech became *con*structive instead of *de*structive. I only wish Larry were still alive so I could tell him once more how much I love him."

*Ever-forgiving Savior, teach me to use my
words to build instead of destroy. Amen.*

Mrs. Potiphar

*"Keep watching and praying that you
may not enter into temptation."*
MATTHEW 26:41 NASB

*P*otiphar's wife had set her cap on her husband's servant.
Scripture tells us that Joseph was a looker, "well-built and
handsome, and after a while his master's wife took notice of
Joseph and said, 'Come to bed with me!'" (Genesis 39:6–7 NIV).

But Mrs. Potiphar had underestimated Joseph's integrity. He
explained that he could never betray her husband's trust. Even
more indicative of Joseph's sterling nature, he said, "How then
could I do such a wicked thing and sin against God?" (Genesis
39:9 NIV). Joseph's relationship with God was so well-established
that he knew a sin—any sin—would be an offense against God.

Mrs. Potiphar wouldn't give up. "And though she spoke to
Joseph day after day, he refused to go to bed with her or even be
with her" (Genesis 39:10 NIV).

Her pride wounded, Mrs. Potiphar decided to punish Joseph.
She waited until the house was empty of servants so there
would be no witnesses, and then she accused Joseph of rape. Her
husband threw Joseph into prison.

Why prison? Potiphar had every right to have Joseph
executed. Did he suspect his wife's duplicity? We never learn
anything more about Mrs. Potiphar, which might be scripture's
way of telling us that we know enough. She was an immoral,
scheming woman who sought to harm a man of God. And yet
God used her treachery for good in Joseph's life. God can use
anyone or anything to accomplish His purposes.

*Lord, guard me against any tendency toward becoming
emotionally or physically involved in an off-limits relationship.
Let me be like Joseph, who stayed clear of temptation.*

Divine Supply

*Your heavenly Father knoweth that
ye have need of all these things.*
MATTHEW 6:32 KJV

Whether it's a new roof or a gallon of milk, there are always needs in a home. For some, the fix is as simple as a quick trip to the grocery store. Other problems take massive renovation. Regardless of what the need is in your home, you can take comfort in the knowledge that God is well aware of it.

Your heavenly Father is an ever-present help in time of trouble (Psalm 46:1). He not only sees the problems that keep you up at night, but He has the solution for each of them. No matter how great or insignificant the need, God has promised to supply it. There is no shortage of His power or willingness to lend a helping hand.

God's time is not your time, and He can see much farther down the road than you can. Be patient while you're waiting for Him to work. Whether you're trying to make ends meet or struggling with your spouse, trust that the Lord is waiting to intervene when the moment is right. Remember that God is bound by His own promise to take care of you and your home, and God keeps His promises.

*Dear God, help me to trust You for the needs in my home,
whatever they may be. Remind me of Your great love and care for
Your children, and help my faith to grow while I am waiting. Amen.*

Your Talents

*God has given each of you a gift from his great
variety of spiritual gifts. Use them well to serve one another.*
1 PETER 4:10 NLT

*A*uthor Leo Buscaglia said, "Your talent is God's gift to
you. What you do with it is your gift back to God."

What's your talent? Is it balancing numbers, writing stories,
being a homemaker, caring for others, making people laugh,
baking sweets, preaching, teaching?

Not sure what your gift is? Well, what are you good at? What
do you enjoy doing? What talent do you feel a burning need to
share? What do you feel God leading you to do? Whatever your
answer is to these questions, that's your gift.

It may be that your gift or talent is not something you can
use on the job. Perhaps it's not even something from which you
can make money. That's okay. Use it anyway.

If you have a way with words, write an article for your church
newsletter. If you have a drive to instruct, teach a Sunday school
class. If you love to cook, begin by trying out some gourmet
dishes on your husband.

Use the gifts God has given you. In doing so, you will find
your life blessed and, at the same time, be a blessing to others.
And, as an added bonus, you'll be giving your gift back to God.
Is there anything better than that?

*Lord, I owe You so much, and although I can never truly repay You,
I can use the gifts You have given me to help others. Show me my gifts, Lord.
And help me find ways to use them. All to Your glory!*

Sarah's Daughters

*Through faith also Sara herself received strength to
conceive seed, and was delivered of a child when she was past age,
because she judged him faithful who had promised.*
HEBREWS 11:11 KJV

Although the popular Narnia series by C. S. Lewis draws attention to the "daughters of Eve," this is not a biblical idea.

While we are daughters of Eve because she was the mother of all living, we are not to pattern ourselves after her. We are never told to be daughters of Eve. Rather, we are encouraged to be daughters of Sarah.

Eve was deceived and fell into a transgression. But Sarah was faithful.

Sarah obeyed Abraham, even in dangerous situations.

Sarah reverenced Abraham, calling him "lord."

Even though Sarah, when told that she would have a son in her old age, had laughed at the idea and then denied doing so, she still had the faith to conceive Isaac. However little her faith was, it earned her a place in the Hall of Faith in Hebrews 11.

How can we be daughters of Sarah?

Peter tells us that we should be in subjection to our own husbands, showing them reverence. We need to display chaste behavior, focus on our inward growth rather than our outward appearance, and have a meek and quiet spirit.

These qualities are lightly esteemed in our modern world but of priceless value to our heavenly Father.

If you would honor Him, be Sarah's daughter.

*Father, it sometimes goes against my flesh to be quiet, meek,
and reverent to my husband. I yield myself to Your Spirit now, Father.
Transform my mind. Silence my mouth. Make me Sarah's daughter. Amen.*

Earth's Dark Glasses

*For now we see through a glass, darkly;
but then face to face: now I know in part;
but then shall I know even as also I am known.*
1 CORINTHIANS 13:12 KJV

*S*he had been married for only a year. Her skin was smooth, her hair thick, her body slim and graceful. She knew her husband loved her, but sometimes she wondered if his love would be as strong when her hair was white and thin and her cheeks were sagged and spotted with age. Looking for reassurance, she studied the other couples in church on Sundays, especially one older couple who sat nearby. This husband and wife had been married for more than five decades, and the years hung heavily on them.

Week after week she watched them, and then it dawned on her. It seemed as if they did not see each other as the rest of the world did. When the wife took her husband's thin arm, she was holding the muscular arm of her young husband. When the husband smiled into his wife's face, he wasn't seeing the wrinkles and liver spots. He was seeing the young woman he married fifty years before.

Soon and very soon these bodies will be discarded and God will give us new ones. Until then, let us try to see each other—and trust that we are seen—as God sees us: spotless and without blemish, covered in the precious blood of the Lamb.

Dear Lord, help me be content with the body You have given me. Thank You for the hope of the resurrection and a new, glorified body in the future. Amen.

Asking for Trouble

*"Therefore do not worry about tomorrow,
for tomorrow will worry about itself.
Each day has enough trouble of its own."*
MATTHEW 6:34 NIV

God's Word is very clear about worrying. God says: Don't do it! Did you know that it is actually a sin to worry? When we worry, we are telling God that we don't trust Him enough with our future.

How often do we worry when it comes to marriage? Almost daily, right? We have a lot of confessing to do then, don't we? We worry about how we're going to pay all the bills, if this person we're committed to will truly be committed to us for the rest of our lives, if one of us will get a life-threatening illness, and on and on it goes. We worry about so much, and God says don't do it! How do we stop?

We have to commit our life, our plans, and our thoughts to the Lord *each day*! Make this the first thing you do every morning. The Bible tells us to give all of our worries over to the Lord because He cares for us (1 Peter 5:7). It also tells us that worrying won't add one single hour to our lives (Luke 12:25). So why do it? When we worry, we're just asking for trouble!

*Father, please forgive me for worrying. Help my husband
and I to trust You at all times. In Jesus' name, amen.*

$\mathcal{L}ife$

Day
287

For whosoever will save his life shall lose it:
but whosoever will lose his life for my sake, the same shall save it.
LUKE 9:24 KJV

$\mathcal{L}$ ife. It's so complex, yet so simple, really. It's simple in that if you give it completely over to God, He will care for the details. The complexity comes because, on the whole, we are not truly willing to be totally surrendered to God. We want some measure of control. We want our way here on earth, but that is not often conducive to our eternal life.

Think about the legacy you are leaving your children or others who come after you. Let's say your husband feels called of God to enter the ministry, but you refuse to be supportive because it would alter your lifestyle or because you have family members who are discouraging you. Your husband knows that the ministry won't be successful unless you are willing to be part of it. Your lifestyle is maintained and your family is content, but what good is that for eternity?

Or what if you feel you are being called to take a missions trip? You're not sure you're a missions-type of person. Not only that, but you're afraid to ask your husband, a nonbeliever, if it's okay with him that you go. Yet you feel that God is truly calling you to do so. If you stay home, you'll maintain your comfort zone, but at what eternal cost?

Think about the many souls who will not be saved because you or your husband weren't where you should have been— because you wanted your way instead of God's way. Wouldn't it be simpler and better to give your life to God?

I surrender my life to You, O Lord. I will go
where You lead and be what You want me to be.

Praise

> *"Give thanks to the LORD, call on his name; make
> known among the nations what he has done, and proclaim
> that his name is exalted. Sing to the LORD, for he has done
> glorious things; let this be known to all the world."*
> ISAIAH 12:4–6 NIV

Have you ever been with a couple who are so in love with one another and God that their lives are a blessing to all they come in contact with? Maybe that describes your marriage. If so, give thanks to God. That marriage exalts the name of Jesus and is in itself an act of worship.

Maybe your marriage falls short of that ideal. If so, we are still to give thanks to the Lord, finding the good qualities in our husbands. Praise God for yours and uphold him before the Lord. Ask the Lord to strengthen your husband's strengths *and* weaknesses. But be prepared for God to change you—to give you a new perspective on the qualities your husband possesses and a renewed love that overlooks his irritating faults (1 Corinthians 13).

Where is your focus? On your husband's failings and shortcomings? Or on the One who can change each of us within and without? Count the blessings in your marriage. Thank Him for the strengths of your marriage partner. God has done glorious things in bringing you together, keeping you together, and blessing you together.

*Father, may I not forget to thank You for my husband. You have prepared
him to be the spouse You would have for me as we complement each other's
strengths and weaknesses. You have indeed done glorious things.*

No Ifs about Love

"This is my commandment: Love each other in the same way I have loved you."
JOHN 15:12 NLT

This verse does not say, Love each other in the same way I have loved you *if*. . . It simply says to love others in the way that Jesus loves us. The truth is that nowhere in the Bible is the mandate to love others with conditions. Yet according to worldly standards, there is no room in marriage for love, forgiveness, or unconditional acceptance. The world says that if your needs aren't being met or your mate isn't perfect, you should split up because you deserve better.

Love, God's way, is the exact opposite of the worldly standard that demands perfection. God's love is offered first, before any action is done to earn it. And we are to follow His example. We are to love to our spouses unconditionally. We are to love them regardless of their actions or whether we deem them worthy.

To love our husbands in the way that God loves us means to love first, love completely, and love without condition.

Jesus, please help me to see my husband through eyes covered with Your blood of forgiveness. Help me to not pick apart his flaws and to offer him my love first, before I expect anything from him. Help me to love him like You have loved and continue to love me. Amen.

Becoming a Follower

> *I will instruct you and teach you in the way*
> *you should go; I will guide you with My eye.*
> PSALM 32:8 NKJV

*S*ometimes life can seem to be careening out of control, so much so that you feel like a fireman running from here to there, extinguishing the fires breaking out in your life or the lives of those around you. Distractions, crises, and interruptions try their best to rob you of your peace, energy, and strength.

But when you accepted Jesus as your Lord and Savior, you were turned inside out. You have the ability to live from your spirit instead of your emotions. The Spirit of God within you wants to guide you and give you something that can't come from your emotions alone—daily peace.

Relax and let the real you—your heart—lead and guide you in all truth. Instead of reacting to your circumstances, stop and respond to the voice of God. Then perhaps you'll still put out fires, but you'll arrive on the scene when the blaze is more manageable, with a clear sense of direction of what needs to be done to bring about the best outcome for your life and the lives of those around you.

> *Heavenly Father, I want to respond to life, not react to it.*
> *Help me to hear Your voice and follow Your lead. Amen.*

And I John saw the holy city, new Jerusalem,
coming down from God out of heaven,
prepared as a bride adorned for her husband.
REVELATION 21:2 KJV

John, Jesus' disciple, recorded extraordinary visions of struggles on earth during the last days, amazing worship in heaven, and the final triumph when Jesus will destroy Satan and live intimately with His people. John described the church as the New Jerusalem, a city resembling a bride who has made herself lovely for her wedding day, ready to live with her Groom forever.

We women can identify with this biblical image! Many of us spent months talking, planning, shopping, preparing, and primping so we would look our very best when we walked down the church aisle to meet our handsome grooms at the altar. Perhaps at that hectic, wonderful time, we didn't stop to think that we, as brides, represented the church.

Years later, we wives still represent the church, the object of Jesus' love (Ephesians 5:25). The efforts we make to look good and spend time with our husbands help build our marriages, which pleases God. Even more, they reflect the desire the church should cultivate in anticipating Christ's return. If we invest similar energy in our spiritual preparations, we'll be ready for our heavenly Groom's joyous smile and a wedding celebration that will continue forever!

Lover of my soul, just as I spend time and energy to enhance my relationship
with my husband, please help me make myself beautiful for You. Amen.

Rachel's Legacy

*Rachel said, "Father, please don't be angry with
me for not getting up; I am having my period."
Laban kept on searching, but still did not find the idols.*
GENESIS 31:35 CEV

*R*achel lived out a halfhearted faith. She was willing to go with her husband, Jacob, to the land of Canaan—but not willing to give up her former ways. Before she left, she tucked a few of her father's idols in her camel's saddle. When Laban, her father, discovered the household gods missing, he accused Jacob and his entourage of stealing them. Rachel lied to her father, using that old ruse of her period. Her lie worked. . .or so it seemed.

That lie revealed the condition of Rachel's heart. She was the daughter of a crafty man and the wife of a schemer and had learned a few tricks from them. But she knew God's ways, too. She could have stopped the cycle of halfhearted obedience that plagued her family, but she didn't. The sin of deception in her family passed from generation to generation, until it came full circle. Jacob's sons sold their brother, Joseph—Rachel's son—into slavery in Egypt and then lied about it.

We must break habits of sins before we pass them on to the next generation. Our lives should show evidence of increasing faith. We don't want to be like Rachel, offering God halfhearted obedience. He deserves our whole heart.

*Lord, forgive me for holding on, excusing, rationalizing,
and coddling my habits of sin. Thank You that Your
Spirit lives in me, leading me in Your Truth.*

Word or Deed

*And whatever you do, whether in word or deed,
do it all in the name of the Lord Jesus,
giving thanks to God the Father through him.*
COLOSSIANS 3:17 NIV

There is no such thing as a Sunday Christian. Bearing the name of Christ is a twenty-four hour, seven-day-a-week proposition. Whether at work, shopping at the grocery store, or playing golf, our lives reflect the One we profess. Once we are united with Christ, our secular and spiritual lives are also united. We should not live one way during the week and then act differently at church on Sunday. People are watching. Inconsistency is quickly recognized. Hypocrisy is offensive.

Although Christians are far from perfect, we are called to be Christ's ambassadors, His representatives. In a world filled with darkness, we have the privilege of being light to those that are lost. By reflecting His glory, we proclaim His truth: Jesus Christ is the way, the truth, and the life (John 14:6).

So whatever you do or say, represent Jesus well. May He be your focus so that others will be drawn to Him. Allow Jesus access to every part of your life, every day of your life. Don't hide your light under a bushel. Let it shine brightly to a world that is lost.

May the light of Christ in you be clearly seen by others. Christ in you is indeed the hope of glory!

*Dear Lord, may I represent You as I should.
May my words and actions be pleasing to You. Amen.*

Gentle Speech

*A gentle tongue is a tree of life,
but perverseness in it breaks the spirit.*
PROVERBS 15:4 ESV

When Joe forgot to take out all the trash and the cat got into the can in her office, Mary's blood boiled. She'd been busy with other household chores—and this wasn't her responsibility anyway!

Mary had a choice: She could blast her husband and make him pick up the trash, or she could pick up the trash and gently but firmly remind Joe that he needed to empty *all* the wastepaper baskets in the house.

She didn't have to think more than a second to know which choice would be better for her marriage. Mary sided with gentleness—and she and her husband were happier for it.

Gentle speech contributes to good communication, while frequent anger, voiced in loud tones, destroys a relationship. People can't hear what we say when we raise our voices and become nasty. All they recognize is the negative emotion behind the words—and they flee from it.

Centuries ago, scripture recognized this truth and advised us to watch our tongues. It's wise counsel. Are we speaking gently today?

*Lord, help me to speak gently to my husband.
I want him to hear my concerns, not be blocked by my anger.
Help us discuss problems kindly and reflect Your Spirit in our speech.*

Home Wrecker

Only by pride cometh contention.
PROVERBS 13:10 KJV

Let's face it. Nobody likes to be wrong, much less admit it. There's a certain amount of shame involved in eating humble pie. But if you want your marriage to succeed, grab the fork and eat up!

The biggest problems between a husband and wife come because one or both are too stubborn or too proud to apologize when they are at fault. They'd rather save face than save their relationship. They refuse to admit blame because they aren't willing to change. Being right is more important than being happy. Such selfishness will wreak havoc on a marriage and kill the love that sealed the union.

The Bible warns extensively about the wrecking power of pride. If the words "I'm sorry" have a bad habit of getting stuck in your throat, it's time to ask the Lord for help. Listen to the still, small voice of your conscience. The Spirit of God will be faithful to let you know when an apology is in order. Obey that Voice and you'll always be right.

Dear Father, I realize that my husband and I will not always see eye to eye. Help me to admit fault when it is mine, to apologize when necessary, and to always be willing to change for the good of my marriage. Amen.

Confidant

Do not be anxious about anything, but in everything,
by prayer and petition, with thanksgiving, present your requests
to God. And the peace of God, which transcends all understanding,
will guard your hearts and your minds in Christ Jesus.
PHILIPPIANS 4:6–7 NIV

*M*aria admired her friend Katie. While the other women bashed their husbands during their monthly lunch, Katie never uttered a negative word about her own. Maria knew Katie did not have a perfect marriage but that Katie took her marriage concerns to the Lord (her Confidant) instead of to the luncheon crowd.

God ordained marriage; however, because of our fallen world, we will always face marriage concerns, worries, fears, or anxieties. God tells us to not worry or be anxious about anything. Instead, God calls us to take our concerns before His throne of grace and pray for them, petitioning them before the Lord. In so doing, we can lay down and exchange our heavy burden for the Lord's light burden (Matthew 11:28–30).

Even better than waiting until we have concerns to take to the Lord, God desires for us to pray daily for our husbands and our marriages. Begin today, asking your husband, "How can I pray for you today?" Be knowledgeable about his schedule and tasks so that you can petition the Lord on his behalf. As you pray for your husband and your marriage, be confident that the Lord, your Confidant, will answer you (Jeremiah 33:3) and provide His peace, which surpasses all understanding (Philippians 4:7).

Lord, my Confidant, thank You that as I present to You my marriage worries,
You will answer me and provide me with peace.

Daily Bread

"Give us today our daily bread."
MATTHEW 6:11 NIV

In our mega-warehouse culture, buying in bulk has become a trend that carries over into the rest of our lives. Who can argue that storing up on dish soap and paper towels doesn't bring some sense of security to our anxious hearts? So with our pantries full, we look toward the unknown with hope for similar assurances. In our spiritual lives, this is an entirely different matter indeed—our hands and hearts need to be emptied before they can be filled. God gives us just enough for one day.

The truth is that no matter what false securities we create, it is God who takes us into tomorrow. In our empty sleep, God refreshes and renews us so that each morning we have what we need to face the new day's demands. His grace is not something we can stockpile but rather something we give away.

Whenever we feel our heart tighten over outcomes we want, we simply need to loosen our grip and take rest in Him. Because we live in a world of independence and self-sufficiency, this faith feels awkward at first until we experience a joy unmatched by anything we can conjure up on our own. It is in these divine moments that we can throw open the cupboard doors of our hearts and give away everything that's there, knowing that tomorrow we will be full again.

Father, thank You for giving us our manna each and every day. Thank You for providing for all our needs as we continually reap the joy of knowing You as the trustworthy sustainer of our lives. Amen.

Our First Love

Taste and see that the LORD is good;
blessed is the man who takes refuge in him.
PSALM 34:8 NIV

*D*id you get married with the hope that your husband was all you ever needed? Did you expect him to always be your knight in shining armor?

God did not design your husband to take care of each and every need you ever have. First He gives us Himself to lean on, and He also wants us to be a part of a church family that will be there for us in any situation.

If you have been living with the expectation that your husband should be your "everything," you are probably experiencing quite a bit of loneliness. . .and your husband has been experiencing quite a bit of frustration.

Even though God designed marriage for oneness, God still wants and needs to be our first love. God has to come before anything else in our lives. . .even before our spouse, kids, church, or career. God is good and we can take refuge in Him anytime. He should be our main source of help, comfort, and security. Revelation 2:4 cautions us about forsaking our "first love." While we should depend on our husbands to love and provide for us, our main source of love and protection should be from the Lord: our "first love" and our refuge.

Dear Father, forgive me for the times when I've forsaken
You as my first love. Help me to come to You first and not
put unrealistic expectations on my husband. Amen.

Honor before Love

*Then Abigail made haste, and took two hundred loaves,
and two bottles of wine, and five sheep ready dressed,
and five measures of parched corn, and an hundred clusters of
raisins, and two hundred cakes of figs, and laid them on asses.*
1 SAMUEL 25:18 KJV

Nabal.
His name meant "fool," and so he was. Although he was a descendant of the faithful Caleb, he was churlish and evil.

Somehow this "son of Belial" had married a daughter of Jehovah named Abigail, who was smart and beautiful and honored God.

The Bible is silent on how this particular pair of opposites attracted, but it does speak on a believing wife's behavior toward her unbelieving husband.

Abigail was a faithful wife to Nabal. She had not left him and did not wish him ill. When his own rude behavior jeopardized his entire household, Abigail interceded. In this way, she honored her husband even though he had acted dishonorably.

Abigail's example of honor for her husband should be a pattern for all wive, and especially those who are married to unbelievers. How we behave toward our husbands is more important than how we feel about them.

Honor for our husbands comes before love. Paul tells us in Ephesians 5:33 that we are to see that we revere—not love—our husbands. Peter says that it is our reverence—not our love—that can win an unbelieving husband without a word (1 Peter 3:1–2).

Honor your husband, and God will bless.

*Father, how often I fail to honor my husband as my head; I don't show
him reverence as I should. Show me how I can honor him today. Amen.*

Decisions

*We put no stumbling block in anyone's path,
so that our ministry will not be discredited.*
2 CORINTHIANS 6:3 NIV

"So what do you want to do on our date night Friday?" Maria asked as she popped a pizza into the oven.

Carl peered over the top of the newspaper. "There's a new Vin Diesel flick out. I heard it's really good. Want to go see that?"

"What's it rated?" Maria wiped her hands on the dish towel.

"Um. . .looks like it's rated R."

"Do you think it's a good idea to go to R-rated movies?"

"Why not? We're way over legal age."

"I don't mean legally. I mean morally. What if someone from church sees us? Wouldn't it look hypocritical that we're teaching our youth group kids to honor God with their brain input while we're filling ours with violence and foul language?"

"It's not like we're going to suddenly start stealing cars and cussing out the neighbors because of one movie."

"Of course not, but isn't that the same defense the kids use when we tell them that listening to gangsta music will gradually lower their sensitivity to right and wrong?"

Carl looked thoughtful. "I guess you're right. Those kids are young in their faith, and they're watching us. I surely wouldn't want to send them the wrong message. If I'd be embarrassed for Jesus to go somewhere with me, I shouldn't be there at all."

What message is your life sending?

Mighty God, help us remember that we are a reflection of You. Amen.

All Kinds of Lies

Do not lie to one another, seeing that you
have put off the old self with its practices.
COLOSSIANS 3:9 ESV

*S*usan didn't tell her husband, Nate, about her visit with an old boyfriend. After all, there was nothing between her and Jack. She loved Nate deeply and couldn't imagine he'd have a problem with her having lunch with Jack. After all, they were in a public place together. Nothing could go wrong.

Until a friend, who'd noticed Susan with another man, told Nate about it. Her husband was wild as he confronted her, and Susan wished she'd never seen Jack.

Lies come in all kinds of guises—the things we don't tell each other, the outright lies, and the little white ones we think protect our spouses from harm. But however they appear, lies can ruin the fabric of our marriages, because trust between two people is built on truth.

That doesn't mean we need to pour out every detail of the cold, hard truth of our past all in one night. Maybe a general description is better than gory details. But we need to disclose enough truth that our husbands can trust us.

Every day, we need to live in truth, putting off that old, sinful self. As truth grows in our lives, our relationship can blossom, too.

Lord, help us live in truth. If we need to share anything
from our pasts, help my husband and me to do so carefully.

Caution, Danger Ahead

If someone is caught in a sin, you who are spiritual should
restore him gently. But watch yourself, or you also may be tempted.
GALATIANS 6:1 NIV

*T*here wasn't much that Carol and Jane didn't know about one another. They had been friends for years and shared many secrets. When Jane found out that Carol had shared an intimate detail about Jane's marriage with a mutual friend under the guise of a prayer request, Jane was understandably hurt and disappointed. But instead of praying about it and confronting Carol directly, Jane spent her time stewing about the issue and discussing it with several of their other friends. Sadly, this long-time friendship deteriorated, leaving both women feeling hurt and betrayed.

As believers, we are called to be accountable to one another. At times it is appropriate and necessary to confront sin in the lives of a brother or sister in Christ. However, the Bible warns of the need to do this prayerfully and in love.

In Galatians, Paul issues another warning: The person doing the confronting needs to be careful not to use the other person's actions as an excuse to sin. Perhaps we are more vulnerable to sin when we see it in the lives of another. Maybe it's while we're busy trying to convince ourselves that we are above such actions that we fall into the trap of sin. Regardless, it is wise to be on guard.

Father, it is never easy to confront sin in the life of a sister or brother.
When the time comes, help me to do so gently and in love—
and to protect my own heart so that I'm not tempted to sin.

The Power of Words

*Kind words are like honey—
they cheer you up and make you feel strong.*
PROVERBS 16:24 CEV

A young pastor's wife often felt unimportant when she compared herself to her husband and his big role in the church. Feeling inadequate, she tended to belittle him in public about things like his messiness, his weight, and his daily habits. Slowly, she began to taint his ministry because people started to see him in the way she was portraying him—as an insensitive buffoon.

As their helpmeet, given to them by God, we wives have the most important role in our husbands' lives. We were created to help them and be a blessing to them. Phrases like you never, you can't, and you're a slob, all speak defeat and failure to our husbands. To speak life, we need to use phrases like Thank you, I appreciate you, I love you, and I want to help you. Similarly, we need to edify our husbands and lift them up before others with encouragement and support.

So avoid those mocking stories intended to incite laughter among your girlfriends at your husband's expense and share only the things that edify and encourage.

*Jesus, I am guilty of dishonoring my husband with my
mouth. Please help me to control my tongue and bring
encouragement to him and honor to You. Amen.*

Who Has Power?

*The wife hath not power of her own body,
but the husband: and likewise also the husband
hath not power of his own body, but the wife.*
1 CORINTHIANS 7:4 KJV

There is no doubt that husbands' needs and desires differ from their wives when it comes to the sexual aspects of marriage. Certainly you've experienced this if you've been married for any length of time at all. You can look at this in a couple of different ways. Unfortunately, too many women take the glass-half-empty approach.

"I would love to take a quiet walk or cuddle on the couch," one wife might say, "but my husband's mind is geared toward the bedroom the moment he walks in the door." This wife is more focused on what her desires are than on how she can meet the needs of her husband.

In another scenario you might find a similar situation, only this wife is first of all glad that her husband still finds her desirable. Secondly she's thankful that she is able to fulfill his needs and that he's not seeking satisfaction elsewhere.

It's no secret that God created us uniquely. That's part of what keeps marriage so fun and interesting, but we must all do our part. Yes, your husband has a role to fill, but it's God's job to see that he does it. God will also help you do your part even in this most personal area of your marriage.

*Thank You, God, for this most beautiful expression of love.
Please help me always to meet my husband's needs.*

Timing

*There is a time for everything. . .
a time to be silent and a time to speak.*
ECCLESIASTES 3:1, 7 NIV

*I*n the middle of Dot and Tom's argument, Tom just walked away. Right out of the room!

Momentarily taken aback, Dot just stood there. *Now what? He can't just leave me hanging. We need to talk this over now!* Furious, Dot stormed after her husband, determined to have it out right then and there.

But then something stopped her dead in her tracks. *Hmm. . . Maybe now isn't a good time to have it out. Maybe we both just need to cool our heads.* With her heart still racing, Dot backed away from the confrontation, resolving to give her husband some time and space. Later that day, they calmly talked through things, and eventually their issue was resolved.

When under stress, women often want to talk about their feelings, about what's happening. But the male animal tends to withdraw into his cave, needing some time to sort through the situation and find a solution to the problem.

Sometimes it's better to walk away from a discussion, taking some time to think through things. God's Word tells us that there is a time for everything, including a time to be silent and a time to speak, after which we can look for a time to embrace.

Lord, I understand that You made both men and women, yet You made us so different. Give me wisdom when it comes to dealing with my mate. Help me to understand him better and to realize that there is a time for everything.

Personalized Prayer

I have hidden your word in my heart.
PSALM 119:11 NLT

*L*ots of Bible verses contain the words *he*, *him*, and *his*. One reason for that is that most of the Bible stories are about men and the deeds they performed, the prayers they prayed, the psalms they wrote and sang. Another reason is that the scriptures Old and New were written from the perspective of a male-dominated society. As a result, sometimes it's hard for us women to get close to a verse, to take it to heart when the references are made to a male and we are definitely female. So what's a girl to do?

Make it personal. If there is a verse that's really speaking to your heart, one that you'd like to commit to memory so that you can pull it from the recesses of your mind when needed, write it down using *she*, *her*, or *hers* (or, for that matter, *I*, *you*, and *we*) where appropriate.

For example, a great verse to store away for those less-than-peaceful moments is Isaiah 26:3. In the New King James, the original verse reads, You will keep him in perfect peace, whose mind is stayed on You, because he trusts in You. Make this personal by changing it to You will keep *her* in perfect peace, whose mind is stayed on You, because *she* trusts in You. Or better yet, You will keep *me* in perfect peace, whose mind is stayed on You, because *I* trust in You.

It's God's Word meant for you. So truly take it to heart by making it your very own. Make it personal. Because if God is nothing else, He's personal.

Lord, I want to make Your Word truly mine. Help me to understand, to make Your Word personal. Let's talk. . .heart to heart.

Making Bread

*Be humble under God's powerful hand so
he will lift you up when the right time comes.*
1 PETER 5:6 NCV

When we reach the end of everything we know, that is
when God rolls up His sleeves and does His best work
in our lives. He waits until we are finished rolling our problems
around like dough, pounding away until there is nothing left
to be done. When we hand our mess over to Him with humble
and sticky fingers, He takes it all and transforms it into a kind of
bread that nourishes us.

There is a story about orphaned children during WWII who
were left homeless and starving. Once rescued, they had trouble
sleeping at night out of fear that they would wake in the morning
and be hungry again. After all attempts were made to ease their
fears, someone came up with the idea of giving each child a piece
of bread to hold during the night. It worked. The children slept
peacefully, holding their bread. We can take a lesson from those
children and hold our bread as a symbol that God was with us
today and He will be with us again tomorrow.

The art of spiritual bread making requires a deep patience
that allows obstacles to rest, quietly covered in His grace so
that they can rise into opportunities that give us strength. He
works in miracles—turning even our most difficult ordeals into
blessings that can heal us.

*Father, You are the Bread of Life. Give us the faith and the
patience we need to allow You to work in our lives. Amen.*

Anger Management

Be ye angry, and sin not.
EPHESIANS 4:26 KJV

No matter how much you love your husband, he manages to tick you off from time to time. And it probably comes as no surprise that you do the same to him. It's impossible for two people to live under one roof without occasionally ruffling each other's feathers.

Anger itself isn't destructive, but how you handle it may be. Giving your husband the silent treatment, the cold shoulder, or throwing a tantrum when he offends you will only make the situation worse. Your job is not to punish him when he upsets you but to work out a solution.

When your husband makes you mad, it's fine to let him know about it, but do it in a constructive way. Talk civilly about your grief and resist the urge to attack him on everything that's ever bothered you about him. Pay attention to your body language. Avoid rolling your eyes, crossing your arms, and clenching your fists. Remember that he is the man you love, not an evil foe. Finally, when it's all said and done, bury the hatchet and move on to more important things. . .like kissing and making up!

*Dear God, help me to be loving and forgiving even when
I am angry with my husband. Teach me to control my feelings
and to handle my anger in a way that pleases You. Amen.*

Three times a day [Daniel] got down on his knees and prayed,
giving thanks to his God, just as he had done before.
DANIEL 6:10 NIV

*L*ike clockwork, Daniel had a custom of praying three
times a day. He left his office, went home, and knelt
by an open window that faced Jerusalem. Taken from Judah
as a young teenager and forced into "friendly captivity" by
King Nebuchadnezzar of Babylon, Daniel excelled in his
responsibilities. In return, he was treated well and rose through
the ranks of Babylon bureaucracy. Eventually he became one of
three "prime ministers" of Babylon! And still he knew who he
was, and he knew who his God was. He never forgot.

Are we praying faithfully for our husbands and children?
Most likely, our record of praying for them is spotty at best. But
are we any busier than a prime minister of Babylon? Daniel made
a habit of regular, effective prayer. It was just as important to him,
if not more so, than food.

We need to develop effective praying habits for our families.
Prayer doesn't have to be locked to a time or a place or a
particular posture. We need to kneel in our hearts, whenever we
sense the Lord's inner promptings to pray.

Lord, forgive me for growing complacent in prayer.
Poke me! Wake me! Remind me to pray regularly for my family,
for their hearts to belong to You for all eternity.

Ask God

What causes fights and quarrels among you?
Don't they come from your desires that battle within you?
You want something but don't get it. You kill and covet,
but you cannot have what you want. You quarrel and fight.
You do not have, because you do not ask God.
JAMES 4:1–2 NIV

Let's be honest: Married life is not always easy. Living harmoniously with another imperfect person requires effort. The marriage relationship is one of give and take. Often we take more than we give, yet we think the opposite is true. Arguments commonly ensue when one spouse perceives an imbalance in this area of give and take. When we're weary and tired, we may blame our spouse for failing to meet our needs. Certainly it must be our husband's fault if we're exhausted! However, Jesus tells us to come to Him, not go to our husbands, when we're weary and need rest. Christ is ultimately responsible for meeting our needs.

Instead of blaming others, why not ask God? We have not because we ask not. Present your needs and requests to Him. He will respond by supplying strength and power. His grace will be sufficient to meet every need you encounter. When you rely upon the Lord, even your attitude will change. Instead of harboring bitterness and anger, rejoice in the Lord's provision! Your relationship with the Lord and your husband will grow closer. Ask God.

Dear Lord, help me to look to You to meet my deepest needs. Amen.

"I Don't Need You!"

Nevertheless neither is the man without the woman,
neither the woman without the man, in the Lord.
1 CORINTHIANS 11:11 KJV

The Women's Liberation movement of the 1960s and 1970s planted many ungodly ideas in the hearts of women around the world. And one of the worst was that women do not need men. Women were told that we were as good as men, that we could be—and should be—independent of them.

Despite America's founding document, independence is not a biblical doctrine.

Although every woman will answer individually to God for what she does in this life, God never meant for individual people or nations to be independent. God's chosen nation, Israel, was a theocracy, a nation under God's rule. They were to follow Him in obedience and be dependent on Him.

Men and women were also not created to be independent. Rather, we are *inter*dependent. Women were created for men, to help them. But women give birth to men. In God's economy, we must work together.

Sometimes, in our foolishness, we may think that we don't need our husbands. Perhaps in anger or frustration we've actually said, "I don't need you!"

Forsake such thinking. Embrace God's plan. And embrace your husband.

Father, I admit it. I have fought sometimes with the desire to
be independent in my marriage. I know this is not Your desire.
Give me the grace to submit to Your perfect plan. Amen.

Inside Out

In like manner also, that women adorn themselves in
modest apparel, with shamefacedness and sobriety;
not with broided hair, or gold, or pearls, or costly array;
but (which becometh women professing godliness) with good works.
1 TIMOTHY 2:9–10 KJV

*I*s it wrong to have a desire to look nice? No! Are women required to walk around looking at the ground or hiding in their husbands' shadows? Absolutely not. The point of this verse is not that women should do their best to look frumpy and unattractive. It *is*, however, to point out that being well-dressed and expensively adorned are completely pointless if inner beauty is absent.

It is possible to be neatly, even stylishly, attired and still be modest. Your makeup and jewelry can be applied neatly and with good taste, but it should not be done in a way that draws unnecessary attention to yourself.

Your purpose is to be godly—to draw people to Jesus. You do this by walking so closely with Him that His beauty is reflected in You. All your designer clothes and expensive accessories are worthless—an artificial beauty—if Christ's love is not radiating through your entire being.

Get your priorities straight. Be sure your heart is beautiful, and external attractiveness is sure to follow.

Lord Jesus, let Your love shine through me.
May my heart be beautiful in Thy sight.

Intimate Communication

The LORD will again delight in you. . .if you obey the LORD your God and keep his commands and decrees that are written in this Book of the Law and turn to the LORD your God with all your heart and with all your soul.
DEUTERONOMY 30:9–10 NIV

*H*ow would we feel if we had to communicate with all our loved ones through a single book? Would we be happy if it was a bestseller among those we loved? But what if our loved ones bought it and never read it?

That's God's dilemma when we ignore His Bible. He wants to share Himself with us, but many of us don't even crack open His Book except on Sunday mornings.

If we communicated with our spouses that little, what kind of marriage would we have? Not very intimate ones. It's the same with our relationship with God. When we don't live in His Word, we end up far from Him.

Read and study your Bible. Draw near to God, loving Him with all your heart and soul. Allow Him the freedom to fulfill His will for your life. Pray for yourself, your marriage, and your spouse. In so doing, you will not only draw closer to God but to the one you've promised to love—forever and ever.

*Lord, draw me nearer to You through Your Word and
closer to my husband and Your will for our lives.
Help me to keep Your commands and seek You each day.*

Demonstrate Righteousness

*"I, the LORD, have called you to demonstrate my righteousness.
I will take you by the hand and guard you, and I will give
you to my people, Israel, as a symbol of my covenant with them."*
ISAIAH 42:6 NLT

*H*ave you ever considered that God has called you to demonstrate righteousness through your marriage? Isaiah 42:6 refers to Jesus Christ and His work on earth. But if we are in Christ, then we, too, are to be examples of God's righteousness to the world.

Paul tells us that marriage is a picture of the relationship Jesus Christ has with His church. Many of the Old Testament prophets liken the relationship of God with Israel as a marriage when they use metaphors of marriage, adultery, and divorce. In fact, God called Hosea to demonstrate God's unconditional love to Israel when He told Hosea to redeem a prostitute and marry her. Hosea stuck with his wife, Gomer, even when she turned her back on him and returned to prostitution.

The marriage covenant we entered into, the vows we exchanged, and even many of the traditions we observed on our wedding day, like the exchange of rings and sharing the cake—all are a picture of the covenant relationship God desires to have with us in Jesus Christ. When we enter into marriage, God calls us to demonstrate His righteousness, love, and grace to others. Knowing that we are imperfect examples, He guards and supports us so His love and righteousness can shine through our marriages.

*Father, I want my marriage to be a reflection of Your grace, Your goodness,
Your righteousness. May others be drawn to You through our marriage.
Amen.*

Freely Give

"Freely you have received, freely give."
MATTHEW 10:8 NIV

*A*s women, it is normal when we devote ourselves to do—and be—as many things as others need. Giving, for us, is as natural as breathing. That is, until we find that we are dancing delicately on a tightrope in a precarious balancing act between what we need and what others want. Despite all our efforts, gravity usually wins as the truth comes crashing down. We simply can't give what we don't have.

It was never God's plan that we spin through life with nothing but a bag of tricks to get us by. Talent and caffeinated energy only work for so long, until the moment comes when we reach into our empty pockets and conclude that we have nothing else to give.

Generous giving begins when we dig into the soil of God's sustenance and find what He has planted for us. We are nourished by this precious truth of who we are in Christ. He fills us with unlimited resources of love, patience, wisdom, and truth. From this place, we are free to give without fear of falling or becoming empty.

Every day the questions laid out before us are these: How can we enter into our day without being connected to the Source who offers His love like a spring? How can we attend to the myriad of demands placed on us without freely accepting the power that God offers first?

Father, help me to begin each day in Your Word so that I can be filled with the Holy Spirit and give from Your strength rather than my own. Amen.

Female Issues

He said to her, Daughter, be of good cheer;
your faith has made you well. Go in peace.
LUKE 8:48 NKJV

When it comes time for prayer requests, nothing can clear a room faster than a woman revealing she has female problems. Even our husbands are sometimes embarrassed when we want to discuss womanly issues that they can't even begin to fathom. Yet Jesus didn't waver when a woman having an issue of blood twelve years (Luke 8:43 KJV) came to Him for help. Talk about issues!

This was one brave woman, considering that Leviticus 15:19 made it clear that any female with an issue of blood was to be set apart from everyone else for seven days. She was deemed unclean, and anything she'd even *touch* would turn unclean.

Yet this particular physically weak woman, who was full of faith, boldly approached the Great Physician, knowing that if she just touched Him, she would be healed!

When she felt Jesus garment, the power left Him and immediately healed her! When He realized what had happened, He wasn't embarrassed or repulsed. In fact, Jesus responded with wonderful words: Daughter, be of good cheer; your faith has made you well. Go in peace. Ah, words to live by. Words that heal.

If you have an "issue" that you are reluctant to share with others, take your faith and bring it to Jesus. He's waiting for you to receive His power, to be healed, to find peace.

Lord, thank You for allowing me, Your daughter, to share
everything with You. I come to You with my issues
and am ready to receive Your power, blessing, and peace.

Let God Work

And without faith it is impossible to please God,
because anyone who comes to him must believe that he
exists and that he rewards those who earnestly seek him.
HEBREWS 11:6 NIV

Would you say that you and your husband are "earnestly" seeking the Lord each day? Maybe you feel like you are earnestly seeking the Lord on your own but your husband isn't and you certainly aren't seeking the Lord together. What can you do about a husband who only believes God exists but doesn't actually care to earnestly seek Him?

You can pray. Prayer is powerful (James 5:16), and it is so much better to have God work things out than for you to try to manipulate circumstances your way. Being unequally yoked can be a difficult and painful process. You won't achieve oneness in marriage until you and your husband are on the same page spiritually.

Let God work on your husband's heart and do your best to live a life of purity and reverence (1 Peter 3:2) while you pray and wait on the Lord. Your husband will be more apt to follow through if he feels that God is tugging on his heart rather than as if you are tugging on his sleeve. So pray rather than pester your husband into action, and let God do the grunt work on this one.

Father, I pray that You would do a great work in my husband's life. Give him the desire to know You more and help me to not get in Your way. Amen.

Transparency

Do not conform any longer to the pattern of this world,
but be transformed by the renewing of your mind.
Then you will be able to test and approve what
God's will is—his good, pleasing and perfect will.
ROMANS 12:2 NIV

*L*ack of communication skills is one of the greatest hindrances to healthy relationships. Most of the time, when we pray, we are seeking change. We cannot change others, but we *can* submit to God's design for our life and marriage through the transformation of the Holy Spirit.

Your words are powerful! They shape the atmosphere of your home and the hearts of all who enter. Your very words build up or tear down relationships. Take a breath and realize that your husband and children have a right to express themselves. Make room for their ideas and opinions even when they are different than yours.

Allow yourself to become transparent to God and to your husband. Ask God to reveal the real *you* to you. When we allow Him to expose the truth of who we are, He brings everything to the light. When we are reproved by His love, then our weaknesses are made visible and He is able to heal the past wounds and hurts that have controlled our behavior and speech.

Focus your words on building up, and when you do need to speak a difficult word, ask the Lord to help you say it with His love.

Lord, teach me to guard my heart with all diligence,
and show me how to speak the truth in love in my home,
in my church, with my friends, and in all my relationships. Amen.

Enduring Love

Put on charity, which is the bond of perfectness.
COLOSSIANS 3:14 KJV

People marry for a host of reasons. Some to gain social status and wealth. Some to please their parents. Some to escape difficult situations or to make a better life for themselves. But the happiest, most functional marriages result from a union born of love.

Love is the glue that holds a marriage together. It is the bond that will last for better or for worse, for richer or for poorer, in sickness and in health. Love will overlook faults and forgive offenses rather than seek revenge. It is understanding, kind, and easy to please. Love doesn't sulk or pout. It isn't selfish or calculating. It is fierce yet gentle, powerful yet meek. It is the single ingredient that will hold your marriage together long after beauty has faded and health has declined.

If you are fortunate enough to love and be loved, consider yourself blessed indeed. Cherish that love. Nurture it. Go out of your way to protect it. Like so many worthy things, love isn't easy. But when the tale of your years has been told, you'll be glad you kept it alive and well.

Dear Father, thank You for giving me someone to love. Help me to do everything within my power to keep my love for my husband strong so that our marriage will last for as long as we both shall live. Amen.

Chill Out

Smart people know how to hold their tongue.
PROVERBS 19:11 MSG

*L*aura, we're going to be late *again!*"

Ow! Laura accidentally poked her eye with the mascara brush and rubbed a huge black smudge beneath her bottom lashes.

Randy's voice called from the living room, "You've got to learn to manage your time better. You knew we had to leave at 6:30; here it is 6:45 and you're not even dressed. What's wrong with you?"

You're what's wrong with me! Laura's voice screamed in her head. *If you had helped bathe the kids, I would be ready by now.* But instead of a blistering retort, she shot a prayer heavenward. "Lord, I don't want to fight. Please soothe my anger and soften my harsh words."

"How much longer, Laura?"

Inhaling deeply, Laura felt supernatural peace calm her anxious heart. "Honey, I know you're frustrated because you had a hard day, but so did I. If we work together, I think we can leave within five minutes. Could you please put the twins in their car seats?"

A moment later, Randy appeared in the doorway holding a chocolate-smeared toddler. He smiled wearily. "Sorry I was crabby, hon. Looks like you've got a little more time while we hit the tub."

Holy Shiloh (Peacemaker), calm my angry retorts before a fire is sparked that blazes into an inferno. Teach me Your gentleness. Amen.

Selfishness:
The Death Sentence
of Marriage

But if you harbor bitter envy and selfish ambition
in your hearts, do not boast about it or deny the truth.
JAMES 3:14 NIV

Ken Blanchard, coauthor of *The One-Minute Manager*, once said, "When we start to get a distorted image of our own importance and see ourselves as the center of the universe, we really lose touch with who we are as children of God. This distorted image of our own importance keeps us out of the lives of others and focuses on what we alone want and think we need."

Selfishness is one of those marriage stresses that will never heal on its own because it can never be fulfilled. Selfishness is never satisfied. If you are a selfish spouse, you control your sex life, you make the financial decisions, and you pout and manipulate until you get your way.

If that describes you, then your marriage will never be what it could be until you and your husband are working for the same things. Rather than selfish pursuits, begin to live for each other, share in decisions—be the partners that God created you to be.

Father, if I've been selfish in my marriage, please show me where
and help me to curb that tendency. Please give me the self-control
that I need to hold back, forsake my own desires, and work with
my husband in the best interests of our marriage. Amen.

Good Things

And the people spake against God, and against Moses,
Wherefore have ye brought us up out of Egypt to die
in the wilderness? for there is no bread, neither is there
any water; and our soul loatheth this light bread.
NUMBERS 21:5 KJV

*A*t this time in their journey of deliverance, the Israelites
had seen many miracles. They had followed a cloud and
a pillar of fire and had been fed with manna. They had seen the
Red Sea part (or had heard about it). More recently they had
seen the earth open to swallow up their rebellious brothers.

Yet when the going got tough and they were without real
bread and fresh water, they complained against God. In fact, they
said they *hated* what God had supplied!

We look back at them and are amazed. How could they be
so dense, so faithless? God was obviously with them. How could
they possibly doubt His love and care for them?

But are we any better?

Believers have the indwelling Holy Spirit. God is *in* us; He is
always with us. He has promised to never forsake us.

Yet when the going gets tough—when our finances and
relationships are strained and when we don't have what we think
we need—we complain just as the Israelites did.

Let us learn the lessons they did not. Let us trust in our
Father, knowing that He cares and is always working for our
good.

How often I complain about the little irritations and miss seeing all the
good things You give me, Father. Have mercy on my fickle heart. Amen.

Team Player

*Therefore encourage one another and build
each other up, just as in fact you are doing.*
1 THESSALONIANS 5:11 NIV

*T*eam players are people who work together with others to accomplish the same goals. On a team, or in a partnership, one selfish person who goes her own way and doesn't consider the needs and goals of the team first will cause failure for everyone. God made Adam and Eve the first partnership. Man leaves his parents and is united with his wife, becoming one with her—the perfect partnership. This is what marriage is!

In marriage, like any real partnership, there is no room for selfishness or single-minded agendas. Each spouse should look for ways to build up each other for the good of the marriage and work together to identify and accomplish goals. When we work with our spouse as a partner, we are helping the marriage become all that God intended it to be. In marriage, our spouse is our partner. Our friends, coworkers, peers, even our children are second to the marital partnership that God has ordained.

*Heavenly Father, please forgive me for the times when I placed my husband last and everyone else first. Help me to partner with him and with You in the unity of marriage that You have designed for us. Please bless our marriage.
Amen.*

God's Plan for Marriage

*All Scripture is inspired by God and profitable for teaching,
for reproof, for correction, for training in righteousness; so that
the man of God may be adequate, equipped for every good work.*
2 TIMOTHY 3:16–17 NASB

*S*ophie often thanked the Lord for her husband and her
marriage, but she knew her marriage was not what the Lord
had ordained it to be. Sophie read every book she could find on
the subject until one day she realized that the only marriage book
she needed was written by the One who designed the institution
Himself.

God's Word tells us that scripture provides everything
we need for teaching, reproof, correction, and for training in
righteousness. God's Word describes God's plan for marriage.
As we desire to become the wife God calls us to be and have
the godly marriage He ordained, we can turn to scripture as
our guide. For example, to learn the way we should love our
husbands, we can turn to 1 Corinthians 13. To learn how to
forgive our husbands, we can read Matthew 6:14–15; 18:35;
Mark 11:25; and Ephesians 4:32. To understand how to interact
with our husbands, we can turn to Colossians 3.

God wants us to apply His Word in the relationship that
is most important to us—our marriage. Find God's Word that
speaks to your circumstances and heart's desires and then pray
God's Word. As you study God's Word and apply it to your
marriage, you will be implementing His plan for your marriage.

*Lord, help me to study Your Word and then pray
it for my husband and apply it to our marriage.*

In the morning, O LORD, you hear my voice;
in the morning I lay my requests before you and wait in expectation.
PSALM 5:3 NIV

No team takes the field without first meeting in the locker room for a pregame talk. No actor takes the stage without first getting into character. It would be foolish to build a house without consulting with an architect and drawing up plans. For any successful endeavor, preparation is key.

Throughout His earthly ministry, Jesus modeled this principle. He was an incredibly busy Man. There were disciples to train, people to heal, and children to bless. No matter what He did or where He traveled, something or someone always seemed to need attention. However, in spite of the many demands placed upon Him, scripture tells us that Jesus got up early in the morning, while it was still dark, and took time to meet His Father in prayer (Mark 1:35). Jesus was perfect, and yet even He knew this discipline was essential to ensure the effectiveness of His ministry.

What is the first thing you do each morning? Many of us hit the ground running, armed with to-do lists a mile long. Unfortunately, this means we try to take off in a hundred different directions, lacking focus, and then falling into our beds each night with a sense that we haven't accomplished anything at all.

While it doesn't ensure perfection, setting aside a short time each morning to focus on the Father and the day ahead can help prepare us to live more intentionally. In these moments we, like Jesus, gain clarity so that we can invest our lives in the things that will truly matter.

Father, help me to take time, each morning,
to focus on You and the day ahead. Align my priorities so
that the things I do will be the things You want me to do.

Stick with Him

*And unto the married I command, yet not I,
but the Lord, Let not the wife depart from her husband.*
1 CORINTHIANS 7:10 KJV

The screen door slammed shut, and suddenly the family room was silent. Stacy didn't know what was worse—the screaming of moments ago or the deafening quiet that permeated the room now that Matt had stormed off. What she did know was that these ridiculous fights were becoming all too common. She didn't know why her husband couldn't just tell her what he wanted for supper instead of waiting until she fixed something else and then getting mad. True, they'd been married for quite a few years, but she was no mind reader. Maybe it was time for them to part ways.

Later, when they'd both calmed down a bit, Stacy brought up the subject. Getting straight to the point, she said, "Matt, our home is constantly filled with fighting. Do you think we should split up?"

Slowly Matt raised his eyes. "When we got married it was for better, for worse—till death us do part," he said. "Let's at least talk to the pastor first and try to work things out."

Stacy nodded. She knew it was the right thing to do, and if Matt was willing to try to fix their marriage she would be grateful. Too many of her friends' husbands hadn't given themselves that chance. She would pray about it then do her best.

*Dear God, for our marriage to work, You have to be in first place.
Lord, please strengthen our relationship each day.*

Glad Service

So he bent over her and rebuked the fever, and it left her.
She got up at once and began to wait on them.
LUKE 4:39 NIV

*O*h, how nice it is to be pampered. Don't we love soaking in a hot bath after a long day, having our shoulders massaged when we're stressed, or having someone bring us something cool to drink on a hot day? On occasion we may even be tempted to allow our exhaustion to be more pronounced just to have someone encourage us to sit down and relax.

Being a servant is a gift and a challenge. Jesus came to serve us, and as those called to do likewise, we should be glad to minister whenever and wherever we can. The problem is we often don't get recognition or even a thank-you from our husband, so we may find it more gratifying to do for others than to be there for him.

God sees each time we sacrifice our own wants and needs to help our spouse. He knows, even if no one else does. We can rest in that, not allowing our pride to dictate how we should be treated. Let us consider our husband and see how precious he is in God's sight. It is a joy to do our best, even when we are tired and worn out, to care for him.

Thank You, Jesus, for setting such a wonderful example.
Help me to serve my husband with a glad heart. Amen.

A Two-Way Street

*You husbands in the same way, live with your wives
in an understanding way, as with someone weaker,
since she is a woman; and show her honor as a fellow heir
of the grace of life, so that your prayers will not be hindered.*
1 PETER 3:7 NASB

In 1 Peter 3:1-6, the apostle Peter tells women to respect, honor, and obey their husbands, as Sarah did Abraham. We are also to let our inner beauty shine forth, to captivate our husbands by a gentle, gracious, and quiet spirit. In this way, we might win our husbands to God. Thus, women are given their direction in the road of life. But, ladies, this is *not* a one-way street.

Husbands are told that they, too, have a definite path to trod. God wants them to *in the same way*, live with [their] wives in an understanding way. . .and show her honor as a fellow heir of the grace of life" (1 Peter 3:7 NASB, emphasis added).

And the best thing about this two-way street is yet to come. We, husbands and wives, are to live this way honoring, trusting, and respecting each other so that our prayers will not be hindered (1 Peter 3:7 NASB). In other words, we need to live peaceably with our husbands in order to keep our prayers unfettered. Wow!

So, ladies, let's not let our prayers run aground. Instead, let that inner beauty shine! And watch your prayers take flight!

*God, may the beauty of Your work in my inner life shine forth,
making my marriage one filled with peace and love. Lord, hear my prayer!*

Serving the Lord

Whatever you do, work at it with all your heart,
as working for the Lord, not for men, since you know
that you will receive an inheritance from the Lord as
a reward. It is the Lord Christ you are serving.
Colossians 3:23–24 niv

God has given all of us some work to accomplish. Whether it's a daily job, raising a family, taking care of a home and a business. . .some of our tasks tend to be tiresome jobs that we wish we could hire someone else to do.

As Christians in today's society, we really need to change our thinking about the little jobs. We need to keep Colossians 3:23–24 in mind anytime we are working so that Christ will be glorified. If we take these verses to heart, our attitudes will change and we will be a strong witness to others.

Try getting up five minutes earlier this week and spending that time memorizing these verses. Write them down and ask the Lord to change your heart and attitude about any grunt work you don't usually enjoy doing. You will see a change in your life and marriage as you take these verses to heart. Your attitude at home will be much better as you mop the floor and clean the toilets because you are doing these tasks as an act of worship to the Lord!

Dear Lord, I want to worship You in everything I do. Change my attitude
about the little things so that I may be a good witness to You always. Amen.

You're on Candid Camera

*Give no opportunity to the
adversary to speak reproachfully.*
1 TIMOTHY 5:14 NKJV

*D*id you ever get the odd sensation that someone was watching you? Did it make you act any differently? You may not realize it, but you *are* being watched every day by your family, friends, and even total strangers. The observers are forming opinions about you and every aspect of your life. . . including your marriage.

People are desperate for good examples, especially when it comes to marriage. It seems that there are far more bad relationships than good ones. Divorce has become so prevalent in our society that people have become cynical of the union designed by God. Too many are deciding to merely live with their companion rather than enter into the bonds of marriage and risk a nasty separation later.

It's up to you as a Christian wife to set a good example for others to follow. The world needs to know that marriages still work and God's design is still best. Show the naysayers that it's possible to be happily married. Be a cheerful wife, extolling the virtues of your husband and home. Make yours the model of what marriage should be and you'll give the observers something good to talk about.

*Dear Father, help me to be a good example of a Christian wife,
and let my home and marriage be an inspiration to others. Amen.*

Sacred Ground

*"Until now you have not asked for anything in my name.
Ask and you will receive, and your joy will be complete."*
JOHN 16:24 NIV

Every day, Jesus invites us to enter into a holy place with Him by praying in His name. So often we ask for things in our daily rush from here to there: "Lord, please give me a parking space close to the door." Or things that do require some miracle making: "Please change my husband." Certainly these prayers, if answered, would make our lives easier, but Jesus isn't talking about prayers that simply make us happier. He is talking about prayers that bring us complete and utter joy.

When we step out of ourselves and into a life with Jesus, we begin to see how this mystery of joy unfolds. Over time, His words take root and weave into our own, until we find ourselves unsure where His thoughts end and ours begin.

And one rainy day, in a crowded parking lot, we see a woman we've never met but suddenly know she needs help getting to her car. Or we gain new insight into the pressure our husband is under and we feel tenderness toward him we haven't felt before. In those moments of clarity when our words and prayers become one with Jesus', the sacred ground on which we walk is the ten steps it takes to offer an umbrella and an extra hand or a loving embrace.

Father, teach me how to enter into a relationship with You so deeply that I can hear Your voice and feel Your joy as I pray Your words as my own. Amen.

Timing Is Everything

"Go and gather together all the Jews of Susa and fast for me.
Do not eat or drink for three days, night or day.
My maids and I will do the same. And then,
though it is against the law, I will go in to see the king."
ESTHER 4:16 NLT

$\mathcal{E}$ sther was an orphan in a foreign land. Suddenly she found herself on center stage as King Xerxes of Persia's new bride. Barely accustomed to her new duties as queen, Esther faced a crisis of enormous proportions. She learned that the king had unwittingly placed all Jews living in Persia, including herself, in jeopardy. Prior to risking her life for her people, she humbled herself by fasting and asking for prayer support from others.

How did God direct her? To wait patiently for the right time to speak. In ancient times, the queen risked her life by appearing in front of the king's throne unless she was summoned. Esther had something she needed to say to King Xerxes, but she paused and prayed and proceeded cautiously and carefully. Xerxes saw her standing in the hall. Pleased, he was in a mood eager to give Esther anything she wanted. Timing was everything.

This is a wise reminder for us to choose our words carefully and to deliver those words at the right time. We want our message to be well received. Is our husband hungry? Tired? Irritable? Distracted? Those aren't the moments for heart-to-heart conversation. What we say matters, but so does how and when.

Lord, give me Esther's restraint. Make me sensitive to Your guidance.
May I learn to practice instant obedience.

Take Heart

Take heart! Don't be anxious or get discouraged.
GOD, my God, is with you in this; he won't walk off
and leave you in the lurch. He's at your side.
1 CHRONICLES 28:20 MSG

When they were first married, Archie and Joan were indifferent about religion. Seven years later, Joan's outlook on life changed. Next thing Archie knew, Joan was being baptized at the local church and taking their little boy to Sunday school. But no matter what, Archie wasn't budging, maintaining his stance that religion was for fools. If his wife wanted to raise their child in a church, she was free to do so. She just shouldn't expect Archie to go along.

Many women find themselves in the same situation. They're called church widows, attending most services and church functions alone, except, of course, for maybe Easter and Christmas. So what are these women to do?

God's Word simply tells them to be good wives. That means being alert and responding to their husbands needs and living a life of holy beauty (1 Peter 3:1–2 MSG). Sometimes this may be quite a challenge. Wives may even, at times, fall short of this goal as tempers or impatience get the better of them. But they cannot get discouraged. These wives just need to take heart, keep the faith, be a good wife, and pray.

Are you a church widow, or do you know of someone who is? If so, pray, asking for God, in His wonderful timing, to someday bring these husbands around to the light, love, and wisdom found only in Him.

Lord, don't let me get discouraged. I know You can do anything.
Help me to live a life that exemplifies You. Forgive me when I fall
short of that goal. And please keep Your eye on my husband,
working Your will in his life. Thank You for hearing my prayer!

Humility Brings Glory

*"For everyone who exalts himself will be humbled,
and he who humbles himself will be exalted."*
LUKE 14:11 NIV

The tree was bare. Every leaf had been shed. Winter had arrived. Yet beyond the barren tree, the sun peeked its head above the treetops. Dawn was breaking. As the sun ascended higher, its rays were visible through the bare branches. Before long, the entire tree was glowing as the sun's radiance shone through it.

Many times our lives seem barren, as if we've been stripped of everything. We find ourselves humbled, humiliated, forsaken, or rejected—standing alone, like a barren tree. But our story does not end there. God's glory will burst forth. Wait. At just the right time, like the sunrise, He makes His appearance. When He does, His light will shine through because our branches are bare. The world will see. Our humility allows others to see the Lord clearly through us because the focus is no longer on us but on Him. When we decrease, the Lord will increase.

Do not view humility with distain. His glory can only be revealed when we are humble. Humble yourself before the Lord and He will lift you up. He will shine through you. You will reflect and make known His glory. May it be so!

*Dear Lord, may humility characterize my
life so that You may be glorified. Amen.*

It's Here Someplace

There is a time for finding and losing.
ECCLESIASTES 3:6 CEV

"Have you seen my car keys?" Matt's voice resounded from the bedroom.

"No, I haven't," Kirsten replied from the kitchen. "It's probably marinating somewhere with my missing rump roast."

Matt appeared in the doorway. "How can you lose a rump roast?"

"I have no idea. It was defrosting in the sink this morning and now it's gone."

"Well, my key needs to appear immediately or I'll miss my meeting. Can you help me look?"

Kirsten resisted the temptation to roll her eyes. Matt was always losing something. . .keys, ties, important phone numbers. He'd even lost his money clip holding one hundred dollars. It had shown up in a pair of ski pants the following winter.

As she backtracked Matt's steps, Kirsten wondered if all wives spent as many hours searching for misplaced items. She couldn't help but wish her husband was more responsible and less scatterbrained. But he did keep life interesting!

"Here it is," Kristen hollered, reaching into the medicine cabinet, "beside your toothbrush!"

"Great!" replied Matt. "And Sherlock found something for you, too, Mrs. Watson!" He led a small boy in a baseball cap down the hall, clutching a slab of raw meat over his swollen, black eye.

"Mystery solved!" Matt grinned. "It's a good thing we're sleuth partners so we aren't like all the couples who say they do nothing fun together!"

Make sure fun is a *fun*damental part of your marital relationship.

*Wonderful Lord, keep my sense of humor intact
throughout this matrimonial journey! Amen.*

Relationship Repair

"For your Maker is your husband—the LORD
Almighty is his name—the Holy One of Israel is
your Redeemer; he is called the God of all the earth."
ISAIAH 54:5 NIV

*D*uring the exile, the prophet Isaiah foretold that Jerusalem would feel totally deserted—the best people of Judah would be taken away and even God would seem to have left them behind. Yet in Isaiah 54, God prophetically compares Himself to a husband who draws His spouse back to His side. He promised to one day end the emotional distance the marked His relationship with Judah. His people's spiritual emptiness would not last forever.

Marriage has its ups and downs. Some days your husband seems wonderful and you're happy that God gave him to you. You seem as close as a couple could be. Other days, pain or disagreements make a space between you and you may feel as desolate as Jerusalem.

Don't despair. Relationships wax and wane, but God doesn't. He always loves both of you. Together you can come before Him and engage in relationship repair. The emotional space that seems eternal doesn't need to be.

But if you feel space between yourselves and God, beware! God never creates space between Him and His people. If you feel a sense of separation, guess who walked away?

Lord, thank You for my husband. Help us to recognize that spiritual downs
need not last. May we always turn to You for relationship repair.

Michal's Choice

As the ark of the LORD was entering the City of David,
Michal daughter of Saul watched from a window. And when
she saw King David leaping and dancing before the LORD,
she despised him in her heart.
2 SAMUEL 6:16 NIV

Nine years earlier, Michal was hopelessly in love with David. She even betrayed her father, King Saul, to save David's life. But today, that love was dead. His abandoned joy only embarrassed her.

Michal couldn't identify with David's joy because she didn't share it. She had no appreciation for the significance of the return of the ark of the Lord to Jerusalem. But to David, it meant basking in the presence of the Lord.

When David returned home, Michal met him at the door, eyes blazing. She blasted him with hot hatred! And he responded by distancing himself from her.

Like most couples, Michal and David once loved each other passionately, but nine stressful years later, that passion had died. Instead of replacing her emptiness with God, Michal let her heart remain. . .empty.

We think passion will be enough to sustain a marriage, but it isn't. Only God can satisfy our heart's deepest desires.

It could have been so different for Michal! She was David's first love. She could have been his last one.

Make God your first choice. Allow Him to fill your heart. He'll keep your love alive!

Lord, may I have a heart like David. He seemed to
intuitively understand that You belonged first in his life.

Relationship Rule #1

Post this at all the intersections, dear friends:
Lead with your ears, follow up with your tongue,
and let anger straggle along in the rear.
JAMES 1:19 MSG

*H*ave you ever had a moment when your husband says something to you and, in response, you lose control, saying something out of line? Instead of listening to his point of view, your anger continues to get the better of you and you speak with resentment that you know you will later regret.

God knows that we experience these occasions in our marriages, at work, at school. In James, we receive some good advice that is difficult to put into practice. Listen first. Listening seems to involve patience, too; we have to give the other person a chance to speak. Only after we have heard the opposing side should we feel free to speak ourselves. However, even while we speak, James tells us to keep our anger away.

While James's advice is certainly difficult to heed, this is a vital verse for healthy relationships, particularly in marriage, when our words fly out more easily that we would sometimes like to admit. Listening to the other side of an argument can be enlightening if we give the other person a chance; speaking calmly, without anger, will lead to much more constructive conversations that will, in turn, build healthier marriages and relationships.

Dear Lord, please give me the patience to listen first, to speak second, and to control my anger. Strengthen my relationships and teach me to love better through Your Word. Amen.

The Greener-Grass Lie

It's healthy to be content, but envy can eat you up.
PROVERBS 14:30 CEV

The grass is always greener on the other side—or so we're told. When your husband fails to keep a promise, when he leaves his dirty socks on the floor again, when he works too much and helps around the house too little, it's easy to look at the seemingly perfect couples around you and desire to have what "she" has. The truth is, there are no perfect couples. And if you actually had what "she" has, you'd eventually not be happy with that either.

The problem is that it is our selfish desires that cause us to fight and rebel against what we have rather than accept and appreciate our blessings. Constant comparison with other marriages, husbands, and families will only lead to disappointment and regret. Instead, focus on the life that God speaks into your marriage when He reveals the gifts He has given to you through the blessing of your husband. Honor God by honoring your husband with appreciation and admiration for his good qualities.

Jesus, please show me the good things in my marriage so that I can focus on them rather than the things I selfishly want. Help me to change my perspective from being so demanding of my own needs and wants to being more concerned with my husband's needs. Amen.

The Dawn of Mourning

"Blessed are those who mourn,
for they will be comforted."
MATTHEW 5:4 NIV

*W*hen dreams become shadows and sadness tramples our heart, mourning becomes the way we learn to breathe again. It is sanity, really, which prompts us to cry out and break the silence that simply absorbs our loss. Giving voice to our grief joins us in song to all those who have suffered before. It releases our sadness and keeps it from settling into and numbing our hearts.

We mourn many things throughout our life. . .loss of loved ones, our health, our ideas, or our expectations. But bemoaning our earthly losses is not the type of mourning Jesus is talking about in the Beatitudes. He is referring to what happens when we are hit with the overwhelming realization that we are spiritually lost beings in need of a Savior. Simply put, we are the walking dead, living a useless life over a fixed amount of time. And the clock is running.

Jesus says that those who grieve over their enlightened spiritual condition are blessed. Yes, blessed because He has great news! He offers us everlasting life with Him through His Son, Jesus. He gives the dead new life. Every time we stumble in sin and fall on our pain, He promises to comfort us and restore us to Him. His love and complete forgiveness turns our mourning into a new day.

Father, thank You for the comfort You give me when
I can't help but see myself as I really am. Thank You for
Your forgiveness and promise of everlasting life. Amen.

How Are You Building?

*Now as touching things offered unto idols, we know that we all
have knowledge. Knowledge puffeth up, but charity edifieth.*
1 CORINTHIANS 8:1 KJV

The success of a building project depends, in large part,
upon the quality of the materials being used. For instance,
pressboard kitchen cabinets might look nice temporarily, but
they won't last as well as solid wood cabinets that were carefully
constructed.

You've probably guessed where this is going in relation to
building your marriage. You have two basic building materials–
knowledge and love—to consider. While knowledge isn't
necessarily a bad thing (in fact it can be quite beneficial), it isn't
strong enough to stand the test of time. You have knowledge;
your husband has knowledge. Pretty soon you both become so
caught up with what's in your head that pride drowns out what's
in your heart. Knowledge can do to your marriage what worn out
pressboard cabinets do to the value of your home.

Love, though, builds your marriage. It is the law of supply
and demand—the more love you get, the more love you will have
to give. Soon it will be overflowing, and yours will be a joyful
home. You see, love does to your marriage what a set of custom-
designed cherry cabinets does for the value of your home.

Now don't quit obtaining and using knowledge wisely. Just
make sure that in your life it is properly balanced with love.

*Everyone wants love and wisdom, dear God. When You offer
me these wonderful gifts please help me to use them properly.*

R-E-S-P-E-C-T

*Her husband is respected at the city gate,
where he takes his seat among the elders of the land.*
PROVERBS 31:23 NIV

The verse above is referring to a woman who takes care of her home, brings in some money, is trustworthy and honorable in all that she does, and works for the good of her family. According to Proverbs 31:23, a woman like that brings honor and respect to her husband from all who know him. A man who is honored and cared for by a woman like the one described in Proverbs 31 is worthy of the respect of his leader and peers. You, as a wife, contribute greatly to the respect your husband receives from others.

Respecting your spouse, and being in a position to be respected yourself, also requires action. Respect involves submission, humility, and appreciation. Mistakenly, many couples believe these things need to be earned, even in marriage. That is true with conditional love, but God's design for marriage is based upon your unconditional love for each other. Respectful ways are a natural part of unconditional love. Respect, in a Christian marriage, isn't offered as a reward; it's given as a gift.

Jesus, please help me to be the kind of wife who earns favor for my husband. And, please help me to respect him first, before I expect anything from him. Help me to love him unconditionally, just as You have loved me. Amen.

Run Home

*But now, God's Message, the God who made you
in the first place, Jacob, the One who got you started, Israel:
Don't be afraid, I've redeemed you. I've called your name. You're mine.*
ISAIAH 43:1 MSG

*R*emember when you were a child and you ran outside to play? When it came time for dinner, your mom called you in. She called you by name. And you stopped whatever you were doing and ran. You ran home. Because at home, your parents (the ones whose love created you) protected you and provided for you. They fed, clothed, and nourished you. They answered all your questions. They gave you direction.

Now you're all grown up. And there is still one who protects you, provides for you, and nourishes you. It's God, the One who got you started. He calls you by your name. You are His! He longs for you to run home to Him!

Listen! Be still. Quiet your thoughts. Do you hear Him? He's calling your name!

Drop whatever you're doing and run! Run into His arms. Allow Him to fill you with His Spirit and peace. Allow Him to love you with an everlasting love. Allow Him to feed you on His Word. Allow Him to hold you tight. He will never let you fall, never let you go. You need not be afraid. You're home!

*Lord, I hear You calling my name! Here I am, Lord!
Hear I am! I'm coming home!*

Behold the Mystery

*This is a great mystery: but I speak
concerning Christ and the church.*
EPHESIANS 5:32 KJV

*M*arriage, Paul says, is so sublime and so sacred that it is the very picture of Christ and His church. As Christ loved the church and sacrificed Himself for it, so husbands are to love their wives; as the church reveres the Lord, so wives are to revere their husbands.

If this is not enough to make us stop to consider our opinion of marriage and our behavior within it, consider this: Marriage is a New Testament type.

In the Old Testament, God gave His people many types, or pictures, of things that would be fully realized in Christ. The sacrifice of Isaac was a type of the sacrifice of Christ. The rock that gave water was also a type of Christ.

God is very jealous of His typology. When Moses struck the rock a second time, he broke the typology, and that kept him from the Promised Land.

Likewise, we must consider the importance of the picture of marriage. Our marriages must reflect Christ and the church. We must not forsake our husbands, because Christ would never forsake the church. We should always honor our husbands, because the church should always honor Christ.

If we want the world to behold our Savior, we must let them behold the mystery of a truly Christian marriage.

*Father, I want the world to see You at work in my life. Let me
show my unbelieving friends the power and wonder of a marriage
that works. Show me new ways to honor my husband today. Amen.*

*And they said to Him, We have here
only five loaves and two fish.*
MATTHEW 14:17 NKJV

*O*ne day five thousand people were sitting on a hillside,
listening to Jesus. But as the day drew to a close, stomachs
began to growl. Knowing that they were faced with an inordinate
amount of hungry mouths, the disciples panicked, telling Jesus to
send the crowd away to buy bread from the surrounding villages.

But Jesus said to them, You give them something to eat
(Mark 6:37 NKJV).

This, to the disciples, seemed like an impossibility! Focusing
on what they lacked, the disciples knew there was no way five
loaves and two fish would satisfy this hungry mob. Yet Jesus
commanded them to bring their meager stores to Him.

Then Jesus took the five loaves and the two fish, and looking
up to heaven, He blessed and broke and gave the loaves to the
disciples; and the disciples gave to the multitudes (Matthew
14:19 NKJV). And here's the amazing thing: They all ate and were
filled (Matthew 14:20 NKJV)! Not only that, but they ended up
with twelve baskets filled with leftovers!

With Jesus in our lives, we dare not look at what we lack
in our marriage, our family, our job, or our church. Instead, He
wants us to take what we have and give it to Him. By doing so,
He will bless our meager store and multiply it. And in the end,
we will find we have more than enough!

*Jesus, help me focus not on what I lack but on what I have.
I know that You can do the impossible. So please take
my meager store, bless it, and multiply it, to Your glory!*

Romance: A Noun or a Verb?

*"Give, and it will be given to you: good measure, pressed down,
shaken together, and running over will be put into your bosom.
For with the same measure that you use, it will be measured back to you."*
LUKE 6:38 NKJV

*M*any marriages end because of disappointment when
the spark fizzles out. We think that love should be like
it's portrayed by Hollywood. But Hollywood portrays scripted
marriages—they aren't real.

Is *romance* a noun? Is it something that you possess,
something that exists for you to own, that one day disappears?
Or is it a verb? Is it something that you must do, work toward,
and maintain?

The hassles of life all take their toll on the "noun" *love*. In
order to nurture romance, we need to realize that it's a verb; it
requires action, and it's a priority. Appreciate your spouse and
show gratitude; learn new things about each other. Give your
spouse your time, your attention, your affection, and your respect,
knowing that when you give, you will receive the rewards of
romance.

Stoke the fires of your romance to keep the spark from
fizzling. Romance is a flame, which, if properly tended, will keep
you warm for a lifetime.

*Father, thank You for my husband. Please help me to remember
that romantic love requires action in order to keep it burning strong.
Help me to keep the fire of my marriage burning brightly. Amen.*

Change and Contentment

But godliness with contentment is great gain.
1 TIMOTHY 6:6 KJV

*H*ave you ever known exactly what the plans for the day were only to have your husband decide to do something different? How do you react to his changes? With anger? Harsh words? The silent treatment? Or do you shrug off disappointment or annoyance and embrace the change to the best of your ability?

Part of being a wife—and allowing our husbands the leadership in the home—is to have adaptability when he redirects how our day will progress. Often what we think we have planned is based on assumptions, not on an actual discussion of what is ahead. Perhaps, too, our husbands have the God-given desire to be the leader in the home yet feel they aren't allowed to lead. Maybe our being flexible is a way to encourage them as they guide our family.

Sometimes we believe we know what God wants for us only to have Him lead us in a different direction. This could mean a move or a new job, maybe even a change in lifestyle because our income decreases. No matter what the direction is, we need to be content to follow God wherever He sends us. When we are willing to do this, we will be blessed with godliness and rewarded with great gain.

*Lord, please give me the ability to be flexible
and content with the changes in my life. Amen.*

To Love Their Husbands

*That they may teach the young women
to be sober, to love their husbands.*
TITUS 2:4 KJV

How much do you truly love your husband? Do you enjoy fixing him a special meal or snuggling with him in front of a good movie or a crackling fire? Do you walk hand in hand, sharing your dreams or concerns as you go?

Oh yes, these are the good times. But what about when he forgets your anniversary? Can you forget the bad and concentrate on the good? What about when he tramps across your freshly mopped floor in his muddy boots? Do you scream and pout or do you quietly wipe up the evidence?

We often forget that, like us, our husbands are human. We are tempted to focus on passages of scripture that command them to love their wives, but we ignore those verses that have parallel instructions for us. We might also give lip service to the admonition, but in our hearts do we truly love the men that God gave us?

Today why don't you challenge yourself anew to love your husband the way God planned? Determine to cherish him for better or for worse. You might be amazed at what it will do for your marriage and family.

*Lord, remind me how to love my husband in a way that
would strengthen our marriage. Help me to be gracious
enough to be the kind of wife You intended me to be.*

Deep Love

*Most important of all, continue to show deep
love for each other, for love covers a multitude of sins.*
1 PETER 4:8 NLT

Let's face it: Marriage is not easy. Combining two lives,
two personalities, two schedules, and two sets of desires
is challenging. Careers take different paths, children are born,
moves occur, and life continually changes. Differences may
arise, and arguments often occur as a result. When events like
these take place, we might confide in our friends, read books on
marriage and life changes, or involve ourselves more in our work
or children.

God has a different—and better—solution. *"Show deep love
for each other."* When we experience differences with our spouses
and arguments become common, the answer is not to distance
ourselves or walk away. Instead, we are to love each other. God
says that love covers over sins. Love allows us to forgive, merge
our differences into a common goal, and accomplish that goal
together with support and encouragement. Furthermore, love
enables us to avoid many of the arguments we might have
had otherwise. By establishing a deep love early and carefully
nurturing it as the years pass, we often avoid arguments because
God is our foundation, our goals coincide, and our primary
concern is the love that we share.

*Dear Lord, please strengthen my marriage every day. Teach us to love each
other better so that we might serve You in a worthy manner. Amen.*

What God Doesn't See

He hath not beheld iniquity in Jacob, neither hath
he seen perverseness in Israel: the LORD his God
is with him, and the shout of a king is among them.
NUMBERS 23:21 KJV

Try has he might, Balaam could not curse the children of
Israel. Instead, he blessed them.

While God had control of Balaam's wicked mouth, he made
an unbelievable statement: God had not beheld iniquity in Jacob
or seen perverseness in Israel.

Really? Just a few chapters earlier, Korah, Dathan, and
Abiram had rebelled and the earth had swallowed them up. Then
the Israelites despised the gift of manna again, and God judged
them with serpents.

There was obvious rebellion and wickedness among the
people, but God said He had not beheld iniquity or perverseness
in His people! How is this possible? The next statement explains:
"The LORD his God is with him."

God is with His chosen people. He sets His love upon them.
He imputes His righteousness to them. Because God was in the
midst of Israel, when He looked on them, He didn't see their
sin—He saw Himself.

Likewise, when God looks upon His chosen now, He doesn't
see our sin. He sees Himself. He sees Christ's righteousness,
imputed to us through the death and resurrection of Jesus.
"Blessed. . .[are] the people whom he hath chosen for his own
inheritance" (Psalm 33:12 KJV).

Father, You have chosen me, saved me, sealed me, and declared me righteous.
I want to yield my whole self to You, as a servant of righteousness.
Show me where I should serve You today. Amen.

Where Are You?

*They heard the sound of the LORD God walking in the
garden in the cool of the day, and the man and his wife hid
themselves from the presence of the LORD God. . . . Then the LORD
God called to the man, and said to him, "Where are you?"*
GENESIS 3:8–9 NASB

*I*magine having a meeting place with God every day at the
same time. He waits for each of us, in our favorite place—in
the shade under a tree or in the coziest chair by the fireplace. For
Adam and Eve, it was in the garden in the cool of the day, after
the sun made its steady decline.

One day, they were gone. The tragedy of sin filled them
with shame and fear so great that they hid. He called out to
them, for He knows that disease grows in the dark and hidden
places of our heart. "Where are you?" was not a question of their
whereabouts, but rather the cry of a Father longing for His
children to come out of hiding and back into the healing light.

Now He calls to us. "Where are you?" Busy days have turned
into weeks of silence. *It's been too long,* we think. *I've drifted too
far.* But with God, no distance is too great. He has already gone
to the ends of the earth to reach us and died on a cross to save us.

*Father, it is hard to believe that You, the Creator of the Universe,
longs to spend time with me every day. Help me hear Your call to come
out of my busyness or despair and spend time in Your Word. Amen.*

God's Gift to Man

*Then the LORD God made a woman. . .
and he brought her to the man.*
GENESIS 2:22 NIV

*C*ontrary to popular belief, man's best friend is not a floppy-eared canine with soulful eyes and a wagging tail. The Garden of Eden was full of friendly beasts, yet none of them could fill the loneliness that Adam suffered. God saw that the man needed a wife—not just to pick up his fig leaves and cook dinner but to be his companion and friend.

Just as Eve filled the void in Adam's life, so you have made your husband complete. You are the love of his life, the sharer of his dreams, the woman he comes home to at the end of the day. You are God's gift to your husband! As such, you are of exquisite value, precious and irreplaceable. You are not *just a wife*. You are the glittering jewel in God's crowning creation.

Shine! Sparkle! Cherish the role that God has designed for you. Be Eve to your Adam and work together to make your home a paradise.

*Dear God, help me to realize my incredible worth as a wife and
to appreciate the role that You intended for me to fulfill. Amen.*

The Eyes Have It

*The God our ancestors worshiped raised him to
life and made him our Leader and Savior.*
ACTS 5:30–31 CEV

The Christmas Cantata was only two weeks away, and the choir director was becoming frustrated. During practice, choir members only occasionally glanced his way. Instead, their noses were buried in their music, focusing on the words and notes. Consequently, joy did not radiate from their faces nor did their voices project as they should. Unity was sorely lacking. It was obvious that all eyes needed to be on the choir director!

Who or what has our undivided attention? Trying hard to live the Christian life, we may forget to look at our leader, Jesus! It is easy to become distracted with worldly concerns—career, family, friends, homes, and so forth. Jesus may get pushed aside or left out altogether. We may even be diligently serving in our church or community. Yet when we take our eyes off of Jesus, we can get caught up in the administrative details and forget the Person we should be serving.

Jesus is our leader. It's imperative that we keep our eyes on Him (Hebrews 12:2) for direction and instruction. How else will we be able to navigate wisely in the world? He will communicate His will for our lives, day by day. He will make our paths straight and show us the way to go. Let's keep our eyes on Jesus so we can follow our leader!

*Dear Lord, help me focus on You. Teach me the
way I am to go each and every day. Amen.*

Which Court?

*Has not the LORD made them one? In flesh and spirit
they are his. And why one? Because he was seeking
godly offspring. So guard yourself in your spirit, and do
not break faith with the wife of your youth. "I hate
divorce," says the LORD God of Israel.*
MALACHI 2:15–16 NIV

When a study by Ben Scafidi of Georgia State University
stated that divorce and children born out of wedlock cost
taxpayers over $112 billion a year, the Web site *time.com* had
its doubts. It quoted another source that sought to blame the
expense on all kinds of other economic factors and discounted
Scafidi because he was supported by pro-life groups.

Maybe we wish to discount reports that call us to account
for our marriages, but can we deny the pain that comes from
divorce? Most of us have had a friend or family member who has
suffered from a broken marriage and know how devastating it is.
Or maybe even we ourselves have experienced a divorce.

God has plenty of reasons for us not breaking faith with our
spouses: It breaks vows made to Him and may lead people into
other sins. Certainly He also hates the pain it causes His people,
who were made to glorify Him through their marriages.

No matter what the world tells us, let's remember God's view
of divorce, seek to keep our vows, and take measures to protect
our marriages. Let's avoid the divorce courts and seek instead the
court of our King.

*Lord, help us to seek You when we disagree,
instead of turning to legal action.*

God's Yoke of Love

*"Come to me, all you who are weary and burdened,
and I will give you rest. . . . I am gentle and humble in heart, and you will
find rest for your souls. For my yoke is easy and my burden is light."*
MATTHEW 11:28–30 NIV

When we first marry, many of us believe that the honeymoon will last forever. Nothing our bridegroom does will detract us from loving the man we married and delighting in him. It's easy to overlook any annoying habits he may exhibit.

Then reality sets in.

Trouble comes to threaten our happiness. Sickness invades our well-ordered lives. Parents grow older and we find ourselves responsible for their care. If children are born into the family or outside interests or ministry increase, we may become weary, weighed down with care and responsibility. If only we could rest and be at peace.

Jesus calls us to come to Him. He longs to carry the heavy burdens for us. He asks us to carry His yoke, to yield to His control. Only when we surrender to His love do we experience the rest we so desperately crave.

As we learn to rest in His love, we realize that His yoke—the "burden" of love—is easy. And as we learn to express our love in acts of service, the burden of responsibility begins to lift.

Jesus, I hear Your call to rest in You, to cast off my burden, to take Your yoke. I desire to experience the rest that comes when I surrender to Your yoke. Amen.

Becoming One

> *God is love. If we keep on loving others, we will stay*
> *one in our hearts with God, and he will stay one with us.*
> 1 JOHN 4:16 CEV

The wife smiled as she looked over the paycheck she held in her hand. Her first. The amount wasn't a lot, but it was hers. Her husband's wages paid the bills. Now she could use this income for some of the extra luxuries she wanted.

Sometimes it's easy to forget that we are one flesh and, as such, all we have belongs to both of us. We find that we consider certain material or monetary goods as belonging to us alone or that are ours to do with as we please. In fact, we must give all we have to our husbands and discuss what they think is right to do with it. This isn't easy to do. An action such as this takes great trust, faith, and humility yet can be so rewarding as our husbands come to realize the depth of our love and sacrifice.

As Christians, we become one with the Lord, too. All we have belongs to Him just as all He has is ours to access. We can't choose when to allow Him to guide our lives. We must continually offer up all we are and all we have. Once again, this sacrifice isn't easy. However, becoming one with our Lord or with our husbands becomes easier with time. Love like this is not a burden but a privilege.

> *Lord, thank You for the gift of love. Help me to truly*
> *become one with You and with my husband. Amen.*

Divine Love

*"So now I am giving you a new commandment:
Love each other. Just as I have loved you, you should love each other."*
JOHN 13:34 NLT

It sounds simple, but rarely is it easy. Loving the people in our life is often our toughest assignment. Isn't that why a part of us is always searching for other people to love who seem less burdensome and more deserving? Many times the behavior of those we live with stirs up confusion and sadness in us. For we each carry a lifetime of experience inside that tells us the painful truth about people. Whether it happens today or years from now, eventually they will let us down.

It is hard to avoid the clarity of Jesus' message to love people to the extent that He loves. Since God is the creator of love, He is the standard by which we are measured. He loves sacrificially, completely, and passionately, without keeping a record of past failures. Can we really love others the way God loves us? Can we love our husbands like that? Try it for just one day; it is easy to see why we need a Savior in the first place.

We may think, *Well, it would be easier if he didn't leave his towel on the floor or slam the kitchen cupboards and doors at every turn.* It's true. Our husbands can make loving them a challenge. But Jesus isn't saying that we should love our husbands as they deserve we should love them in the way *He* deserves to be loved.

*Father, help me to love my husband the way You do.
Please show me how. Amen.*

The Devil's Triangle

*For all that is in the world, the lust of the flesh,
and the lust of the eyes, and the pride of life,
is not of the Father, but is of the world.*
1 JOHN 2:16 KJV

For all the complaining we do about the things we don't
have, we sure miss out on a lot of the blessings of the things
we do have. Our prayers are more focused on complaining to
God than they are on praising Him. Why is this? Often it's
because we're trapped in the devil's triangle. Our hearts are filled
more with lust for things we don't possess and on sinful pride
rather than on love for God and others and joy in the blessings
He has bestowed on us.

This triangle has caused a rift in many marriages because it
is self-centered and doesn't seek the best for each partner. It's a
dangerous enemy because Satan displays it so prominently and
makes it so attractive.

The lust of the flesh doesn't have to trap you, though. Be
aware that it is present, and arm your heart against it. As humans
we *are* susceptible, but as Christians we *can* overcome. We must
engross ourselves in the Word of God and let the Holy Spirit
do a work in us. We need to daily crucify the old nature within
us and let Jesus form us into new creatures. Once our hearts are
habitually filled with true praise to our Creator, it will be easier to
live in His love rather than in the lust of the devil.

*Father, I praise You for Your greatness,
for You alone are worthy.*

Silent Night

*But Mary kept all these things in her
heart and thought about them often.*
LUKE 2:19 NLT

*A*s a woman, Mary must have fretted about things like
dusty straw, flea-ridden livestock, and splintery wood in
her baby's birthplace. But she was likely comforted by knowing
that the Son of God had the best beginning humankind could
offer—a loving family and parents devoted to one another.

Despite Joseph's initial inability to comprehend the most
unusual circumstances surrounding Mary's pregnancy, amid
raised eyebrows and scandalous gossip, he married the woman
he loved. The couple was probably avoided by neighbors and
shunned in public places.

Nevertheless, Joseph treated Mary with tenderness and
respect throughout her pregnancy (Matthew 1:19–25). Upon
their arrival in Bethlehem, Joseph urgently sought shelter and
provision for his wife, miserably "great with child" (Luke 2:5 KJV).
He no doubt scurried around the stable, tidying up harnesses,
dung buckets, and stray lambs, while Mary labored in childbirth.

Can't you picture an exhausted but radiant Mary cuddling
baby Jesus, smiling at the straw sticking out of Joseph's hair as
he hovered nearby? Words could not express the fullness and
gratitude of her heart as her eyes drank in God's immeasurable
gift of family.

*Lamb of God, as we celebrate Your birth, we thank You
for the special blessing of family. Help us, like Mary,
to treasure these precious moments in our hearts forever. Amen.*

Simple Prayer

*Be assured that from the first day we heard of you,
we haven't stopped praying for you, asking God to give
you wise minds and spirits attuned to his will, and so acquire
a thorough understanding of the ways in which God works.*
COLOSSIANS 1:9 MSG

*D*o you pray for your husband? Do you stop to think about what his day is like and the types of challenges he encounters? Often men are faced with spiritual challenges and temptations on the job and deal with ungodly people and situations. One of the best things you can do in support of your husband is to pray for him.

You can pray for physical safety, for peace of mind, for spiritual protection, for strength to withstand temptation, and for a happy heart. You can pray that he will be a good leader, deserving of respect. If he's a believer, you can pray that he will be a good Christian example. If he's a nonbeliever, pray that the Holy Spirit would open his heart to God.

You can pray for new opportunities for him, for renewed passion for his work, and for excitement in his day. Most of all, pray for God to guide him and for his openness to that guidance. Lifting him up in prayer over the daily things of life is the best support you can offer.

*Father, please guide my husband, today. Lead him in the paths of
righteousness and help Him to be strong in You. Bring peace and
happiness to his heart and mind. Thank You for all You do for him. Amen.*

A Teachable Heart

Day
361

"My son, do not despise the chastening of the Lord,
nor be discouraged when you are rebuked by Him;
for whom the Lord loves He chastens."
Hebrews 12:5–6 nkjv

How we appreciate our husband's telling us when our slip is showing or when we have something in our teeth after a meal. We don't want to be embarrassed in front of our friends by something we don't realize is wrong. However, when our husbands gently correct us in other areas or ways, we tend to get defensive and try to justify our actions or words.

Just as when God disciplines us, we need to understand that our husbands are doing so because they love us. Sometimes they may not be as gentle in their correction as God is, or as humble, but their intent is usually right. It is our pride that often keeps us from accepting any rebuke, no matter how well-done it is.

Having a teachable heart is a gift from God. We must pray that He will help us see the changes we need to make. God can also show us how to love our husbands even when their correction isn't what we agree with or want to hear. Instead of defending our actions with poor reactions, let us take a step back and pray that God will teach us what we need to know.

Lord, thank You that You care so much for me.
Thank You for my husband and his love for me, too. Amen.

Heaven's Exchange

*Because by one sacrifice he has made perfect
forever those who are being made holy.*
HEBREWS 10:14 NIV

*I*t sounds like a riddle, but it's true. We are a living work in progress all the while the final work in us has already been finished. We are forgiven and spiritually perfect at the same time we are living through the process. When this becomes too much to comprehend, just remember that we live inside Earth's time bubble, separate from eternity.

Jesus has completed the work needed to guarantee our future in heaven by dying on the cross for our sins. He has made us complete in Him by beating death and rising from the tomb. He stands in our place with a sinless record and trades our life's work with His. Because of that heavenly exchange, we are free to become who we were created to be here on Earth.

Too often we are fooled into not trusting this promise, believing that what Jesus has done is not enough and we must take matters into our own hands. We have been trained to find ways to secure our future and earn our own way, but Jesus tells us that in life's greatest ambition, we have already won the ultimate prize.

So before you face the day ahead with all its troubles, reflect on the power of this verse. Our strength lies in accepting its truth and living as we really are in Christ.

Father, thank You for taking my place on the cross and securing for me eternal life. Help me believe that You have completed a good work in me. Amen.

*And though a man might prevail against one who is alone,
two will withstand him—a threefold cord is not quickly broken.*
ECCLESIASTES 4:12 ESV

*M*any married women believe that they are better off working alone. They go by the old saying, "If you want something done right, you have to do it yourself!" They could not be more wrong in marriage. Partnering with a spouse creates strength in unity that can stand against the wilds of the world. Ecclesiastes 4:12 explains that two people working together can withstand the things that come against them but that even stronger are those who are partnered together with each other and with God in a three-strand cord.

God joins two people together in the covenant bond of marriage because they complete each other with their strengths and gifts. When not partnered together, those two people are only working with half of the strengths that God has given them. Rather than battling and fighting against partnership, why not join with your spouse as one unit, together with God, to take on the world together?

*Father, please forgive me for my sometimes-controlling ways
and for dismissing the partnership of my husband so that I can
"just do it myself." Help me to join together with my husband and
You as a three-strand cord that cannot be easily broken. Amen.*

Sing Praises

Sing a new song to the LORD!
Sing his praises from the ends of the earth!
ISAIAH 42:10 NLT

*W*hat blessings has God brought you today?
Maybe your husband appreciates what you do to support him, to provide a safe environment for him, to enjoy and delight in him. For those kinds of husbands, it's easy to sing a new song to the Lord, to sing His praises to the ends of the earth!

On the other hand, your marriage might be a difficult one. Your husband shows little appreciation for you, doesn't help with the chores or childcare, or is never home. You may wonder if he really loves you. It's hard to find the blessings in anything.

Yet the psalmist encourages us to sing a new song to the Lord. . .no matter what our circumstances are. Each day is a new opportunity to praise Him, to thank Him for His blessings, even when life is difficult and not as we anticipated or hoped it would be. When we offer the sacrifice of praise, God rewards us with strength and joy.

Nehemiah faced severe opposition when he obeyed God's call and traveled to Jerusalem to rebuild the walls of the city. Yet he proclaimed, "The joy of the LORD is your strength!" (Nehemiah 8:10 NLT). He learned that rejoicing in who God *is* affected his perspective of his circumstances, and he was able to bear the difficulties with joy.

Lord, may I seek each day to praise You for Your abundant
blessings in my life. May my life be a sacrifice of praise to You. Amen.

Foil the Boil

*It's smart to be patient,
but it's stupid to lose your temper.*
PROVERBS 14:29 CEV

"*Y*ou asked your mother to spend *how long* with us?" Amy's voice squeaked incredulously.

"Just three weeks. I thought she would enjoy watching the kids decorate for Christmas and then stay for our New Year's Eve party. Why? Is that a problem?" Don asked nonchalantly.

Amy swallowed hard. *Is that a problem?* Memories of previous holiday visits flashed through her mind: Mom offering suggestions on how to make better stuffing, the two-hour mall traffic jam during Mom's last-minute shopping excursion, Mom's wrapping paper and Christmas cards covering the kitchen table for a solid week.

Amy could feel her blood pressure rising like a teakettle about to boil. How dare Don impose on her like that! Didn't he realize how much effort his mother required?

"She's been so lonely since Dad died," Don continued. "I know she misses the huge family gatherings she used to host—family has always meant everything to her."

The boiling teakettle reduced to a simmer in Amy's chest. She was awfully glad it hadn't whistled out loud. Okay—time to think with her heart instead of her head. Her own mother was gone and Don's mom was eighty-three. How many more years would they have together? Wasn't family *worth* extra effort?

"Three weeks it is, then," Amy said, smiling.

*God of patience, please give me more.
Temper my temper to Your glory. Amen.*

Days of the Year Index

Hyatt, Gale
1, 24, 36, 55, 77, 89, 104, 116, 133, 146, 162, 180, 193, 199, 212, 219, 231, 247, 261, 282, 295, 308, 319, 330, 352

McQuade, Pamela
13, 23, 46, 58, 63, 88, 92, 115, 123, 137, 151, 166, 179, 186, 204, 229, 233, 255, 271, 272, 294, 301, 313, 336, 354

Maltese, Donna
11, 31, 51, 67, 79, 97, 117, 130, 155, 156, 184, 206, 209, 222, 232, 242, 268, 283, 305, 306, 316, 328, 333, 343, 345

Middlebrooke, Helen Widger
8, 18, 27, 34, 50, 66, 87, 96, 106, 124, 138, 153, 174, 189, 211, 221, 236, 248, 260, 284, 299, 311, 322, 344, 350

Nydegger, Mandy
21, 30, 47, 78, 108, 141, 172, 208, 252, 277, 338, 349

O'Dell, Nicole
17, 41, 56, 75, 94, 120, 132, 136, 157, 160, 182, 210, 217, 249, 264, 267, 289, 303, 321, 323, 339, 342, 346, 360, 363

Parrish, MariLee
5, 19, 37, 45, 62, 86, 110, 161, 185, 201, 218, 240, 258, 269, 286, 298, 317, 329

Phillips, Rachael
7, 26, 35, 64, 73, 90, 107, 119, 135, 148, 164, 183, 198, 214, 230, 243, 262, 276, 291, 307

Quillin, Rachel
9, 29, 38, 44, 54, 72, 93, 100, 113, 127, 142, 158, 188, 190, 207, 223, 246, 265, 287, 304, 312, 326, 341, 348, 358

Rayburn, Julie
2, 25, 49, 60, 83, 105, 134, 145, 176, 192, 216, 225, 253, 270, 293, 310, 334, 353

Vawter, Margie
12, 32, 53, 69, 82, 95, 101, 118, 139, 163, 168, 181, 200, 224, 245, 259, 288, 314, 355, 364

Contributors

Joanna Bloss is a personal trainer, writer, and student living in the Midwest. She is a coauthor of *Grit for the Oyster: 250 Pearls of Wisdom for Aspiring Authors*.

Debora M. Coty is an internationally published freelance writer, columnist, and author who also teaches piano and is children's church coordinator. Look for her historical novels *The Distant Shore* and *Billowing Sails* for ages 12 and above.

Tina C. Elacqua, PhD, teaches, writes, and publishes in journal articles, books, conference papers/presentations, and technical reports/presentations. She is a mom of two small children and lives with her husband in Tennessee.

Nancy Farrier is the author of twelve books and numerous articles and short stories. She is married and has five children. She lives with her family in Southern California.

Suzanne Woods Fisher's historical novel *Copper Star* and its sequel, *Copper Fire*, are inspired by true events. Fisher writes for many magazines and is a wife and mother and a puppy raiser for Guide Dogs for the Blind.

Laura Freudig has lived most of her life on islands along the Maine coast. She enjoys reading, hiking, and singing with her husband and three (soon to be four) children.

Shanna Gregor is a freelance writer, editor, and product developer. The mother of two young men, Shanna and her husband reside in Tucson, Arizona.

Sarah Hawkins is an English and Bible teacher to junior high students and has often taught a women's Bible study. She lives with her husband and son in Northern California.

Gale Hyatt has been writing since the third grade. She and her husband live in Valrico, Florida with their two handsome sons and one precious princess.

Pamela McQuade is a freelance writer and editor in Nutley, New Jersey, who has worked with numerous publishers. She enjoys spending her spare time knitting, quilting, and fly-fishing.

Donna Maltese is a freelance writer, editor, and proofreader; publicist for a local Mennonite project; and the assistant director of RevWriter Writers Conferences. Donna resides in Pennsylvania with her husband and two children.

Helen Widger Middlebrooke is a homemaker, home educator, and the mother of nine. She is a freelance columnist and the author of Lessons for a Supermom.

Mandy Nydegger lives with her husband, David, in Waco, Texas. She loves Christmas, snow, and the Indianapolis Colts.

Nicole O'Dell, wife and mother of six, is an accomplished writer of books, devotions, and Bible studies. She has been a Bible study leader and teacher for over fifteen years.

MariLee Parrish lives in Colorado with her husband, Eric, and young son, Jake. She's a freelance musician and writer who desires to paint a picture of God with her life.

Rachael Phillips (www.rachaelwrites.com), an award-winning fiction and humor writer, is also the author of four biographies published by Barbour Publishing. Rachael and her husband live in Indiana.

Rachel Quillin and her husband Eric and their six children live on a dairy farm in Ohio. She enjoys gardening, writing, and spending time with her family.

Julie Rayburn is a public speaker and an area director for Community Bible Study. She lives in Atlanta with her husband, Scott. They have two grown children and one granddaughter.

Margie Vawter is a full-time freelance editor, proofreader, and writer. She lives with her husband in Colorado and enjoys hiking and snowshoeing near their cabin with their two adult children.

Scripture Index